W9-AHO-328

THE LOYAL AND THE DISLOYAL

We, *who are as good as you, swear to you, who are not better than we, to accept you as our King and sovereign lord, provided that you observe all our liberties and laws; but if not, then not.*

Oath taken by subjects of KING OF ARAGON

Men . . . *may talk of patriotism; they may draw a few examples from ancient story, of great achievements performed by its influence; but whoever builds upon it, as a sufficient Basis for conducting a long and bloody War, will find themselves deceived in the end. We must take the passions of Men as Nature has given them, and those principles as a guide which are generally the rule of Action. I do not mean to exclude altogether the Idea of Patriotism. I know it exists, and I know it has done much in the present Contest. But I will venture to assert, that a great and lasting War can never be supported on this principle alone. It must be aided by a prospect of Interest or some reward. For a time, it may, of itself push Men to Action; to bear much, to encounter difficulties; but it will not endure unassisted by Interest.*

GEORGE WASHINGTON *from Valley Forge, 1778*

THE LOYAL AND THE DISLOYAL

Social Boundaries of Patriotism and Treason

By MORTON GRODZINS

THE UNIVERSITY OF CHICAGO PRESS
CHICAGO AND LONDON

Library of Congress Catalog Card Number: 56–7201

THE UNIVERSITY OF CHICAGO PRESS, CHICAGO & LONDON
The University of Toronto Press, Toronto 5, Canada

Published 1956. Second Impression 1967. Printed in the United States of America

This volume is affectionately dedicated

to the members of my family,

separated by generations, geography, and styles of life,

yet all loyal to the group:

Esther and Jack and Beb

Gil, Maxine, Martha, Barbara, and Carol

Kel, Di, Jim, and Josh

Jerry, Joy, and the young Nicholas

Mitch, Ann

and at the center

Ruth

Table of Contents

PART I
Most Men Are Patriots

1 Introduction: The Competition of Loyalties

An indignant thief called the New York office of the Federal Bureau of Investigation to confess that he had just stolen a suitcase in Grand Central Station.

"It's full of blueprints and other stuff that looks like secret military information," he said. "I've checked it in one of the public lockers and I'm mailing you the key. I'm a thief. But I'm a loyal American thief."

National loyalty is asserted in this way by almost every resident of every nation, no matter what his vocation, no matter what his social position. Our age is an age of patriotism. One of our principal fears is the fear of traitors. The policy of nations is to encourage patriotism and to root out treason.

The difficulty in the policy is the difficulty in knowing what makes for loyalty, what produces treason. If thieves can be patriots, can traitors be honest men? The answer by almost any standard is "Yes." Americans should easily understand this. If their revolution for independence had not ended in victory, the name of George Washington would today mean perfidy in the English-speaking world.

Disloyal persons, until they act, are very much like everybody else. The twenty-one Americans who refused to return home from Communist prison camps following the Korean hostilities looked just like any other group of G.I.'s. Some were poor, some well off; some religious, some not; some single, some married. None carried any discernible mark of Cain when taking his oath of allegiance. And so it is throughout history. Above all—and contrary to many popular beliefs—the poor and downtrodden are not conspicuous among the traitors. Under many circumstances treason is a more likely occurrence among happily married and successful businessmen than among skid-row bums.

This book asks: Why are most people loyal to the nation in which they live? Why are some people disloyal?

The usual answers given to these questions are unsatisfactory. In many cases the questions are not asked at all, and loyalty to the nation is assumed to be a natural thing, constant and unswerving among "good" citizens, lacking among the "bad."

When the questions are asked, answers come in contradictory terms. We are told that loyalty to the nation is a coolly rational choice, individuals having concluded that one way of life, one nation, is superior to others and therefore worthy of allegiance.* On the other hand, it is also asserted that national loyalty is no more than a conditioned reflex, individuals—like Pavlov's dogs—reacting blindly but certainly to cues and symbols manipulated by their political masters; some-

* Sources of quotations, other references, and an occasional technical aside are collected in the Notes, beginning on p. 265.

times this view is extended, and patriotism is described as pure mystique, an ingredient of the blood stream.

Both extreme views are rejected in this volume. National loyalty is neither purely intellectual nor purely irrational. It would be foolish to describe marriage or divorce or delinquency or crime in such a shorthand fashion. It is equally foolish so to consider patriotism. We look at loyalty and disloyalty in precisely the same way that observers of social life look at other social facts.

Patriotism, as an ordinary and commonplace social fact, must be regarded in ordinary and commonplace terms. This means that patriotism—and treason—must be analyzed as the products of social situations and of human reactions to those situations. The joys and ills of life, related to a person's own nation and to other nations, are the stuff from which patriots and traitors are made. We are concerned, in other words, with establishing the social sources and social boundaries of loyalty and disloyalty to the nation. We are concerned with how human responses to life-situations become the source of patriotism and treason.

It is a contradiction in terms to speak of a man without loyalties. He does not exist. The human qualities that distinguish man from other mammals are the products of his social life. One with all the attributes of man, including his brain, is, in isolation, not a man. He is a beast, less than a beast, because even animals cannot live alone.

This only says that when you scratch man you touch loyalty. For man means society. And society—social structure of every sort—rests upon loyalties: upon attitudes and actions directed at supporting groups, ideas, and institutions. Loyalties sustain and are sustained by mutual rights and duties, common beliefs, and reciprocal obligations—all essential ingredients of social life. To accuse a person of being devoid of loyalty can have only one meaning: his loyalties are antagonistic to your own.

Loyalties are a part of every individual's life because they serve his basic needs. They function as a part of his indispensable habit patterns. Loyalties provide him with a portion of the framework upon which he organizes his existence. In the absence of such a framework, he could establish no easy, habitual responses. He would be faced with the endless and hopelessly complicated task of making fresh decisions at each moment of life. He would soon degenerate into wild and random inconsistencies or into a brooding state of confusion and indecisiveness, conditions that merge into insanity.

The propensity of man to structure his activities is apparent in every phase of life. His very perceptions are so organized. Even what a man sees or smells or hears is determined in very large part by predisposing frameworks. This has been demonstrated in laboratory experiments, and these experiments are duplicated daily in ordinary life-situations. Drivers of cars which have collided have very different stories to tell. Two readers of the same book derive from it support for widely different points of view. Chinese music and Mohammedan paintings are displeasing or unintelligible to those who have not acquired the framework necessary to make them beautiful and meaningful.

These simple and well-known facts form the basis of the various tests of personality based upon so-called "projective" techniques. The ink-blot designs of the Rorschach test evoke a wide variety of responses. Yet there is a high degree of consistency among the responses of given individuals and among groups of individuals. This consistency shows that perception is highly selective and thus supplies, almost incidentally, new tools for the analysis and classification of personality.

Life itself is an ink blot, full of undifferentiated masses, sinuous twists that have no ending, interlaced and opposing lines, jagged blank areas—the whole without boundary or definition. Just as the individual puts meaning into experimental ink-blot cards, so he must put organization and structure into the larger, undefined mass from which life is made. This structuring of life's enormous range of potentialities begins to take place even before birth. During the first years of life, when individuals are most easily influenced, the family is the dominant molding agency. Later, play group, school, church, job, social class, government, all take important roles—sometimes parallel, sometimes conflicting—in shaping an individual's career, attitudes, and personality.

These groups that so crucially affect existence are the groups that demand and receive loyalty. They become the eyepieces through which a person views his life and its relation to society. They literally determine what he sees, what he likes, what he considers his life-goals. Without the aid and comfort of these group ties, an individual would find existence impossible.

The functions of loyalties are thus easily understood. They are given in return for gratifications received. They organize the life of the individual, reducing the area of his uncertainty and anxiety. They allow him to move in established patterns of human relations, confident of the actions expected of him and of the responses that his actions will evoke.

One is loyal to the groups that provide gratifications because what serves the group serves the self; what threatens the group threatens the self. There is no self outside group activity. "In so far as one identifies himself with a whole, loyalty to that whole is loyalty to himself; it is self-realization, something in which one cannot fail without losing self-respect."

Complete identification between an individual and a group does not often exist. Totalitarian governments aim at this complete identity between the state and the individual. They attempt to attain it by destroying all intermediary loyalties or by fusing the activities of all other groups with those of the state.

In the democracies, except in periods of extreme crisis, freedom to form and maintain group ties is cherished and encouraged, and individuals preserve strong loyalties to many non-national groups—to family, friends, neighborhood, church, ethnic society, job, class, and a host of other institutions, groups, and idea systems. Such loyalties exist most frequently in situations that bring the individual face to face with others who share his views and situation. The relative strengths and weaknesses of these numerous loyalties change with age, with shifts in life-situation, with new experience, and especially under the stress of crisis. They change as old relationships no longer serve biological needs or as they no longer supply satisfaction and security to the individual in the total network of his social existence.

The nation as the capstone of other loyalties and as the largest entity to which most men under most circumstances give effective allegiance is a modern phenomenon. Though rooted deeply in the past, the nation emerged in its modern form no earlier than the eighteenth century. Yet the nation's primacy as a focus of loyalty is now widely assumed. When the existence of the nation is threatened, it is expected that other loyalties will be sacrificed, at least temporarily. "The supreme loyalty of man is . . . due to his nationality, as his own life is supposedly rooted in and made possible by its welfare."

Before the Christian Era—in both Greece and Rome—strong political allegiances, of course, existed. Citizenship in both cases was limited to relatively few of the total population, in marked contrast to modern states, and the most important life-role of those who qualified was their role as citizens. Philosophers and poets, moralists and artists, were, first of all, soldiers and senators, statesmen and strategists. Duty to the state was a moral duty of the highest order, patriotism taking precedence over all other obligations. Thucydides, Herodotus, and Plutarch parade before their readers a procession of great patriots and great traitors. Plato advocated a community of wives in the ideal Republic largely in order to make certain that children would be attached more firmly to their civic duties; and Cicero asserted the same unqualified primacy of nation over family.

These ideas may sound somewhat extreme to residents of modern democracies; to the early Christians they were completely alien. Christian practice and dogma gave little support to the idea of loyalty to city or state. Prayers were permitted for the welfare of the Roman Empire, but the emperor could be obeyed only if his commands were consistent with the law of God. Indeed, according to Westermarck, no men in the whole Roman Empire "so entirely lacked patriotism":

> They [the early Christians] had no affection for Judea, they soon forgot Galilee, they cared nothing for the glory of Greece and Rome. When the judges asked them which was their country they said in answer, "I am a Christian." And long after Christianity had become the religion of the Empire, St. Augustine declared that it matters not, in respect of this short and transitory life, under whose dominion a mortal man lives, if only he be not compelled to acts of impiety or injustice. Later on, when the Church grew into a political power independent of the State, she became a positive enemy of national interests.

Christians learned to serve temporal masters before many centuries passed. Nevertheless, when Machiavelli in the sixteenth century declared that "he preferred his country to the safety of his soul, people considered him guilty of blasphemy." As late as the seventeenth century, a Jesuit general called patriotism "a plague and the most certain death of Christian love."

Machiavelli's ideas mark the birth of the modern national state. They caught one of the first dim images of a popularly supported government, powerful at the center and wielding authority over a unified territory and a single culture. But from the decline of the Roman Empire to Machiavelli, roughly a thousand years, there was no such thing as national loyalty. The mass of people were generally regarded as scum, and generally regarded themselves as unrelated to larger secular institutions. The dominant ethic was a universal one which recognized no significant distinctions among Christian souls, wherever they resided. Nations did not exist. Throughout this period—five times more lengthy than the present era of supreme national loyalties—the church remained the object of most men's largest allegiances.

The "country" of the man of the Middle Ages, if it meant anything, meant the neighborhood in which he was born, worked, lived, and died. Men's loyalties were thus confined to either very small or very large objects: on the one hand, to a town, a feudal manor, a guild, or a family; on the other hand, to the entire human universe or at least the Christian part of it. Always serving his God, a person's first earthly duty was to local objects: town, guild, lord. No strong bond existed among the various lords of a given area. A man might be the vassal simultaneously of the king of France and the king of England. Frequently a nobleman sold his services and those of the people he commanded to the enemies of the kingdom in which he lived. Patriotism had little place in medieval codes of chivalry.

Throughout the entire Middle Ages, loyalty was effectively demanded, as it had been in the pre-Christian era, by some ruler or ruling group—city, small republic, or lord. And there was throughout a growing consciousness of national differences. This was stimulated, among other things, by the development of vernacular languages, the Crusades and their aftermath, the military efforts of strong western European monarchs, and the slow but steady growth in commerce. Modern historical research tends to push back the dating of emergent nationalism.

Tudor and Elizabethan England and the strong monarchs of fifteenth- and sixteenth-century France produced prototypes of modern nations and modern national loyalties. But universal, mass loyalties came much later, with the decreased power of the universal church; the growth in the division of labor; the revolutions in commerce, communications, and industry; and the widening of the popular base of political participation, not least of all participation in mass armies. English developments again preceded those in the rest of the Western world. The deep benchmarks are recent—the American and French revolutions. Rousseau's argument in favor of a "civil religion" as a substitute for Christianity was an argument for patriotism. Not until the eighteenth century can one find ideas that match those of Roman times concerning the primacy of political institutions over other groups. "Children belong to the general family, to the republic, before they belong to particular families. . . . The spirit of private families must disappear when the great family calls. . . . You are born for the republic and not for the pride or the despotism of families." This is a statement of a French revolutionary leader. The history of strong national loyalties for the masses is a history of less than two hundred years.

When the heavyweight boxing champion, Joe Louis, was asked why he was happy to serve in the United States Army during World War II, in view of American discrimination against Negroes, he responded, "Man, whatever is wrong with my country ain't nothing Hitler can fix." Mr. Louis was saying that he saw no alternative to his national loyalty. Yet alternatives exist as at no other time in history. The industrial age which has made the nation-state has also provided a multiplication of alternative loyalties. Developments that have produced nations and national loyalties have the potentiality of destroying them.

Technical advances in communication and transportation have greatly aided the growth of the national state. They have expanded the areas of effective governmental control. They have dissipated parochialism. They have been crucial in advancing common interests and common understandings over large regions. They have provided essential tools for building strong nations and, simultaneously, the means for expressing strong national loyalties.

The same developments can reverse the process. Now the whole world is every man's neighborhood. Aside from political barriers to the flow of communication, there is no limit to the images in words, pictures, and sounds that can be transmitted from one place to another. When oceans are crossed in a matter of hours, those on the opposite shores lose their awful strangeness. Faraway places are no longer menacing if they are populated on week ends by refugees from the boredom of week-day life in one's own home town. Patriotism lives largely on differences. The revolutions in communication and transportation have transformed the strange to the familiar and have effaced many imagined and feared differences among the peoples of the world. To that extent, patriotism is weakened by the very factors that made it strong.

The same dual effects can be traced through many other social processes. Greatly increased literacy has expanded the effective area of state power and has strengthened the hold of national political leaders over diverse population groups. The same literacy, however, is the source of sensitivity to alternative political appeals and a medium of protest for those whose political docility was once based on ignorance.

The great state services—ranging from the supervision of the newborn to the care of the aged, from the fixing of wages to the allocation of scarce minerals—have made more and more people dependent upon the state. The fostering of dependency is one way of fostering loyalties. But if state services are promised and then not produced, loyalties turn sour. The state draws to itself strong allegiances by virtue of its services; it also makes itself a universal scapegoat if those services do not meet the expectations of the populations served. In the latter event the state runs the risk that its citizens will seek other sources of satisfaction and, in the process, transfer their allegiance.

Before the industrial revolution, Western man lived his life in a network of relatively inflexible social, largely family, relationships. He was fixed geographically by the lack of transport and by his ignorance of opportunities elsewhere. He was fixed occupationally and socially by a relatively closed class system and by traditional modes of thought and action. He was not a free, individual agent; he had not, in Maine's famous phrase, moved "from status to contract."

His status was established by virtue of his membership in a family, a community, a guild, or a manor. He was bound by tradition, and his activities were under the careful surveillance of those whose community he shared. Living his whole life with a limited number of other persons, all similarly bound by status and tradition, his actions were severely controlled and limited. Class hatreds burgeoned and occasionally were expressed violently. But, under most circumstances, whatever an individual's discontent, his only opportunities to vent grievances were private; and even drunkenness or wife-beating were controlled by rigorous community prohibitions. He could not shift his loyalties to new communities, new leaders, or new causes because these alternatives were simply unavailable to him.

This is an oversimple and schematic view. Yet it is sufficiently accurate for comparison with the situation today. Life no longer revolves around a single community, tradition is no longer controlling. Populations are fluid through space, through occupations, through social classes. Continuous personal relationships with the same people in all aspects of living have been replaced by the segmentation of life. Neighbors may be strangers or the closest friends; association with fellow-workers may end at five o'clock or be the basis of the strongest political ties; church brethren may meet only on Sunday morning or may define for one another a complete way of life.

All this means that modern man has a variety of groups, causes, and leaders to choose from. His loyalties are as fluid as his career and as numerous as the segments of his life. Within the nation the diversity of the social structure has produced a diversity of loyalties, and the competition of these non-national loyalties may be an important source of national disloyalty.

At one stage of industrial development, the newly mobile middle classes were the prime promoters of national power. The alliances between nation and commerce, between enlarged free markets and industrial enterprise, were natural. They are still strong. Yet modern life increasingly places national loyalty in competition with other-nation and cross-nation loyalties. Scientists, professional workers, artists of all kinds, and even businessmen may find their strongest colleagues in other nations. They may find loyalties to such colleague groups antagonistic to national loyalty; they may find national boundaries confining. More importantly, there are few population groups of any kind who suffer discontent simply because of their ignorance of an alternative national loyalty. The Communist appeal is universally known in democratic nations, just as the promises of democracy are known, despite curtains of iron and bamboo, in other parts of the world. Every state attempts, sometimes by policies of suppression and violence, to prevent its citizens from transferring their allegiance to another state. Yet at no previous time in the short history of national states have the attractions of an alternative national loyalty been so widely advertised or so widely known.

Developments in social process and social structure affect, and in turn are affected by, developments in social personality. In Riesman's terms, the personality change has been away from the "tradition-directed" and "inner-directed" to the "other-directed." Attitude, outlook, and cues for action no longer came mainly from community tradition or age-haloed precedent; they no longer spring from inner moral conviction, fostered by a Protestant "calling," and strong even in the face of contrary opinions of friends and associates. For the modern industrial man, attitude and action are influenced primarily by his peers—the groups with which he associates. He is "other-directed" in the sense that he fits his views to theirs. He finds this easy because their esteem is what he most desires.

To the extent that a person is "other-directed," his loyalties are relatively soft. He holds to causes and institutions without moral fervor and without consciousness of the strength of tradition. He is less concerned that his loyalties are good and proper, in any absolute sense, than that they are acceptable. Cross-pressures from different groups sometimes make his life difficult. But he can be loyal to many causes, even to contradictory ones, as long as he finds favor with the appropriate colleague or friendship groups. The segmentation of his life encourages such multiple attachments and discourages any uneasiness concerning their possible antagonisms.

The "other-directed" personality, if appropriate group support is forthcoming, chooses with relative freedom among the alternative loyalties that social process and social structure make available. If social pressures strongly reinforce one another in encouraging loyalty to the nation as the supreme loyalty—and this is most frequently the case—the other-directed individual will be highly patriotic. But he does not hold loyalties, not even loyalty to the nation, passionately or with unshakable conviction. His sensitivity to group opinion makes him less likely to be the bold traitor but more likely to be the easy collaborator. He tends to follow his crowd, even if his crowd is traveling the route to treason.

Loyalties sustain man by making society and social life possible. This is why "all serious political writing regards the quality of loyalty as a good thing." Yet judgments about the "goodness" or "badness" of national loyalty, in both short and long perspectives, are difficult to make. Within the framework of national loyalties, the modern world has been made. But the nation as the object of largest loyalties has been attacked by a variety of hands in a variety of ways for a variety of purposes. A surprising consensus has been achieved. Patriotism is condemned as an archaic trait, twisting good purposes to evil ends, standing as a barrier to the higher organization of human institutions and energies. These voices have become numerous and powerful since the advent of the hydrogen bomb. Like E. B. White's observant child, they ask whether they are "pledging allegiance to a flag or to a shroud."

Time plays tricks in altering judgments about acts of loyalty and disloyalty, and the perspective that history gives is a sobering one. Patriots become scoundrels; an act of treason becomes a feat of national heroism. The most staid Americans belong to a rebellious nation. "Our whole history is treason . . .

our creeds are infidelity to the mother church; our constitution treason to our fatherland."

The passage of years may caricature the national heroes of today and may endow our traitors with national halos. This commonplace of reversed judgments merits emphasis only because it is difficult to project it into the future. Consider only an extreme case, that of William Joyce, "Lord Haw-Haw," hanged for treason by order of a British court following his broadcasts for Germany during World War II. Legal considerations clouded the claim that Joyce owed formal allegiance to the British Crown. This issue aside, there can be no reasonable doubt that his broadcasts were designed to be detrimental to the British war effort, that by every current definition Joyce was a traitor. So the public thought, so the courts decided, and so the man was hanged.

Yet Joyce's place as a traitor in the span of history is not secure. "God bless dear old England," he wrote after his capture. It would need no renaissance of Joyce's brand of fascism to elevate him to heroic stature. On a simpler and more immediate level, it could be claimed, as he himself was anxious to do, that he labored to strengthen Britain, to achieve amity between Britain and Germany, and to preserve the strength of the West against the expanding peril of the Soviet Union. The argument seems less pointless a few brief years after it was made than it did during Joyce's day in court. It may acquire even greater dignity according to the accidents of history.

All this illustrates how social judgments vary with the position of the judge and those judged. Such judgments have validity only in particular situations at particular times. The same act at a given time may be loyal in one context, disloyal in another; it may, without variations in place but with the passage of time, be judged in contradictory terms.

Beyond judgments of particular acts are larger conclusions

concerning the utility of national loyalty. Marxists view the nation-state as a weapon in the hands of a ruling class and patriotism as an evil device to divert the force of valid discontents. Thorstein Veblen, in a similar fashion, believed that modern nations were parochial islands in a world-wide network of technology and that patriotism was "a patent imbecility," contributing nothing to the welfare of the common run of men. The patriotic spirit never rose "to the consummate pitch of enthusiastic abandon except when bent on some work of concerted malevolence . . . its highest and final appeal is for the death, damage, discomfort and destruction of the party of the second part."

These words are reminiscent of Mark Twain's: "The spirit of patriotism is the spirit of the dog and the wolf." And Twain's contention that patriots could only be alleged, not real, Christians is put to a hard reverse demonstration by thousands of practicing Christians who take their religion most seriously and cannot therefore be patriotic. Religious objectors to wars are a case in point. The pacifism of Quakers, Mennonites, Brethren, Jehovah's Witnesses, and Christian Socialists testifies to the continuing religious questioning of national policies and values.

The age-old quest for a world government has always received impetus from religious forces. In more recent times these forces have been augmented by all variety of men, including those who fear destruction, those who seek world-wide minimum standards of living, and those who hold that salvation lies in universal standards of law. There are legions who believe that the achievement of peace, the dignity of man, even the continued existence of the race, depend upon the reduction of national pride and the diminution—or the elimination—of national loyalties.

The same skepticism and the same doubts can be reached

from still other paths. The good patriot is not necessarily the good man. Aristotle was explicit on this point; we have had his view bleakly corroborated in recent years by good German citizens burning their fellow-citizens alive in gas ovens as a patriotic duty. Furthermore, patriotic activity may be only a disguise for selfish ends or for failure in other areas of endeavor. A multitude of personal sins can be hidden behind a waving flag. "The love of one's country . . . is in many cases no more than the love of an ass for its stall." "Patriotism," Dr. Johnson said, "is the last refuge of a scoundrel."

If the good patriot may not be the good man, the good man may not always be the good patriot. We have Emerson's word that "good men must not obey the laws too well." Ignoble loyalty can be matched by noble disloyalty. Not only does this occur when time gives new definitions to old acts; it is also true in more immediate situations: as in the case of Germans who plotted to assassinate Hitler; as in the case of Robert E. Lee, who chose the Confederacy over the Union with noble resolve and sore heart.

2 National Loyalty as the Supreme Loyalty

National loyalty is relatively new, and it must compete with many other loyalties. This sharply raises the question: What makes national loyalty so strong?

Loyalties, as we have seen, function dynamically. They are demanded by and given to institutions and persons that provide life-satisfactions. They are means by which individuals organize and give meaning to their existence. Individual satisfactions are related to national loyalty in an infinite number of ways. The strength and universality of national loyalty rest upon the ease and the force with which this positive connection between nation and happiness can be established in the mind of the individual. The whole social structure tends to promote the relationship, binding human satisfaction to national welfare.

On one plane the relationship between individual and nation is direct. There are satisfaction and delight in attaching one's self to a larger cause. Inner doubts are dissipated because the cause gives purpose and direction to life. The meanness and pettiness of everyday existence become more tolerable because the nation is involved in enterprises of grandeur.

The mechanism is one of identification: of accepting the nation's symbols and achievements as one's own, of feeling personal satisfaction as a consequence of institutional accomplishment. This identification is fostered because the nation directly satisfies personal needs by governmental programs that more and more tend to touch more and more people. Fulfilment of needs aside, the nation is looked upon as a good in itself. Ritual and myth, just as they do for religion, reinforce this definition of the nation as good and endow the definition with emotional force. The nation thus dissipates actual and imagined discontents and weaknesses. It simultaneously crystallizes a common faith in a way of life, a common system of ideas, and a common view of the world—attributes that philosophers and politicians, sociologists and seers, hold essential to successful group life.

The direct strand of patriotism is expressed by a necktie salesman (or a professor or a cab driver) when he says: "We ought to pull out of the UN," or "We ought not let the Russians take over Germany," or "We ought to send troops to Formosa." When citizens say or think "we" in referring to the actions of government, even the most abominable official acts are difficult to condemn. Condemnation under the circumstances is self-damnation; and to avoid this kind of injury to self, prodigious mental feats may be performed. So German citizens refused to believe that "we" slaughtered political enemies by the millions, and so Russian citizens argue that "we" must slaughter political enemies today in order to make possible the better world of tomorrow.

"We" usually refers to the nation because the world is

organized, territorially and to a large extent functionally, into national units. This very organization permits a complex flow of simple emotions to be woven into the sentiment of national loyalty. At the same time, the nation-states and the institutions within them conspire to promote and sustain this loyalty.

The tendency of man to prefer the familiar to the unfamiliar is universal. Even those who search for new experience and delight in the exotic seek reassurance in the familiar and the habitual. As the world is presently organized, the familiar and the habitual are principally equated with the national, sometimes directly, sometimes through the further identification of family and community with nation. So affection for the scenes and experiences of childhood is linked to the benevolence of the state. The familiar language, the familiar food, the familiar humor, the familiar interpersonal responses—including, as Kipling wrote, the familiar lies—all are affectionately related to nation.

Familiar misery is frequently more attractive than promised or actual, but unfamiliar, bliss. This is a function of what social anthropologists call "ethnocentrism," the habit of judging foreign practices by familiar standards. Even the mean and savage regard their own way of life as the best and all others as subhuman or at least distinctly inferior. The same mechanisms operate in more complex societies. North Americans are crass money-pinchers in the eyes of most Argentineans. The Germans are still *Boches* to the French, Russians are barbarians to the Germans, the capitalist world is rotten bourgeoisie in at least the official Russian view.

Anatole France described this interaction in classic terms. The Porpoise philosopher, Gratien, was engaged in conversation with a Penguin cottager in idyllic surroundings:

"Delightful inhabitants of a delightful country [Gratien said], I give you thanks. . . . Everything here breathes forth joy, concord, and peace."

As he said this a shepherd passed by playing a march upon his pipe.

"What is that lively air?" asked Gratien.

"It is the war-hymn against the Porpoises," answered the peasant. "Everybody here sings it. Little children know it before they can speak. We are all good Penguins."

"You don't like the Porpoises then?"

"We hate them."

"For what reason do you hate them?"

"Need you ask? Are not the Porpoises neighbours of the Penguins!"

"Of course."

"Well, that is why the Penguins hate the Porpoises."

"Is that a reason?"

"Certainly. He who says neighbours says enemies. . . . Don't you know what patriotism is? For my part there are but two cries that rise to my lips: Hurrah for the Penguins! Death to the Porpoises!"

The modern world network of communications and other technological factors tend to weaken the force of ethnocentrism. But it remains potent because it lives on difference, real or imagined. It is strengthened by the structural qualities of the nation-state system. The great hostilities generated within nations are, to every extent possible, siphoned off into regulated channels, as in prize fight and business competition; at other points these hostilities are suppressed by the nation, not always with success, as criminal statistics testify. And, by every means available, hostilities within the nation are turned outward, finding outlet in bursts of patriotic fervor directed against other national units. Man's love of community—his "aim-inhibited libido," to use Freud's term—is encouraged to stop at national boundaries. The ills of own person and own culture are then projected to others: we are peaceful, they are aggressive; we are kind, they are cruel; we fight for justice, they for conquest.

These mechanisms prompted the sardonic Sumner to comment that "the masses are always patriotic." They inspire the antagonisms and animosities that are basic to much patriotic endeavor. The process is self-generating and circular. National boundaries and patriotism to the nation establish convenient ethnocentric battle lines; the belligerencies so evoked add to patriotic fervor; and the heightened patriotism produces new belligerencies. Thus patriotism can pour meaning into otherwise empty lives. The price may be individuality itself; but this seems cheap to those glorifying and suffering for great causes.

The nation is not the only focal point for mass loyalties. Just as loyalty to nation competes with loyalty to family, job, and friends, so it must compete with loyalty to race, religion, and class. The nation's advantage is based not only on the processes just described: to some degree those energies are also available to other causes. National rather than other loyalties are also partly the result of objective facts—common language, common traditions, common suffering and sacrifice, a common territory. Finally, national loyalty is built strong as the result of the active role taken by social institutions in building a firm, direct tie between individual and nation.

The institution of government is of first importance in this effort. By laws establishing limits of freedom and control, government defines general guidelines for life-activities. Through direct and indirect control of the schools, government has a crucial lever for encouraging some character traits and discouraging others and for molding individuals to standards of thought and action. Through its multitude of programs, government purchases conformity and allegiance. By enforcing service in the armed forces, government transforms citizens into soldiers and, in the process, brings about similarly striking changes in attitude and outlook. As the source of major news developments, government commands a large portion of the words and symbols transmitted to the public by press, radio, television, and film. By the encouragement of national holidays and festivals, government pounds home myths of national might and images of national glory. By fostering patriotic organizations and activities, government enlists citizens in active demonstrations of patriotism.

There are great variations in the extent and manner that governments utilize the power they possess for building patriotism. There are even greater variations in the size and composition of the groups to which governments are responsible and thus in the ends for which patriotism is utilized.

Totalitarian governments attempt to create situations in which individuals receive all their cues for action from a state or state-party agency. They do this by capturing or destroying all other institutions and groups—religious, professional, and social—that guide and control human action. The terrible effectiveness of this fully mobilized state-controlled system cannot be doubted. Under certain circumstances, it makes the state even more powerful than the family as a molder of attitude and action. It drastically alters the direction of the culture and the very personality of the people.

Democratic values and traditions do not countenance this ruthless exploitation of individuals by the state for the state. The power structure within democracies makes such exploitation impossible; it occurs only at the price of changing the character of the state itself. In the United States and in other democracies, therefore, there is no total mobilization of state resources and state institutions for the purpose of constructing strong national allegiance. Yet state activities move strongly in this direction. Only a small portion of these activities aim at building direct emotional ties between individual and state. School programs illustrate this attempt, as do bond drives, ceremonies dramatizing the might of armed forces, the display and symbolic care of the flag. But in the democracies, unlike the totalitarian nations, the major impact of state activities is an indirect one: it strengthens national loyalties by strengthening the numerous voluntary groups through which so much of the life and politics of democratic people is organized and directed.

The effects of these programs do not, of course, stop with the voluntary groups. These groups have a vitality of their own, and they direct the emotions of group members toward the nation. Virtually all groups contribute to national allegiance. Their members minimize or efface antagonisms between their own group and the nation. They identify group and national welfare. "What is good for business is good for the nation," advertises the National Association of Manufacturers. "High wages mean national health," responds the Congress of Industrial Organizations.

All these voices and forces accumulate and produce the religious—more properly, the sectlike—quality of patriotism. It is a quality for which totalitarian nations strive continuously and which is known to democracies largely in crisis. It is "an element of worship, of willing sacrifice, of joyful merging of the individual life in the life of the nation." Here the direct nation-individual linkage is most graphically expressed.

To the modern national state, as to the mediaeval church, is attributable an *ideal*, a *mission*. . . . The nation is conceived of as eternal. . . . She protects her children and saves them from foreign devils; she assures them life, liberty, and the pursuit of happiness; she fosters for them the arts and the sciences; and she gives them nourishment. . . . Nationalism is sentimental, emotional, and inspirational.

Patriotism cannot long be maintained by the direct tie to nation alone. No man has expressed this idea more clearly than George Washington, whose view is quoted on the title-page of this volume; and Washington's view was shared widely by those who founded the United States government. They believed that patriotism was given toughness by "a prospect of interest or some reward." "Interest," in their conception, was largely monetary or commercial. The definition need not be so narrow. But Washington's point is basic.

Nations cannot exist unless they provide satisfaction for their citizens. Life-goals must be approximately achieved or achievable. In the democracies these satisfactions and achievements are principally realized in areas where there is little or no direct nation-person relationship. Here the indirect link binding nation and individual is forged. One early American settler put the matter bluntly:

> What attachment can a poor European emigrant have for a country where he had nothing? The knowledge of the language, the love of a few kindred as poor as himself, were the only cords that tied him: his country [America] is now that which gives him land, bread, protection, and consequence: *Ubi panis ibi patria* is the motto of all emigrants.

In democratic states, the principal life-satisfactions are experienced in the face-to-face relations of everyday living, in pleasurable experiences with friends and neighbors, in the achievement of expectations in marriage and career. A person's relationships to the nation are transmitted or filtered through these experiences. To the extent that they produce a satisfactory life-situation, the individual's identification with the nation is positive, and his loyalty may be presumed. Where the individual's life-situation does not produce a balance of gratifications, his identification with the nation may waver. His national loyalty is more easily eroded.

Leon Trotsky once remarked that revolutions were not caused by the poor. If they were, he said, there would be revolutions going on all the time. This is a valuable reminder that "life-satisfactions" or "life-goals" are not fixed or static concepts. Individuals define these terms in very different ways. To say that loyalty is dependent upon the achievement of life-satisfactions is therefore not to say that the poor are disloyal and the rich loyal. The individual's definition of satisfaction is of crucial importance, and even the same person's ideas of "satisfaction" change with changes in time and circumstance. Social status, public esteem, freedom, power, skill—all may be as important as wealth. The fat men who do not make easy converts are those fat in satisfactions, not necessarily in body or other material possessions.

Life-satisfactions are pursued and life-goals are achieved within the framework of groups. The happy man in isolation does not exist. He may—and most frequently does—take his terms of reference, his cues for action, his definitions of the good and desirable, from the small face-to-face groups with which he comes into most intimate contact: family, friends, business associates, fellow-workers. Or these cues for life may be influenced by larger, less visible groups with which he identifies himself: professional association, social class, the universal church, the workers of the world. In these latter cases and even where frames of reference are derived from such apparent abstractions as "the good of mankind," there is usually a face-to-face group in existence, functioning to define and to clarify abstract goals in terms of day-to-day activity.

These are the sources of life's principal joys in a democratic state, and these are the objects of man's primary loyalties. The very existence of such groups provides possibilities for sharp clashes between national and other loyalties. But, paradoxically, these other loyalties are also the most important foundation of democratic national loyalty.

The nation is the only group with which all persons in a given geographic area are associated. It gives all citizens a common point of reference. A threat to the nation is interpreted as a threat to groups within the nation and to the gratifications derived from those groups. The satisfactions springing from smaller groups are thus related to the nation and to national loyalty.

The American's conformity, like the Englishman's, is a self-generating achievement. His patriotism results less from the direct internalization of national ideals than from linking to the nation the love and joy he derives from all the diverse activities of life. "Neither a central or political body nor a representative social group enforces [it]. Yet so far as the social and psychological process of integration is concerned, this society transcends the boldest dreams of fascist or communist revolutionaries. . . . [The Englishman's] dictator is installed in his heart."

The welter of non-national loyalties makes a direct national loyalty a misnomer. It does not exist. Loyalties are to specific groups, specific goals, specific programs of action. Populations are loyal to nation as a by-product of satisfactions achieved within non-national groups, because the nation is believed to symbolize and sustain those groups. From this point of view, one is loyal not to nation but to family, business, religion, friends. One fights for the joys of his pinochle club when he is said to fight for his country.

So national loyalty has a variety of roots. It springs from direct involvement in the nation's grandeur, from direct response to the symbols of the nation. It is an indirect product of satisfactory private life, loyalties to voluntary groups being transmitted to, and culminating in, national loyalty. In both these cases national loyalty fulfils a function of structuring human existence, providing "economies" among the many choice-points of life.

At the same time, this loyalty leads to positive attitudes and action. In Royce's term, loyalty is expressed as "the willing and practical and thorough-going devotion of a person to a cause." This loyalty is accompanied by conviction. Even sacrifice in the nation's service is accepted willingly.

Many people derive no joy from the religious quality of patriotism; many do not achieve satisfactory life-situations; some do neither. And still others may be perfectly satisfied without in any way relating their happiness to the state. Apathetic or critical, beaten by life's circumstances or isolated from the nation by private joys shared privately with others, this large segment of the population must be included among those considered loyal to their nation. They may not support the nation in any active fashion, and their brand of loyalty plays no important role in the organization of their lives. Rather, their loyalty is residual. These persons are loyal because they are *not disloyal.* And they are not disloyal because the entire weight of society repels them from open acts of national disloyalty.

One of the greatest weights is that of social inertia. Lord Bryce argued that indolence was the most important force that kept men under government. He was pointing to the fact that "most of us hate trouble and like to choose the line of least resistance." He believed this to be a great force (greater than fear or reason or deference or sympathy) in bringing about social conformity.

Even where indolence is not controlling, disloyalty is difficult. Many acts of social protest and adjustment, short of disloyalty, are readily available. Within the framework of national groups, there are a great number of attachments available to man in democratic states. If he does not like one lodge, there are others. If he is bored with his job, he can quit and, at least in good times, find another. If he is dissatisfied with his neighbors, he can move. If marriage palls, divorce is possible. If pastor or church become distasteful, other leaders and other denominations exist in great number. Some of these avenues to sense and satisfaction in life take a psychological toll and carry social penalties, but they are prescribed and accepted social processes. They are carried on within the nation, not against it.

Some protests against life-situation are neither easy nor socially acceptable. They run the whole gamut of deviant behavior: alcoholism, arson, bank robbery, embezzlement, hoboing, whoring. In the extreme, the individual may withdraw himself from all meaningful human contact. Eventually he may find himself under the wheels of a streetcar or in an asylum.

These protest methods for seeking integration and meaning for life often meet with deep social disapproval. Yet many of them, especially within the great urban centers, are readily at hand. They may be utilized without discovery and therefore without penalty. They may result in intense guilt feelings that frustrate their aim, though men have infinite abilities to appease their consciences and rationalize their behavior. Even if their behavior is brought to public light, the community wrath aroused hardly compares with that called down upon the head of the traitor.

The dissatisfactions of life may be met passively. Some persons thrive on defeat. They react to ills and misfortunes with complacency, not revolt. They are low in energy and are characterized by inner tiredness and resignation. They are not disloyal, because they do not define their situation as an unhappy one or because they do not relate their misery to politics or because they have no will to protest.

Another possible response runs in the opposite direction, in demonstrations of superloyalty. Here are patriots with nothing else to do. They are hyperactive in programs celebrating the flag, the Constitution, and the Bill of Rights. They may have no ideological commitments beyond the fact that the nation provides them with a career, and they may find support for their own mediocrity because of the respectability of the causes they pursue. Patriotism can be a vocation because of failure or boredom in other spheres of life, because it satisfies the need for dependence, or because it allows for the legal expression of animosities and aggressions.

In the political sphere, democratic society allows for easy protest. The existence of political parties channels discontents into socially approved forms. Inside and outside the formal party structure, special-interest groups offer many opportunities for action within a wide spectrum of political beliefs. Politics within non-political institutions—business, labor union, or club—attracts the energies of many. When local or national problems appear parochial, movements for world betterment challenge attention.

Outside the acceptable protest channels in politics, there are wide marginal areas between loyalty and disloyalty in which individuals can express dissatisfaction and seek happiness. These areas exist because of giant ambiguities in the meaning of both loyalty and disloyalty, ambiguities known only in democracies. Here are found all manner of people, from the food-hoarding housewife to the materials-hoarding manufacturer. Virtually every citizen finds himself at one time or another on this fringe of disloyalty.

The clearly disloyal acts—treason, sabotage, espionage—are

an altogether different matter. For one thing, they are rarely available. This is true on a relative scale: the very multiplicity of other opportunities for deviant behavior makes the openly disloyal act less enticing. It is also true on an absolute scale: the traitorous act usually requires a combination of circumstances not easily achieved. Confederates may be needed, and they are not always available. Joint activity involves ideological and personal sacrifices that are often extreme. Foresight and planning may be demanded. The time must be propitious.

Furthermore, acts of open disloyalty are not usually relevant to the frustrations and deprivations that individuals commonly face. Relationships between deprivation and protest are not always direct: witness the man who kills his cat because he cannot kiss his wife. Usually, however, the connection is more apparent. And only as the state increases its functions and demands more and more from its citizens do acts of disloyalty become immediately pertinent. The very increase in state functions thus provides new opportunities for disloyalty. If national conscription did not exist, there would be no draft dodgers. Historically, programs of the democracies have been relatively light in their impact upon the lives of citizens. Only within recent years have government programs made the disloyal act a relevant protest for many people for many reasons.

Even where government programs might realistically inspire protest, other considerations become potent. Satisfactions in the non-public spheres of life—on the job, in the home—constitute both an opiate and a deterrent. He who is completely involved in his job may find no time to become sensitive to political effrontery. This is an ignorance imposed by limitations of time and energy. It is simultaneously an ignorance of great political convenience. Most people are "too busy" to acquaint themselves with matters they might find completely distasteful. The penalties for violent protest, especially protest that is clearly disloyal, strike at the very roots of happiness. Job, family, friends, comfortable existence itself, are in this sense all hostages insuring loyalty.

Indeed, it is often more attractive to join your enemies than to fight them, especially if they occupy the benches of legality and the seats of power. The most recent striking illustrations of this occurred during the Nazi regime. Those abandoning protest solace themselves with the thought of achieving reform more effectively from within. In the interim, they do not jeopardize many spheres of happiness and need not surrender their hostages.

The scales are thus heavily weighted against disloyalty. Even under the darkest circumstances, individuals can always look to better things in the future. They can channelize their protests within institutionalized processes, however narrow they may be, and believe in fullest sincerity that no more is possible. And they rationalize their action in terms of higher loyalties: the nation must be preserved for all time, the current government must therefore be suffered; socialism (or Mother Russia) must triumph, Stalinism is only a temporary evil.

Finally, disloyalty is rare because of the stigma attached to it. In the eyes of his contemporaries, the traitor or otherwise openly disloyal person is more venal than the murderer or the rapist. He runs the risk of losing his place in all social life. Since men depend upon society for sustenance in no less certain a manner than they depend upon food, this risk is one that few are willing to take. If a person takes it, he does so either without regard for the social consequences or because he has found a new social environment in which to act.

These obstacles to disloyal acts operate in an ever tightening circle. The lack of traitorous opportunities and the irrelevance of treason to most of life's ills mean that there are few traitors. The few who exist, when exposed, suffer the concentrated wrath of society. And this stigma, in turn, constitutes a new deterrent.

The alternatives to national loyalty increase with advances in levels of education and communication. But it remains true that these alternatives are relatively limited. Traitorous acts stand in a poor competitive position with all the other opportunities for deviant behavior.

In sum, the state has become modern man's largest point of reference. It supplies him with psychic security and religious-like joys. However poor the conditions of his life may be, he is molded to conformity by the forces of ethnocentrism, by the powerful antagonisms of the strange and unknowable, by social inertia, by the satisfactions that even suffering sometimes brings, by the utilization of patriotic activity as a substitute for other joys, by the relative absence of alternatives to national conformity, and by the social vengeance that follows the traitorous act. To these factors must be added all the positive steps taken by society to identify the individual with his nation. Government, family, neighborhood, church, school, and business all push in the direction of strong national loyalties.

Life may be hell. But disloyalty is the last way out. By inclination or by default, most men are patriots.

PART II
Democratic and Totalitarian National Loyalty

3 One Life, Many Loyalties: The Democratic Allegiance Network

The anthropologist Linton has observed that the last thing a dweller in the deep seas would discover is water. "He would become conscious of its existence only if some accident brought him to the surface and introduced him to air." Modern man has similarly learned the uniqueness of his own culture by discovering the cultures of others. The complex that is culture—knowledge, art, custom, law, belief—establishes the broad outline for the total pattern of life. The culture, in Sumner's words, "can make anything right and prevent condemnation of anything."

So it is that epileptics are honored in one society, scorned in another; that milk drinking is encouraged by Americans, looked upon with horror by the traditional Japanese; that sexual relations between young males and elderly females are taboo in most of the Western world, required on occasion among certain West Africans. Man's culture, within the limits of biology and the physical environment, is the most important factor that establishes definitions of good and bad, proper and improper, honored and despised.

Inside the broad boundaries of cultural definitions, there lie—as if in smaller concentric circles—other influences of action. Government itself is such a subcultural force. And there are many others, all giving cues for action, all defining what the individual can or cannot properly do, all tending to fix a person within a routine of acceptable action and expectable reaction.

This network of social force and counterforce contains a network of loyalties. Loyalties are common to all cultures. Loyalty to nation cannot be understood without understanding how other loyalties confirm or contest it. In proper perspective, the problem is one of competing subcultural allegiances.

In many cases multiple allegiances support one another. There may be, for example, direct relationships between business success and the tax policies of governments, between a flourishing church and state policies that guarantee religious liberties. In these and other cases, loyalty given to the non-national group may be expressed as national loyalty. On the other hand, conflicts between national and other loyalties arise frequently—for example, when the individual believes that national programs run contrary to the welfare of his family or his union. If forced to choose between nation and family, he may choose the latter. Family loyalty may be expressed as national disloyalty.

Non-national loyalties thus play a paradoxical role. Their very strength is the strength of national loyalty. They promote and encourage patriotism. But in conflict situations they also compete with national loyalty. Their very strength may become a threat to the nation. Non-national loyalties are simultaneously the bricks out of which democratic national loyalty is built and the brickbats with which national loyalty may be destroyed.

Individuals derive their greatest satisfactions and pay their most direct allegiances to primary groups: the groups, best exemplified by the family, whose members frequently come face to face and strongly identify themselves as a unit, whose rules of behavior are relatively informal, and whose solidarity remains high despite the existence of strong internal dissension. Members of the same primary group tend to look at fellow-members with love and affection; they share the group's joys and sorrows without asking, "What's in it for me?" Wherever we turn to pinpoint those elements in the larger culture that compel obedience, we discover the primary group.

In industry, for example, the primary group of workers is of supreme importance both for work output and for work satisfaction. Production tends to increase independently of other factors, such as opportunity for increased wages and the physical conditions of work, so long as a face-to-face work team is congenially organized and congenially supervised. The informal work group, if well organized and so inclined, cuts absenteeism and minimizes labor turnover. It can also restrict work output and frustrate management-defined production goals.

Play groups are like work groups in this respect. The Swiss psychologist, Piaget, has clearly demonstrated how the face-to-face relations within children's groups lead to the establishment of rules of conduct that in many cases are stronger than those imposed by any other source, including parents. Warm friends have been transformed into bitter enemies by the simple device of splitting one play group into two; and then foes became friends again when the two groups were reorganized into one. Among adolescents, striving for identity with the face-to-face group results in drastic alterations of demeanor and outlook on life. "If conformity to . . . [group] norms is achieved by ruthless competition and individualism, [the adolescent] does his level best to be competitive and individualistic to the limits of his capacity. If the norms of his group put a great premium on being co-operative, he does his best to be co-operative."

As with play, so with delinquency. Virtually every adolescent crime is a crime committed in a group. The delinquent is one who successfully becomes a member of a delinquent group. He meets the demand of his gang. If he is a non-delinquent in a delinquency-ridden neighborhood, he is a failure in the eyes of this primary group and frequently in his own. This has been demonstrated in studies by social scientists and is graphically stated in an autobiographical novel:

> I . . . have been, am still, a criminal. But there is a sense in which I have been an almost abjectly law-abiding person. From my very first years I adapted myself whole-heartedly to the community I lived in, accepting its values, obeying its imperatives, observing its customs. Submissiveness could go no further. If, then, law-abidingness is acting according to the dictates of the community you were born into, there never was a more law-abiding person than myself.
>
> But, unfortunately or otherwise, the community I was born into was a small one at variance with the larger community containing it. In obeying the laws of the criminal quarter I incurred the disapproval of the law courts.

Even the hardened criminal feels he belongs to a group to which he pays loyalty and which demands of him a code of honor and, in some cases, extreme sacrifice. There are few lone criminals. They work in groups. A man of character in a criminal group is defined by gang norms, and "a stigma is . . . attached to legitimate employment." To be called a "thief" is regarded as an honorific. The thief's "distress is mitigated, his isolation reduced, and his professional life made possible because he has a group of his own in which he carries on a social existence as a thief, with a culture and values held in common by many thieves."

Nor is the situation of criminals, in this respect, any different from that of businessmen. The morals of business are the morals of special groups, and they differ radically from one group to another. What is approved for dealers in junk is forbidden to dealers in bonds, and vice versa. Even within a single vocation, there are variations in acceptable standards of conduct, in each case defined by different face-to-face groups.

Perhaps the most dramatic demonstrations of the loyalty given to primary groups come from military life. An army, more than any other group, is rigidly structured; each person has his appointed place, and each is tied into a command chain that, in theory, squeezes from him the utmost of directed energy. If one were to look for niches in the society where informally organized, face-to-face groups were particularly powerless, the military would be a natural place to turn. But even in the armed services, the influence of the primary group is great.

The high morale of German troops was not to any great extent the result of convictions concerning the larger Nazi cause or the "ideological possession" of German soldiers. The real locus of Nazi military effectiveness was the face-to-face group. German soldiers surrendered more easily where this group was weak, tended to fight on without surrender where the face-to-face group was strong. Military effectiveness was great where the small group was cohesive, even when members of the group had no great conviction concerning the justness of war aims or ultimate battle success.

American infantrymen in World War II did not fight well because they were inspired by the idea of democracy, the four freedoms, or the evils of totalitarianism. Military morale and effectiveness, as with the German army, emerged from loyalties to immediate comrades, from the confrontation of common dangers by the face-to-face group, and from the mutual interdependence of men in small groups. Nor were American Air Force personnel any different from German and American foot soldiers:

> The . . . force necessary to keep the men's determination to continue in combat at a high level stems from the effects of the combat group, and is recognized as group morale. . . . It is the result . . . of the intense loyalty stimulated by the close identification with the group. The men are now fighting for each other and develop guilty feelings if they let each other down. . . . The men seem to be fighting more *for* someone than *against* somebody.

Of all primary groups, the family is the most important. The individual in a well-integrated family is responsive to that group to a far greater extent than he is to any other. The family is the first molder of the child, and the child as parent transmits this influence to succeeding generations. A persistent theme in all literature, since Abraham's concern as he prepared to sacrifice Isaac at Jehovah's command, is the theme of conflict between loyalty to family and other loyalties. Abraham's choice was the extraordinary one. In most cases loyalty to family comes first. This can be demonstrated in many ways and perhaps most dramatically by evidence from disaster situations.

In the famous Halifax disaster of 1917 the earliest community leadership was exerted by those who were visitors to the city. Those normally expected to exercise this leadership "as a rule ran first to their homes to discover if their own families were in danger." Exactly the same reaction was noted during the 1947 explosion in Texas City, Texas, and in three Oklahoma tornado towns. In almost every case where family and community presented conflicting demands, the individual obeyed the family. "Much of the initial confusion, disorder, and seemingly complete disorganization reported in the disaster communities was the result of the rush of individuals to find and rejoin their families."

Though there were some exceptions, most of those who served the community as workers and leaders did so because they were not faced with the family-community conflict. One civic hero in Texas City said he could give undivided attention to his official duties because "he knew that his family was safely out of town, visiting relatives, at the time of the explosion." And one volunteer fireman of a tornado town promptly went about the business of fire-fighting and later explained: "All the rest of the firemen had relatives that were hurt, and they stayed with them. Naturally they looked after them. *If it hadn't been that my wife was all right, this town probably would have burned up.*"

Loyalty is also given to groups in which the individual does not come face to face with other members or where face-to-face contacts are sporadic and unimportant. A person becomes related to such groups for many reasons: sometimes because he is born into membership (a Negro, an Irish American) or arrives there as a consequence of other accomplishments (a doctor, a veteran); sometimes because membership is sought as a good in itself or as a step to other desirable ends (a Fascist, a world federalist, a Rotarian). The important factor is not simple membership; it is how and to what extent identity is established between an individual and a group. When a person acts *with reference* to group demands, the group is important to his life. Membership groups become important, in other terms, when they are also reference groups. Obviously, many membership groups are not important at all for some individuals (Harvard alumnus), and others are important only sporadically (Red Cross blood donor) or for minor events (Dodger fan). Some membership-reference groups establish a complete life-way (Mormon).

Not infrequently a person feels himself a part of a reference group without achieving actual membership. Where face-to-face group membership is unsatisfactory or where several primary groups exert conflicting pressures, the individual tends to look elsewhere for his comforts. A familiar example is the young second-generation American, unhappy in lower-class surroundings and ashamed of his parents' language difficulties and food habits. He strives to identify himself with middle-class ways of life. The whole process of immigrant assimilation is an example of shifting identification away from face-to-face groups and toward reference groups. The American ideal of a "classless" society and the opportunities that exist for upward mobility encourage this kind of shift. It is truly successful when, after molding one's actions and attitudes in anticipation of acceptance by the new group, acceptance is actually achieved; when, in shorthand terms, the reference group becomes the primary group, or at least a membership group. The *nouveaux riches* may paint their walls dark green, but they do not become members of the desired primary group until they are invited to join tea tables and foursomes at the country club.

In other situations, the reference group remains potent not only despite, but for some people because, it never leads to continuous face-to-face relations. Certain professional associations control their members' activities in spite of contrary primary-group demands. A common complaint, for example, is that state and local public health officers are not "reliable" in supporting local or state programs when those programs conflict with national ones. Doctors, even when working for state or local governments, do not automatically follow the line of their face-to-face associates. Instead, they identify themselves with their professional group and adhere to standards defined by that group. And they do this despite charges of disloyalty by their immediate work companions. The loyalty of doctors to their professional group, in opposition to the demands of other groups, is also notable in other areas. The doctors' lobby against prepaid group medical plans—"socialized medicine"—and even in some places against the free distribution of polio vaccine are cases, perhaps pathological cases, in point.

Many other factors can operate to cement the identity of individual and reference group: ethnic or racial similarities, religious beliefs, sectional interests, or even more generalized values. In extreme cases the reference group to which an individual pays allegiance need not exist in actuality at all. As William James noted many years ago, the group can be strong enough to dictate action, even though it lives only in the imagination. Coming close to this definition are groups devoted to "the good of mankind," those opposed to "enemies of individualism," those seeking "the unity of all religions." Persons on the periphery of respectability or beyond the edge of practical action appeal for justification to unborn generations.

The groups to which one is loyal supply "the sort of sympathy and mutual identification for which 'we' is the natural expression." And it is in this feeling of "we"—of feeling at one with the group—that the individual finds "the chief aims of his will." Fellow-members of these groups are those who really matter. To borrow G. H. Mead's phrase, they are the "significant audiences." Their opinions are the important ones, their disdain most feared, their appreciation most sought. These groups are the sources of conscience, guilt, and shame, of duty and of pride. When groups are most effective, a member internalizes their rules: he accepts them as his own. The "we" groups are powerful because, without them, there would be no "I." Personal happiness is achieved through them. To lose identity with such a group is to lose a portion of self-identity, and this is more damaging than any other blow the individual can sustain.

All the groups, therefore, possess weapons to enforce conformity and to punish disloyalty. Or, to say the same thing in a different way, all the groups supply gratifications to their members, gratifications which, however mean, are preferred to the penalties the group can impose. In the face-to-face group, association is more intimate and more continuous than in any other situation. Gratifications are more immediate and more profound. And this group's weapons for inspiring and enforcing conformity are tremendous and terrible.

These weapons are ever present and pervasive, in contrast with the infrequent penalties of the law (you're not punished unless you're caught) or the demands of some hard-to-define and difficult-to-sense "public opinion." Within the primary group, escape from group norms or evasion of group demands is difficult: group contacts are continuous, group projects are shared, group penalties are applied immediately. The pressures and penalties may take a visible form: "sending one to Coventry" (the schoolboys' equivalent of the wife's "silent treatment"), physical coercion in some cases, expulsion from the group in the end. But it is the subtle and continuous pressures that are the most powerful ones: a word, a grimace, a shrug, a lack of cordiality, a change in voice inflection—indications imperceptible to the outsider but therefore all the more powerful to the insider. These unceasing and virtually inescapable weapons, wielded by those who mean most to the individual, make the primary group a principal locus of power over action. They result in the strongest affectionate identification between individual and group.

Yet an injunction to action found in a book is not essentially different from the same type of injunction from parent or friend. Moral precepts derived from speculation may guide conduct just as certainly as those derived from church membership. Even individuals devoted to intellectual causes; even those who place doctrine above men; even those who give their lives to causes that seem beyond practical attainment, all are acting in ways that bring satisfaction and gratification to their lives. They are, in this respect, no different from those serving immediate groups with whom they are in intimate contact. In each case, loyalty functionally serves the individual's needs, expectations, and aspirations.

So the individual gives his allegiance to many groups. He identifies himself for different purposes with different models. Guided by material interests, the quest for status and security, and other biologically and socially defined objectives, his numerous loyalties are sometimes mutually compatible, sometimes opposed. He is a father, a scientist, an industry consultant, a member of the German-speaking Union, a golf enthusiast, a Republican; he belongs to the world federalists and is a member of the Catholic church. He owes loyalty to each of these groups with which he identifies himself. And he is also a loyal American citizen.

The individual, Cooley remarked, is a point through which pass numerous arcs, each arc representing a different group membership. James was making the same point when he said that a man has as many social selves "as there are distinct groups of persons about whose opinion he cares." Difficulties arise when these groups make conflicting demands upon the same person.

Such conflicts among loyalties are very numerous. Family loyalties may conflict with professional loyalty: the scientist leaves his sick child in order to finish work in the laboratory, or a workman "scabs" on the job because of the need for wages at home and thus earns the undying enmity of his striking comrades. Church- and peer-group loyalties clash: the golf player skips Mass on Sunday morning in favor of eighteen holes on the course, or mother cooks dinner for the sodality and is cut socially by her poker-playing neighbors. Loyalties to friends become incompatible with institutional allegiances: the consulting engineer "covers up" the inefficiences of his former classmates on the job, or workers slow up productivity in the face of company demands for greater output. At a higher level the individual must meet and in some way resolve the conflict between the Christian ideal of universal brotherhood and the business ideal of universal otherhood. The list is virtually never ending. At each point that a person acts in conformity with one group, he runs the risk of penalties from another. The allegiance network, for all the comfort it provides, sometimes leads to contradiction, confusion, and pain.

4 The Strength of Democratic National Loyalty

How are conflicts between national and non-national loyalties resolved? What happens when family says yes and nation no; when church demands right and nation left; when profession decrees stand and nation orders move?

The nation, as a membership and reference group, possesses unique powers to attract and enforce allegiance and unique abilities to utilize the force of loyalties given to many other groups. We must do more than explain the reconciliation of national and other loyalties. The larger problem is to specify how loyalties to non-national groups are energized and expressed as national loyalty.

One answer is that they are not. For some men the conflicts are irreconcilable. Definite choices are made against the nation and in favor of non-national or other-national causes. For others, the alternatives are not clearly understood, and individuals aimlessly drift into national disloyalty.

For most men under most circumstances the strains that exist among loyalties are easy to tolerate. Overt conflicts may never arise: antagonisms between non-national and national loyalties may exist and not be perceived; or they may be perceived and either ignored or readily reconciled. The capacity to rationalize inconsistency is very great and very comforting to the people concerned.

These processes are aided by a giant ambiguity. It is by no means clear in a democratic state what the "nation" is to which loyalty is required. Is it the government in power? Is it the system of government? Is it the moral creed or the historic ideas on which government rests? Is it the duly elected leaders? Is it the enduring cultural complex? Is it, in the United States, the legislature or the executive; in Britain, is it the Crown? The answer is that national loyalty is all these things and more. Except in periods of crisis, individuals and groups define for themselves to which of these "nations" they owe their allegiance. And they are not loath to shift definitions with changes in time and circumstance.

It is thus possible for all manner of activity to be defined as loyal by all manner of men. A businessman hoards steel during a wartime crisis, telling himself that his business is more important to the national welfare than those businesses to which steel is allocated. He curses the stupidity of bureaucrats that makes his deception necessary and pockets his profits with a good patriotic conscience. The coal worker strikes during wartime: the freedom of labor is a democratic principle more sacred than wartime "strike-breaking" laws. Moreover he has once fought in the nation's army, and his son is now in service. Who can doubt his allegiance? The conscientious objector goes to jail rather than serve in the armed forces: the Christian ethic transcends national boundaries, and what in the long run could be more advantageous to the nation than a pacific world?

Organized groups also take advantage of the ambiguous nature of democratic patriotism. The Poles in Chicago urge condemnation of Russian aggression in Poland: whatever the risks of immediate war with the Soviet Union, America should not be the appeaser and should not cavil at affronting the godless Bolsheviks. When organizations mobilize their members in opposition to a program of government—real estate operators in opposition to rent controls, for example—they argue that their cause is in the national interest: "The free market is the American way." Even when groups seek to tear away the very roots of a system of government, they are mindful of the need to justify their action in terms of great national symbols. The British Union of Fascists insisted that new members swear to uphold "His most gracious Majesty . . . the established constitution . . . and the British Empire."

Loyalty is defined formally—that is, in law—only negatively. No constitutional provision or statute attempts to set forth what loyalty is. The legal documents define *disloyalty:* treason, espionage, sabotage, and related crimes. And these definitions tend to be narrow ones in a democracy, except when international tensions and national fears become dominant: the Smith Act of 1940 produced a definition of disloyalty that included *conspiring to "teach,* advocate, or encourage the overthrow or destruction . . . [of the government] by force or violence."

Crisis and fear similarly tighten the informal definitions of loyalty and disloyalty. Some population groups after World War II attempted to label as "disloyal" all persons belonging to organizations whose membership included Communists or ex-Communists. But under most circumstances the public view of "loyal" action is elastic. Traditions of freedom in democratic states make them so. Indeed, there is no simple public view at all; rather, there are as many views as there are separate publics to support them. Only crisis reduces the number of these publics. And the ambiguities concerning the meaning of national loyalty, in the absence of crisis, render all their definitions equally right and equally wrong.

The ambiguity makes possible another mechanism for reconciling national and other loyalties. This is the near-universal process of *legitimation,* of making other loyalties right and justified by equating them with national loyalty. Private and special interests are given the prestige of the national interest. Some persons and organizations argue that their own goals are—or should be—the nation's goals; others take up national programs as their own. In this fashion, prohibition and a high level of beer sales, Ku Klux Klan racialism and Urban League equalitarianism, high-tariff policies and the doctrine of free trade, European intervention and national isolation, are all conceived by their advocates as policies promoting the national welfare.

Diverse roles in other spheres of life are thus justified and given prestige. They are blanketed with national symbols. Not only does this allow a wide variety of actions to be considered righteously patriotic, but, at the same time, all the loyalties that accrue to non-national groups become, to the persons and groups concerned, expressions of national loyalty.

In addition, loyalties normally extend to compartments, not to the whole, of life. The role demanded by each of several loyalties is limited. Modern life is lived in discrete segments. "No tolerably normal person is totally absorbed in any group in which he participates." Loyalties are rarely exclusive.

The very segmentation of life makes it typically easy for individuals to reconcile the different kinds of action demanded of them by their various group loyalties. Indeed, the very multiplicity of roles and the apparently conflicting behavior they demand may be looked upon as the challenging and exciting aspect of one's life. A lady will keep her lover waiting until she finishes ironing her husband's shirts. A businessman will work hard to win a citation for efficient war production, including among his labors purchasing copper on the black market. In refutation of the once-popular song, men can get drunk on Saturday night and then go to church on Sunday morning.

This does not say that reconciliation of conflicting loyalties is always easy. Sometimes it is impossible, and sometimes it is possible only if one cuts loose from certain demands by dropping the groups that make them. But the difficulties, in any case, do not often center upon the demands of democratic governments.

The segment of life traditionally controlled by these governments is small. "To take a hand in the regulation of society," De Tocqueville wrote, "is the American's biggest concern, and, so to speak, [his] only pleasure." In looking at the American scene today, one can only doubt the accuracy of the French visitor's observations or marvel at the changes a century has brought. Because the contemporary fact is clear: the American round of life is played with little political concern. Barring acute international crises and presidential elections (whose mechanical four-year spacing discourages continuous political involvement), politics do not loom large in the activity or thinking of most Americans.

The waking hours of Americans are concerned with family, job, business, hobby, entertainment. Their politics are largely played within the groups organized around, and concerned with, these major life-activities. Their views in the larger political scene—state and national—are presented through the interest groups with which they are identified. These tendencies are fostered by the economic dogma which holds that society is best served by individuals pursuing their own goals. A citizen can be exclusively concerned with private affairs, and he can still assume that he fulfils his role as citizen. He may vote—though more than half of those eligible usually do not —and he may pay his taxes—though tax evasion is widespread. The center of his life and the center of his interests are rarely the nation.

The nation's demands can thus be put into a pigeonhole alongside other pigeonholes. The segmentation of life makes possible the segmentation of loyalties. Expressions of loyalty to the nation seldom conflict with the expression of other loyalties.

Democratic governments make it easy for individuals to reconcile national and non-national loyalties. At the same time, these governments have immense resources for forging direct nation-person ties.

The government, by definition, owns a monopoly of legal force. Even in the many spheres of life where force is not apparent, its very existence makes orderly society possible. The numerous groups that provide the joys of life exist because of the state's protection. Citizens come easily to believe that the state is a shield against internal foes and, more crucially, against foreign ones. They believe that family life is destroyed by fascism, that private enterprise and privacy itself disappear with communism. They believe free association and free thought are inconsistent with any type of totalitarianism. So direct loyalties are given to the nation. And so, simultaneously, loyalties given to non-national groups are linked to the nation's strength.

The state takes active steps to bring about this linkage. It has many tools for the task. They range from a Prussian monarch wielding his umbrella on the heads of the citizens of Berlin, shouting "You must love me, you must love me," through great programs of civic education, to Franklin Roosevelt, buying the support of organized labor at the expense of big business.

The Roosevelt tactic is a typical one. The state performs services of all sorts for various population groups: tariffs for businessmen, price supports for farmers, minimum wages for workers, and compensation for the unemployed; education for the young and institutional care for the sick and aged; parks and recreational facilities for vacationers and safety inspection for laborers; loans for homeowners and subsidized projects for those without homes. There are programs for the whole mass of people (price controls for consumers) and for tiny groups (technical advice for date farmers). There are great protective projects (as in food and drug inspection) and services aimed at regional groups (as in land reclamation). There are, as in the case of religious freedom, negative services performed: the government takes no action.

All these services produce national allegiance. Government programs are in almost every case the product of group agitation, and they are in every case directed at satisfying some group demand. State programs become a sale price of national loyalty. Frequently the advantage given to one group by a state program is the disadvantage of another. The very essence of democratic government is the running equilibrium of the groups advantaged and disadvantaged so that no large group of citizens or no coalition of smaller groups becomes permanently estranged.

Democratic government is party government. That parties ultimately control the government is of fundamental importance to national loyalty in democratic states. Control of the government is freely given to the groups mobilizing sustained majority public support. The members of organized groups can view government as a creature, not a master; as a prize to win, not a threat to avoid.

Moreover, the struggles for government power are through the organization and activity of parties. The distinctive party function—indeed, the basic party function—is the attempt to gain control of the government through making appeals for the support of groups around which non-national loyalties cluster. Parties out of power make promises to these groups, and parties in power institute programs to preserve and widen group support. In both cases the effect is to align national loyalties with non-national ones.

The freedom with which parties contend for the control of government keeps protest within lawful and institutional channels. It is not by accident that the British party out of power is called "Her Majesty's Loyal Opposition." This very phraseology highlights the interparty compromises and the general commitment to a common market place of political ideas and political programs. The American party in power connives with the party in opposition so that the latter will have sufficient time in Congress to criticize the former. Under such circumstances extremism is discouraged. Both parties are equally committed, and neither can completely condemn the other.

It is frequently said that party government cannot exist without a common acceptance of basic rules and basic values. This statement is true. But it is also true that the party system, and particularly the two-party system, encourages, and does not merely reflect, these basic agreements. This is only another way of saying that the party system builds national loyalty.

Services directed at groups contribute principally to the indirect nation-person tie: members of the groups concerned are conscious of the nation's contribution to their welfare, and their non-national loyalties are simultaneously expressed as national loyalty. The democratic state also forges direct links between nation and individual. These contribute to what we have called the religious quality of patriotism and, at the same time, make the transfer of allegiance from smaller groups to the nation all the more natural and all the easier.

Public education in the United States is a state and local function. Among the major activities of government, education has been least affected during the last century by insistent trends toward national financing and national supervision. One would suppose that this is the hard example, that patriotic themes here would be difficult to find. Nothing could be further from the truth. Patriotism and national service are consistently and insistently encouraged.

These themes are found not only in the daily pledge of allegiance, the singing of the "Star Spangled Banner," exercises commemorating national holidays, or history lessons extolling military heroes. The same emphasis appears in even the most simple reading texts, art exercises, and geography lessons. In the nineteenth century, authors of arithmetic books advertised the lessons of patriotism contained in the reckoning of sums. Such claims are no longer publicized, but the patriotic motif is still dominant.

The schools, Merriam concluded after an extensive comparative study of American and European practices, have to a large extent replaced the family, the church, and the army as the agency of civic education. An investigation of four hundred texts used in American schools revealed that they are "permeated with a . . . patriotic spirit." Attitudes displayed toward other nations "redound to their ignominy in contrast with the glory of America."

The effectiveness of this educational process is increased by virtue of the longer number of years now spent in classrooms. The four-year-old kindergartener is indignant that his parents do not know the identity of "Richard Sands"; and the parents remain ignorant until the school's invariable opening exercise is dutifully repeated: "I pledge allegiance to the flag of the United States and to the republic of Richard Sands." The college Senior at twenty may find his most memorable impressions in a course concerned with great issues of American history, if not on ROTC maneuvers. All ages in between are subject to similar experiences. They are leavened only slightly and for relatively few individuals, by undergraduate skepticism or by left-wing, pacifist, and internationalist movements.

The total impact of the schools is designed certainly, if unwittingly, to conform to Rousseau's dictum: that education should direct the opinion and tastes of men so that they will be "patriots by inclination, by passion, by necessity."

Similar effects could be traced for government information programs, encouragement of patriotic demonstrations on national holidays, and other activities. The end result is plain. From the individual's very earliest years he is identified with the nation. The nation protects him from both foreign foe and domestic harm; it is his parents writ large. It binds all its citizens together in a great and powerful family. Whatever its shortcomings, it is good in itself, and it makes possible the good things in life.

The government's task of weaving and reweaving the two strands of national loyalty—direct and indirect—is facilitated by the binding qualities of national values and the national symbol system, as well as by modern technology. The very historical tendencies that produced nation-states have also tended to produce national ideologies, common ways of observation and valuation that have a remarkably sustained vitality. The American's regard for material success and the American's penchant for looking down on—rather than up to—political leaders are commonplace examples. This sharing of viewpoints is both a cause and a result of the national symbol system.

A nation's flag, objectively, may be no more than a piece of cloth, designed asymmetrically and colored in doubtful taste. To most citizens it is a thing of beauty. And its symbolic quality—its representation of the good and greatness of the nation—moves poets to tears and soldiers to feats of heroism. Napoleon said: "Give me a button and I will make men die for it." Flag, seal, song, drawing of Uncle Sam, silhouette of hammer and sickle—these are the obvious national symbols. Their efficacy in evoking a nationalistic spirit cannot be doubted, even though some claims made for their effectiveness are certainly fictitious.

The most effective symbol systems promoting national loyalty are probably the least apparent ones. The ceremonial calendar of the United States performs this function; the ceremonies are symbols which function "to draw all people together to emphasize their similarities and common heritage, to minimize their differences, and to contribute to their thinking, feeling, and acting alike." The rituals of Memorial Day, for example, are a symbol system that integrates the entire community by emphasizing the sacredness of those who died for the nation and by expressing the common faith in the nation's strength. The ceremony builds national solidarity because it relates the reverence for the dead of each individual—members of separate churches, regional groups, ethnic organizations—to the cause of the nation and its greatness. The sacrifice of each was for the whole country.

Memorial Day ceremonies, described by W. Lloyd Warner, start with different groups, each separated in space and time and each paying homage principally to its own dead. But the ceremony becomes a common one—in time, place, and content—when the residents of the town gather for common prayer and to hear a speaker urge "better and greater devotion to our country and to all that our flag represents."

Here we see people who are Protestant, Catholic, Jewish, and Greek Orthodox involved in a common ritual in a graveyard with their common dead. Their sense of separateness was present and expressed in the different ceremonies, but the parade and the unity gained by doing everything at one time emphasized the oneness of the total group. Each ritual also stressed the fact that the war was an experience where everyone sacrificed and some died, not as members of a separate group, but as citizens of a whole community.

The symbolic calendar is a long one. Its unifying effects are supplemented by less sacred, common events, such as motion pictures, and less formalized processes, such as reading the daily newspapers. All these events and processes combine to bridge differences, to supply common vocabularies, to give mutuality to lives lived in compartments. The technical virtuosity of an industrialized age—a possible audience of seventy-five million people watching a presidential inauguration on television—gives strength to this process. It is a potent factor in bridging the schisms created by non-national loyalties and in tying those loyalties to the nation. The symbol system makes it natural for an individual to believe that General Motors' wealth is his wealth, that the strength of American business is his strength, that the power of the American press is his power. By such a process, "the least among the citizens . . . can instantly tower . . . into a very big and great and happy personage."

The inclusiveness of the national framework is apparent to the people. They live their lives within the nation. Economic activities are made possible by a common national currency; cultural life is fostered by a common language and hedged by common definitions of style. Resignation or expulsion from the nation is difficult. Resignation at the least involves emigration and the disruption of a complete pattern of life; it also involves the acceptance of some new national scheme of things. Expulsion is effectively carried out only by the prison terms or death sentences handed out to those convicted of overt disloyalty. In days past, traditions of sanctuary for political refugees made both resignation and expulsion relatively easy. Today, political dissenters find foreign havens only when they serve the ends of the host nation. (The exceptions, as in Switzerland, are relatively unimportant.) The world is otherwise too small to give them refuge.

At other periods in history the church competed with the nation as the most inclusive group with which persons identified themselves. Calvinists of the seventeenth century legitimated their business roles in terms of salvation, not nation. But this is no longer the case. Though church identifications for some population groups are still strong, churches in most parts of the world and at most times are effective, even if sometimes reluctant, handmaidens of national policies.

The greatest challenge to the democratic nation for the individual's largest group identification comes, of course, from international communism. In some parts of the Western world the challenge is an important one. Yet it is notable that Communist parties always claim that their values are the nation's values. This is true of American Communists. The party is no challenge to the "Frenchness" of Frenchmen, and strong nationalist views are held by Italian party members. Even where the party controls, it has worked to strengthen national allegiance—thus the nationalism of Tito's Communist Yugoslavia; thus, paradoxically, the fervent patriotism of the Soviet Union. Lenin himself was wroth to note that "scratch a Communist and you will find a Great Russian Chauvinist." Despite internationalist dogma, the course of Soviet history is a development of ever increasing nationalism.

Even the strength of the Communist appeal cannot compete

with the great service programs of government, the development through time of national values, the binding effects of national symbol systems, and the consequences of populations sharing in common the good things in life. These factors elevate the nation-state as the largest group with which most people identify themselves. This is the way the world is presently organized, and, unless new organizational forms are evolved, one must perforce fit all other allegiances into the national scheme of things.

The non-national groups, small and large, play a crucial, independent role in the transference of allegiance to the nation. For one thing, they are the means through which citizens are brought to participate in civic affairs and national ceremony. If the state did not have their resources for mobilization, little could be accomplished. Press announcements do not produce social action.

The organization of a war-bond drive illustrates the point. A Treasury Department office sets goals and concerts efforts. But the advertisements are designed and paid for by an advertising or magazine owners' association, and the radio programs are sponsored and produced by the association of broadcasters. Direct appeals to purchasers are made through divisions organized by industry, by workplace, by neighborhood group, by church organization, by fraternal bodies, by school competition, by union locals. The crucial face-to-face solicitation is within very small groups, in which worker talks to worker, clubwoman to clubwoman, friend to friend. The national government's program is implemented only because of the concerted effort of the whole society. The organizations within the society have brought their power to bear so that virtually all citizens participate in patriotic endeavor.

The nation at times calls directly upon its citizens and enforces its demands with legal penalties for non-compliance. Even here, the power of the primary and secondary groups is controlling. Kriesberg has shown that the responses of businessmen to government price policies for metals resulted not from government demands and penalties but from the business groups themselves. Government action was in some measure important in establishing a given group's policy, but the crucial enforcement was by the groups themselves. And different groups within the same industry established different policies, to which their members adhered.

Similarly, the government defines draft-dodging as a penal offense, and this stigma has great importance in determining the attitude of primary and secondary groups. But it is the opinion of family and friends that largely influences action. The important rewards and punishments are exercised in the face-to-face situation, by those whose opinions are crucial to the individual's inward ease and largely control his career as neighbor, friend, spouse, and worker.

In theory, at least, the chain is an endless one. For if the dictates of government are enforced by the sanctions of the smaller groups, the smaller groups in turn establish the governmental policies they enforce. This is one hallmark of democracy: populations effectuating the policies they determine. Where population groups believe—or understand—this dual role, their patriotic performance is all the stronger.

The individual need only feel what is easy for him: first, that he is directly identified with the nation's cause and, second, that a strong link exists between national benevolence and private joys. Yet the larger point is that citizens will perform patriotic duties even in the absence of any direct identification with the nation. As with American soldiers in World War II, they may be literally incapable of explaining their action in terms of the national welfare or of their own contribution to the national cause. Their patriotic services are no less effective.

Immigrant groups in the United States, for example, are frequently shaped into distinct and separate communities. They can easily, under most circumstances, claim a dual national loyalty: to their country of origin as well as to the United States. But the group's primary interest is its own preservation:

> The Pole in this country sincerely claims to be equally loyal to America and to Poland—and he certainly is, because both loyalties are really only indirect. In fact, if not in theory, his ultimate and fundamental allegiance is to the Polish-American society, and both Poland and America are appreciated rather as the natural and necessary allies of this national group to whom the latter as a whole owes gratitude for its culture [and] for its economic and political security.

The immigrant community tends to lose significance with the second and third generations; and dual allegiance becomes a sore trial when the old nation becomes the new nation's enemy. For large numbers of immigrant Americans, however, it is plain that loyalty to the immigrant group is what makes for loyalty to the nation.

The mechanism is by no means limited to immigrants. A college student from the West Virginia coal fields asserted in 1940 that "I'll slash with my fingernails the throat of any man who tries to get me into a uniform." Yet he subsequently fought with distinction as an officer in the Army Air Corps. His valor was no consequence of changing views concerning the effectiveness of war as national policy, the evil of Germans, or the just cause of the United States. Rather, his college friends and fellow-workers all served in the armed forces; his fiancée was involved in Red Cross work; his father served on the local draft board. All the several worlds in which he lived were geared for war. All expected the same of him. Without some group to support his own opposition, he had no alternative available. He had to fight to live, and the immediate threat to his living came not from the nation's enemies but from his friends, colleagues, and family. Once in service, loyalty to immediate comrades, the need for self-preservation, and the satisfactions of doing the job well were sufficient to insure his fidelity.

Individuals, in short, act for the nation in response to the smaller groups with which they identify themselves. The larger group, the nation, need only establish the goal. The citizen may or may not participate in this goal definition, may or may not agree with it. Except in rare cases, he will nevertheless supply the force through which its achievement is attempted. His loyalty to smaller groups insures his doing it. These groups stand or fall with the nation. They perforce must support its causes, especially when, as during war, the very existence of the nation is at stake. So it is that mothers tearfully send their unwilling sons to war. So it is that loyalties to smaller groups supply the guts of national endeavor, even when that endeavor has no meaning to the individual concerned.

We have accounted for the great number and variety of non-national loyalties and explained how these non-national loyalties become activated as national loyalty. Democratic nations could not exist if this reinforcement were not possible. If any single lesser loyalty were completely exclusive, there would be none left over for the nation.

The economy of allegiance is similar to Freud's economy of the libido. Just as children compete for the love of parents, so groups and organizations—including the nation—compete for the allegiance of citizens. Just as Freud saw conflict resulting from simultaneous love-demands of family and community, so it is that conflicts may exist as the nation and non-national groups compete for the individual's loyalty. And just as Freud saw that culture could not exist if some love were not diverted from family to community, so it is that the nation could not exist if the allegiance demands of non-national groups did not leave some loyalty for the nation.

Loyalty is akin to love. But there is no fixed quantum of either. Lavishing allegiance on non-national groups does not necessarily decrease allegiance to the nation. As the preceding discussion has made clear, the allegiances may be reinforcing. And this multistrand allegiance leads to the strongest national loyalty.

Military discipline is weak, Hans Speier has written, where there exist "strong family ties and strong religious beliefs in the sinfulness of killing." Here we see group directives at odds with one another. But military morale is highest where military orders are also religious orders, as in Cromwell's army, or where family influence is minimized through adherence to celibacy or homosexualism, as in the armies of ancient Greece. Here group directives are reinforcing.

So with national loyalties. An individual in all his various roles—as father, businessman, Democrat, deer hunter, church member, Irish American, and United States citizen—can find all these roles in parallel. He relates the whole structure of his satisfactory existence to the benevolence of the state. His national loyalty is many-faceted, multiple-compounded, and stoutly secure.

Such a model of the perfect patriot seldom exists in reality. The demands of all roles seldom run consistently in the same direction, and some individuals feel no direct allegiance to nation at all. Nevertheless, this is the drift of things, and it is this relationship between non-national loyalties and the nation which produces strong allegiances to democratic nations among most people most of the time.

5 One Life, One Loyalty: The Totalitarian Manipulation of Life

The essential difference between democratic and totalitarian national loyalty is this: the major ties of national loyalty in a democracy are indirect; in a dictatorship the most important tie is direct. Loyalty to nation in democracies is built upon the non-national loyalties to family and other primary groups, to church and other reference groups. Loyalty to nation under totalitarianism is forged directly between individual and state, between the led and the leader. In democracies the direct strand of loyalty exists, but, except in crisis, it is relatively unimportant. In dictatorships, crisis is endemic, and non-national loyalties are regarded as a danger to the nation; if these loyalties cannot be controlled, the state makes every effort to smash them.

States labeled "totalitarian" are not all alike. The extent and severity of government controls differ markedly from one totalitarian nation to another, and different groups within the same dictatorship are differently affected by the state. The Jew in Berlin in 1936 had little in common with a Bavarian farmer on an isolated hillside; and neither of them faced the same problems now faced by a Ukrainian student in a Moscow university. Some totalitarianisms are less total than others. Some groups escape the impact of even the most total. These differences are important. But they do not efface the essential similarities of the totalitarian way of government.

"Fascism," Mussolini said, "takes a man from his family at six, and gives him back to it at sixty." This epitomizes the totalitarian view. Its essence, the first principle of totalitarian organization of society, is to destroy—or to incorporate within the state or state-party—all independent social organization. The goal is clear, though it is never completely achieved: to replace free pluralistic loyalties by a "monistic, total, authoritarian organization."

Leaders of totalitarian states have uniformly recognized that free identification with non-national groups can weaken national loyalty. They have uniformly been unwilling to risk this prospect. Their programs, however glossed in terms of racial strength, national glory, or classless brotherhood, have been designed to make strong the direct tie between individual and state, to obliterate every social relationship not controlled by the state.

It is not true, as some have claimed, that this is a strategy of the "atomization of the individual." The totalitarian leaders know the power of group life and group activity. They do not approach individuals as isolated persons. Hitler consciously manipulated individuals as members of groups. He knew that "a man without group ties is like a crab without its shell." His principal technique of social action was to disorganize and disrupt the groups—family and church, fraternity and union, soccer team and officer corps—from which people gained stability and satisfaction for their lives. At the same time that the shell of these protecting smaller groups was cracked, the disorganized individuals were offered direct, gratifying ties with the state.

This is the course of action in all totalitarian states. Every effort is made to blast the individual from his non-national identifications. Then he is offered the single identification with the state. He is not atomized, not robbed of group identification. He is synthesized, forced into a single group, which is the nation.

To this end, the state brings to bear the whole terrible arsenal of modern means for social control and individual intimidation. This is more than simply the use of propaganda, the systematic terrorization of individuals, and the build-up of the leader. The state attempts completely to control the entire society, to shape all social intercourse so that there can remain only the single strong tie to the nation. If other group ties exist, they must serve the state, or they must exist in secret.

The totalitarian government's fear of strong family ties has been recorded in the modern utopias. In *Brave New World* children were produced in mechanical assembly lines, and unrestricted promiscuity combined with efficient contraceptives was substituted for love relationships. In *Nineteen Eighty-four*, the important workers of Oceana were taught to abhor sex, intercourse being regarded as "a slightly disgusting minor operation, like having an enema." The important reason has already been suggested: "to prevent men and women from forming loyalties which [the party] might not be able to control."

The Nazis, in official propaganda, honored the family as an

institution of first importance in a social system based upon the "blood" principle. In fact, however, the Nazis "suspected and attacked the family as a shelter against mass society. They looked on it as a virtual conspiracy against the totalitarian state." Where the Nazi party was strongest and busiest, it attempted to destroy the family as a self-functioning social unit.

The state and party apparatus reached directly into the home. Children were trained to put the precepts of the state before those of parents. Even if children did not inform the authorities against their parents, as they were frequently instructed to do, parental control was sorely compromised. Parents feared that their injunctions would be interpreted as being contrary to state dogma. The children came to know that their parents lacked authority, and this knowledge was a further invitation to enlist in state-controlled programs.

The Nazi state approved—indeed, encouraged—extramarital childbearing. The organization of Nazi youth, with "its feasts, its farm years, and hayloft nights," maximized the opportunities for children without families. Party approval efficiently smothered parental disapproval. And the Nazi courts gave more or less full legal sanction.

The attributes that make the family the strongest primary group—and the recipient of strongest loyalties—were sorely weakened. By its voracious timetable of activities, the state denied family members their traditional periods of lengthy face-to-face contact. By its use of family members as informers against one another, the state undermined the intimate informal rules and moral precepts that are characteristic of successful primary groups. By replacing the family as the formulator of life-rules, the state robbed it of an essential social function. "What is the ideal German family?" a story current in Nazi Germany asked. "It's a family in which the father is a member of the party, the mother a member of the Association of Nazi Women, the daughter belongs to the Association of German Girls, and the son is in the Hitler Youth—they meet once a year at the Nazi Congress in Nürnberg."

What the Nazis aimed to accomplish with the German family is a model for what dictatorships attempt to do for all social organization. The history of labor unions in the U.S.S.R. is a similar history of the destruction of group autonomy and the twisting of group functions for state purposes.

Immediately after the revolution, Soviet workers attempted to control industrial production directly through their local organizations and various hierarchies of workers' groups. The attempt was demonstrated a failure within a year after the revolution began. From the chaos that followed, a triangular direction of industrial affairs emerged, reaching a highly developed stage in the late 1920's. Workers' committees shared control with political representatives of the Communist party and with industrial experts appointed as plant managers. During this period the unions still possessed very real power. Lenin himself stated that they had an "absolute duty to defend the interests of the workers," and they were active in raising living standards, correcting inequities in pay, and criticizing management.

In 1929, however, the trade-unions were broken when virtually every prominent labor leader, including the entire leadership of the Central Trade Union Council, was purged. Since then any tendency of labor leaders to take steps for the special interest of workers is repudiated as "opportunist" or "trade-unionist." Union committees cannot, under an injunction of the party Central Committee, "intervene directly in the running of the plant or endeavor in any way to replace plant management."

Subsequently, the unions' task has been defined as that of increasing production and improving labor discipline. The latter end was implemented in 1930 by a system which evicted workers from "living space" if they gave up their jobs without cause or if they were dismissed for a breach of discipline. Subsequent decrees have made the possession of a labor book mandatory, thus rendering impossible any free movement from job to job. Those who now work within the system are faced with the exploitation inherent in piecework competition; those who do not, have the alternative of forced labor.

Unions have no authority in hiring, no influence in the fixing of wages, no voice in controlling conditions of work. Union contracts have not been written in the Soviet Union since 1935. The piecework rates of compensation, which characterize the system, are fixed within limits established by larger plans on the initiative of plant managers and party representatives.

Various union committees still retain the privilege of making suggestions and offering criticism. Under close supervision from above, the unions also perform a number of welfare functions. But their prime responsibility and the principal focus of their activity are in the maintenance and improvement of production standards. Even here they are subordinate to Stakhanovites, shock brigades, foremen, and industrial technicians. Having lost power to plant managers and party, the unions have no semblance of authority. They are, quite simply, agencies of the state for furthering state objectives. They have no independence outside those objectives and very little within them.

The political is but a segment—most frequently a minor segment—of democratic life. This leaves for the democratic citizen very wide areas of action without political reference. Few of his actions, however good or evil they may be, can be clearly labeled as either loyal or disloyal. Even political acts fall into a twilight zone, where their effect upon the ambiguous "nation" is a matter of public controversy.

The totalitarian contrast is sharp. All actions of all people may have political content. Soviet youth are told that "all . . . life must be subordinated to the great aim—the struggle for Communism"; that "it is completely correct to say that personal existence is politics"; and that it is "profoundly incorrect and pernicious" to believe that an individual can live his personal life as his own concern. Treason in Russia, as it was in Nazi Germany, is found in slack work habits or disapproved sexual behavior; in listening to prohibited radio programs or in idle gossip; in unacceptable statistics or undesirable jokes. When every action is state-controlled, all action contrary to the dictates of the controllers becomes treasonable.

This accounts for another contrast between democratic and totalitarian national loyalty. In democratic states it is easy to maintain loyalty because the meaning of national loyalty is ambiguous. But the ambiguities are drastically reduced with totalitarianism. There is no way by which individuals can openly justify action contrary to the government by appealing to the national cultural complex, national ideals, or the sacred fatherland. The rulers make full use of these concepts in their effort to promote patriotic endeavor; and many individuals and groups are able to serve a hated leader by convincing themselves that they really serve the fatherland. But no opposition can be based upon unapproved definitions of the nation. If individuals or groups distinguish the nation demanding loyalty from the totalitarian government in power, the distinctions cannot be made public. Those who make them are traitors.

The importance of terror as a weapon for enforcing obedience in totalitarian states can be easily overestimated. Under most circumstances for most individuals it is not needed. The satisfactions offered by the regime are in themselves sufficient to insure allegiance. If a regime rested exclusively upon terror, it would not last very long.

Like garlic in a salad, a little terror goes a long way, and therefore it is also easy to underestimate its importance. It is certainly a foundation stone for all totalitarian governments. At least, no such government is willing to risk testing its chances of existence without benefit of violence.

Violence, above all, is the ready tool of the totalitarian rulers for effacing opposition. Here it works most crudely and least effectively. Converts are not made by killing them.

But the example of those liquidated has a powerful secondary effect. It deters deviation. Those who find it difficult to square their consciences with the activities of the regime comfort themselves with the thought that conformity is a desirable alternative to torture and death. Even the prison-like controls of totalitarian government are preferable to the horrors of an actual prison or labor camp. Violence in the hands of the governors silences those who otherwise might dissent and simultaneously provides them with solace for their silence.

There is a further multiplier effect. The threat of violence quickly mobilizes the powerful, non-violent social sanctions, quickly endangers the joys of life provided by friends and colleagues. He whose actions are an invitation to the secret police finds few to share his vodka.

Winston Smith, in Orwell's *Nineteen Eighty-four*, had inherited from childhood one great terror: rats. He was brought to complete capitulation only when faced with a cage of them, fixed in such a way that they might escape their cage by eating through his face.

By itself pain is not always enough [his tormentor explained]. There are occasions when a human being will stand out against pain, even to the point of death. But for everyone there is something unendurable—something that cannot be contemplated. Courage and cowardice are not involved. If you are falling from a height it is not cowardly to clutch at a rope. If you have come up from deep water it is not cowardly to fill your lungs with air. . . . It is the same with the rats. For you, they are unendurable. They are a form of pressure that you cannot withstand, even if you wished to. You will do what is required of you.

Every man has his own rats. It may be doubted that the totalitarian rulers have the subtlety and prescience, the *savoir faire* in violence, attributed to them by creators of horrible utopias. But they have been aided immeasurably by psychological tools of refinement and efficiency. "Brain washing," based upon utter fatigue, and the use of family members as hostages are usually effective against even the most resolute. Like other aspects of violence, their greatest utility is in their threat; they dry up the sap of dissatisfaction before it can begin to swell.

Violence attracts as well as repels. The ruthless are admired as well as hated by the cowed. And those who control the violence are cemented to their own controllers by the strongest ties. These are a very small fraction of the entire population, but a fraction whose existence colors the entire process of government. Their defection is unthinkable because they have no point of escape. They face only the revenge of their former victims or the bite of their own tools in the hands of former colleagues. Their loyalty is the utter loyalty of the damned.

Caprice gives totalitarian violence its greatest effectiveness. The bulk of the population, willing to follow where led, sees only that the old legal institutions still operate. But a new kind of law enforcement also appears. "The task of the totalitarian police is not to discover crimes, but to be on hand when the government decides to arrest a certain category of the population." When this happens, orderly processes of law disappear. No predictions concerning the gravity of given offenses can be made. The offenses themselves are not definable, the "potential enemy" and the "possible crime" providing adequate cause for repression. Special courts are established for different cases and different people. A judge's decision is based upon neither statute nor precedent. Punishment without law becomes common.

So violence is established in a way that confounds all Western concepts of orderly institutions. In democracies, violence is a punishment for a limited number of defined, serious, social derelictions, the end result in an orderly process of law. For dictatorships violence is a tool for terror. It is all the more terrible because it is established within no system of orderly law and confined by no orderly process for redress or appeal. This, as much as anything else, distinguishes the totalitarian from the democratic state.

The habit of the democratic citizen—doing what he likes, avoiding only the illegal—is too expensive a habit for the totalitarian citizen. The latter tends to do only what he is told or, at least, to do only what is known to be legal and approved. Even more, justice is not expected. One hopes not for justice but for luck and for mercy. It becomes an asset to possess sensitivity to the latest currents of what is officially desirable. When disobedience is drastically punished and when rules change sometimes without official announcement, the people must search for those rules. They search to conform.

Capricious violence produces few people who love the state in addition to obeying it. Yet the totalitarian states uniformly consider loyalty-as-attitude less important than loyalty-as-action. Their aim is to insure reliable behavior. Attitude is important only if free choices are available. And it is a first point of totalitarian policy—by regulating the tempo of life, by controlling the means of livelihood, by granting rewards and imposing punishment, by the caprice of violence—to make free choices impossible. Violence, above all, compels obedience. This is essential to political action. And there is only a shadowy line dividing obedience built upon fear of violence and obedience built upon a true personal identification with the state.

The manipulation of life is by no means a life of complete terror. The state attempts to fill the gap left by the relative destruction of voluntary groups and the relative disappearance of privacy. It does this and masks its terror by filling the life of its citizens with state-controlled activity. And it enjoys a considerable measure of success, as an extreme example, concerning a child of Lidice, illustrates.

Lidice was the Czechoslovakian village which the Nazis utterly destroyed in 1942. All adult males of the village were shot, the village itself plowed into the earth, and most of the women and children sent to concentration camps, in which they eventually met death. A few of the children, however, were declared to be "Germanizable," after crude measurements were made of their height, body structure, and eye and hair color.

Marie, aged nine, was in this manner declared to be capable of becoming a member of the master-race. She was first processed through a German Race and Settlement Office in Poland and then sent to a Polish home school. At the school she was given a few lessons in German, prohibited from speaking any other language, and beaten whenever she lapsed into Czech. She was taught German history and German songs.

Marie was subsequently sent to a German home—that of the Schillers—in Posen. She was given a new German name, and she soon decided that it was more suitable than her real one. Herr Schiller told his wife that the party had "ordered us to make a German woman out of her, and we are going to do it." Frau Schiller told Marie that "if I ever hear the word

'Lidice' in my house, I will beat you half dead." And as time went on, Marie became accustomed to her new home and called Herr and Frau Schiller "Father" and "Mother." She told Nazi visitors to the Schiller house that she liked the Reich.

When liberated in 1945, Marie was a German. In the three years since her father had been shot and her mother sent to a concentration camp, the German state had profoundly changed her personality. Her aunt came to get her in Berlin after the war. The aunt later said:

"Here I come all the way to Berlin to get my niece, happy that at least one of the children in our family had been saved, and what do I find? A German girl! You should have seen her hair. She wore it long, like those Hitlermädchen, and she wouldn't talk Czech to me. Said she didn't understand. Mind you, she wouldn't even come with me. She hung on to that Schiller woman and cried, 'Mutti, Mutti, I don't want to leave you!' . . . One more year and that girl would have been a real Nazi!

"She didn't want to listen to me. When it was time to leave, she started to whisper with that Schiller woman. Later she confessed to me that she had promised her she would come back to Berlin as soon as she could. . . . I bought her some decent clothes and took her to a hairdresser to have that silly long German-style hair cut off. Somehow it got around that Marie was a Lidice child. A crowd began to collect in front of the hairdresser's. . . . They looked at her as if she were a saint, and an old man wanted to kiss her hands, and there she sat, shouting—in German—that she didn't want to have her hair cut, *nein, nein, nein!* You should have seen the stunned faces of the people! . . . The old man who had wanted to kiss Marie's hands got mad and said they should send her back to Germany, where she belonged, but a woman took his arm and said, 'Don't you understand, Jan? This child isn't guilty. It's the Germans who are guilty. Not only did they take our children away from us but they even tried to change them inside so they would never be ours even if we ever found them.' "

Marie's experience represents with a vengeance the ability of the totalitarian state to destroy and to rebuild human lives. She was set loose in the world. Her original human and physical contacts completely disappeared. It was therefore easy to mold her to the state's desire, all the easier because of her youth and because of the availability of a new family and new friendship groups to capture her love and to direct her energies according to the state's dictation.

Totalitarian leaders enjoyed advantages over Marie that they are unable to duplicate for others. Marie nevertheless represents the totalitarian ideal: the destruction of all human activity not controlled by the state and the construction of a new life in the state service under state direction.

6 Attractions of Totalitarian Loyalty

One road to disloyalty is through alienation: the loss of understanding of what life is about, the decline of joyful personal contacts, the reduction of persons to the point where they seem to become pawns rather than personalities. Industrialization and the concentration of people in large cities are forces that encourage alienation for some population groups and, in the process, erode traditional loyalties.

But disloyalty to one cause and loyalty to another are two views of a single act. The alienation that disrupts old loyalties can be seen as a step toward building new ones. And the policy of totalitarian states is precisely the policy of *controlled alienation* as a means of achieving strong national loyalty. This is the policy that seeks to destroy the joys and privileges of independent families, friendship groups, churches, and professional organizations—depriving people of the standards, goals, and satisfactions most highly prized in democratic societies. It is a policy of putting steam behind the cultural drift that threatens alienation to many groups in an industrialized culture.

But the totalitarian states have a cure for the social disease they induce. This is the cure of state direction and state control. Voluntary groups do not disappear; rather, their energies are absorbed and controlled by the state. The individual neurotic takes pleasure in his discomfort; the totalitarian state attempts to create satisfactions for its masses manipulated into alienation.

Those whose lives in voluntary groups give them security, status, and a sense of well-being need no love for a ruler to sustain national loyalty. But, once individuals are blasted from their smaller groups, they are ready to seize other means of achieving sense and stability for their lives. Dictators offer themselves, and there are joys in follow-the-leader.

Populations must be ripe before leaders of mass national groups can be effective. The leader cannot manufacture the necessary social conditions for mass frustrations, though he certainly can make individuals more sensitive to their unhappy state and to happy alternatives under his guidance. This has been one role of mass leaders—religious, military, and national—throughout history. Once in command, the modern dictators have demonstrated that policies of controlled alienation can give added strength to the very forces that originally made possible their rise to power.

Thus some population groups "escape from freedom" happily. The leader, as Hitler himself pointed out, can "burn into the little man's soul the proud conviction that, though a little worm, he is nevertheless part of a great dragon." Once constructed, the bond between leader and led is strong and difficult to break. After all other bases for allegiance to Nazi

Germany were swept away, many German citizens maintained an intense personal devotion to Hitler. This was one of the important factors in prolonging German army resistance. Even in defeated postwar Germany, large numbers still preserve a great love for Hitler, believing that the excesses and faults of his regime were committed by false or inept subordinates, in some cases against the Führer's own orders.

The use of intermediate leaders as targets for criticism is institutionalized in the Soviet Union. Primary loyalty to such leaders is officially intolerable. This is partially the result—and partially the cause—of endowing the supreme leader with godlike qualities. Stalin, like Lenin before him, was presented as a person of superhuman stature. He was a scientific genius, a person of unlimited love, and a man of implacable will. In this way, all dictators are made to serve as the primary focus of popular loyalty. The dictatorships here again take on the characteristics of a militant religious sect. The savior is identified, and religious ritual and enthusiasms glorify him.

Out of love for the leader and the enthusiasm of the elect, there emerges the dogma which, as we have seen, reduces the sphere of private action and gives a political cast to more and more of life. Thus there is a Communist biology, a Communist statistics, a Communist literature, and a Communist music. Furthermore, totalitarian leaders do not believe that politics is a matter of trial and error; rather, there is only one truth. This is political messianism: "It postulates a preordained, harmonious and perfect scheme of things." True believers in the system, like religious fanatics, are more dangerous than sinners: they are bothered by no guilty consciences. They can regard their opponents neither as innocent fools nor as honest but wrongheaded gentlemen. Rather, all who oppose are heretics. And heretics cannot simply be defeated; they must be exterminated. Compromise is dangerous to the regime and no favor to those who cannot see the truth. Bellarmine remarked that it is good for the heretics to be killed, since the longer they live, the more damnation they acquire.

To those impoverished of life's joys, there is great comfort in giving up the individual struggle and in following leaders who promise a glorious future. To embrace a leader and his cause is one way to give meaning to an empty life. To be free of decision-making is to be free of care. Life is good because life is active. Life is meaningful because ends are determined and are defined as desirable and necessary. Life is happy because one derives joy from service. Life is full because the state leaves no moment undirected.

There is no sense of sacrifice in giving up freedom when freedom means only emptiness or bewilderment or sore worry. There is no humiliation for those serving great causes. There is no failure to find a role in life for those enlisted in the state's service.

Whatever frustrations are encountered as the result of control from above may be discharged against those below. The hierarchy of statism guarantees this for almost all classes, the roles of ruler and ruled being shifted on many occasions. Those in the lowly occupations of janitor and trash-collector, for example, may play leading political roles as informers. Even those consistently at the bottom of the scale are strengthened because of their identification with the state. "Man in Fascism," Mussolini wrote, "is individual, nation, and country all at once. . . . Fascism affirms the state as the true reality of the individual."

Hostilities, nevertheless, still proliferate, and these are drained off against the nation's ever threatening enemies. Where such enemies do not exist, they are manufactured. They can usually be easily identified, as in the Soviet emphasis on the ever present threat of the "rotten Western bourgeois democracies." Where identification is more difficult, the enemies can be tagged, as when the Nazis put yellow arm bands on the Jews.

These near-clinical terms obscure the real joys and privileges of the loyal totalitarian citizen. His is the full life. Sir John Maynard put his sensitive finger close to the crux of the matter. The state provides a joyous "release of energy" in the service of a great cause:

> The Russian worker is freer than the British from anxiety, because of the absence of unemployment. He stands higher in the comparative scale of human values. . . . He has no cause (other than personal indolence) for restricting output, and has a feeling (which the British worker lacks) that he is working for himself. His wife works hard, but is economically freer, and is largely emancipated from household drudgery. He lives in an obviously advancing and improving world, which breeds hope.

These words were written more than ten years ago. Whatever may have been the truth of the matter at that time or changes in the objective situation since, there is no doubt that this is what very large numbers of Soviet citizens believe. They are enlisted in a great enterprise. As official Soviet philosophy and psychology strive to demonstrate, it is an enterprise in which private and social goals become one. As long as individuals give up large areas of free choice, they have many opportunities for a satisfactory life. It is a life hateful to those who prize democratic freedoms but no less happy for those involved.

Many citizens of the totalitarian state do not give up anything. Life for them becomes better, not worse. For residents of a small German town who were members of the party, the Third Reich, until the war, was a place of joy:

> The lives of my nine [ex-Nazi] friends—and even of the tenth, the teacher—were lightened and brightened by National Socialism

as they knew it. And they look back at it now—nine of them, certainly—as the best time of their lives; for what are men's lives? There were jobs and job security, summer camps for the children and the Hitler Jugend to keep them off the streets. . . . So things went better at home, and when things go better at home, and on the job, what more does a husband and father want to know?

In the experience of members and sympathizers, the party watched over their entire lives, "not spying on them, but caring about them." Whether one was unemployed or sick or penniless, the party was always ready to help. "No one in Germany was alone in his troubles."

The horrors of the regime, if known, were the responsibility and worry of others. The strict laws that controlled large areas of activities were not felt to be binding. In fact, many of these laws did not touch their lives at all. "It is dangerous, in Nazi Germany, to go to Communist meetings or read the *Manchester Guardian,* but who wants to go to Communist meetings or read the *Manchester Guardian?*" Anti-Nazis, the Nazis admitted, were unhappy under naziism; but Nazis, at least plain "little" members of the party, had a great deal to be happy about.

Every social upheaval creates career opportunities. When the old social fabric is destroyed, there follows a wholesale shuffling of leaders and led. The poor are risen, the mighty trodden into the dust. Revolutions leading to the modern totalitarian states have produced this characteristic change of elites. The actual change of government may be accomplished by relatively few, but in the wake of those few, millions have seized the opportunity to achieve power, status, and income. They have pledged their loyalty in return.

Three factors have made this process easy and widespread. For one thing, no qualms of conscience are suffered by the individuals who find advantage in serving the new regime.

They do what they do by direction and with the approval of those above; and they do it not for themselves but for the larger cause. One damns a factory supervisor because he has failed to maintain a sacred work schedule; if the damner replace the damned, so much the advantage to the fatherland and, only incidentally, so much the better for the new factotum.

Second, the necessity of closely controlling the entire population mass means that large numbers of new dignitaries must be created. All receive preferred treatment, political privilege, higher income, increased social esteem. There is more to do for the state, and more are needed for the jobs. One small oligarchy does not simply replace another. The modern revolutions are mass movements in more than a single sense.

Third, as already noted, lowly jobs can be given new wisps of glory. Janitors and garbage-collectors can be endowed with important political tasks. This has twin advantages: it makes ordinary dirty work more palatable, and, since it capitalizes on the envy and frustration of such workers, it eases the job of finding personnel for extraordinary dirty work of a political character. So those in lowly occupations have been easily recruited as the internal spies of all modern totalitarian nations.

The more the state can involve a person in state-controlled enterprises, the more his loyalty is secured. The more completely involved he is, the more congruence between his interests and those of the state. But the regime controls many other jobs whose incumbents need feel no national identification. In the Soviet Union, indeed, the economic theory and the labor-book practice give to the state control of virtually all economic activity. The whole population is dependent upon the state for its livelihood. One must express loyalty to eat.

Work is crucial in establishing life-satisfactions and dissatisfactions, and the propensity of totalitarian governments to meddle in the sphere of work has produced defections in loyalties to those governments. Furthermore, opportunities for upward mobility decrease as the new social system grows older. This kind of freezing is already apparent in the Soviet Union, with its increasing disparities in income, the labor draft, fees for higher education, inheritance and tax laws, and repression of cultural minorities. And this blocking of career lines as the result of regime stabilization is probably not appreciably counterbalanced by the periodic political purge, despite Hannah Arendt's suggestion that many are willing "to pay the price of a considerably shorter life for the assured fulfillment of all their career dreams."

Whatever the long-run impediments to rapid career advancement in totalitarian states, they are relatively unimportant over the moderate span of years. Taking advantage of natural shifts in status that are the essence of all revolutions and of the unique mass character of modern revolutions, totalitarian states use the work situation in a positive and effective fashion for promoting national loyalty. They manipulate the entire symbol system, and they manufacture honors and social prestige just as they exact penalties and social disgrace. They reward the most deserving with jobs, wages, power, prestige, and living quarters—preferments that in other societies are largely controlled by non-political forces and mechanisms. These are potent tools for building and maintaining national loyalty.

Intellectuals and political leaders alike are fond of saying that participation in governmental affairs distinguishes citizens of democratic nations from those of totalitarian states. Nothing could be further from the truth. The totalitarian organization of life makes possible a degree of popular participation in civic affairs that is unknown to democracy. Except for periods of sleep, the totalitarian ideal is unremitting civic activity.

Great joys and benefits accrue thereby to large segments of the population. The program fills life and effaces other desires. Even play—the German "Strength through Joy" and the Italian *Dopolavoro*—becomes purposeful. And the surrender of private self-will for a cause that demands love and activity produces unity, purpose, and stability for life. Josiah Royce, the American philosopher, had no idea how accurately his description of thoroughgoing national loyalty would be realized in the totalitarian states: "Honor . . . means submission, and to obey means to have one's way. Conformity is no longer opposed to having one's own will. One has no will but that of the country."

Unceasing civic participation tends to produce the unenthusiastic totalitarian: to convert even the reluctant into true believers. The more complete the autocracy, the more intensive the participation demanded, and the more difficult it is to preserve a segment of life immune from politics. On those occasions that the regime demands active opposition or active participation, opposition invites death. So participation is essential. Once caught in a round of even reluctant compliance, people find it difficult to know whether their action is the result of fear or of conviction. Though there are many exceptions, the regime becomes attractive even to its opponents.

For many situations, the modern totalitarian state will not willingly tolerate a person's silence or allow him the comfort of simple acquiescence. He must actively show his agreement: in some German cities during the Nazi period an individual was expected to salute and say "Heil Hitler" at least 150 times a day. But to go through the motions of compliance without believing them robs the individual of his integrity and takes from him the very self-respect upon which his original opposition is based. "In order to be a perfect actor one not only has to act, but to mean, to live the role. Only by becoming the perfect subject of the totalitarian state can one feel sure that one obeys all its orders."

Thus hatred for the regime soon may turn into hatred for one's self. The individual can finally protect himself only by accepting what he abhors. He can keep the secret of his dissatisfaction only by hiding it from himself. The alternative is destruction. So the paradox, the unwilling patriot, is produced.

The totalitarian state is not uniformly successful in creating loyalty to nation as a product of enforced political participation. Population groups have methods of frustrating even the most absolute leaders, of avoiding civic participation, or of making it meaningless. More than this, pivoting all social life on the state leads to a brittleness of social structure that is one of totalitarianism's greatest frailties.

Despite these qualifications, devices for encouraging and enforcing continuous civic participation are of the greatest effectiveness in promoting national loyalty. They fill the lives of the citizen and constitute a principal means of maintaining his happiness and draining off his aggressions. They make the life of the non-believer always difficult, often impossible.

In one perspective, differences between democratic and totalitarian patterns of loyalty can be traced to historical factors. In the nations where democracy and self-government have had a long period of development—Great Britain, Switzerland, Sweden, the United States—non-national loyalties do not often run counter to national loyalty. Rather, as we have seen, the two kinds of loyalty mutually enforce each other. On the other hand, in those nations where national development has been recent or where it has been drastically disrupted, non-national loyalties tend to be divisive:

> The citizens have shared enough national feeling to bring the nation-State into existence, but that common feeling has not

covered a sufficiently wide range of subjects for them to succeed in managing the affairs of the nation-State by democratic methods. The subsidiary associations . . . in a time of emergency . . . *have had on the citizens a disintegrating rather than a consolidating effect.* . . . a really thorough common feeling can only be produced by a long and gradual process, for which an intense and self-conscious growth is not an adequate substitute.

The history of Soviet family policy illustrates how the totalitarian regime, as it becomes established and integrated, may depend less upon its own controls and more upon the collaboration of voluntary groups. During the early days of the Soviet Union, "the Communist movement fought the family as an enemy of the new social order, a bulwark against change, a seedbed for anti-state tendencies." The traditional autocratic Russian family was weakened by a host of laws that, among other things, minimized the responsibilities of spouses, recognized common-law marriages, established full rights for illegitimate children, and legalized abortions. As one theorist of the day rhapsodized, the family would no longer be "a chain for the working man and woman." Instead, marriage would become a "union of affection and comradeship, a union of two equal members of the communist society, both of them free, both of them independent, both of them workers."

From 1936 onward, however, the whole course of development changed. Every effort has been made to strengthen the family as a basic social institution. Abortions have been severely limited, aid to mothers with large families increased, punishments provided for the non-payment of alimony. All this was underlined in 1944 with laws establishing "motherhood medals" and an order of "motherhood glory"; most significantly, divorce was made difficult and costly.

Soviet leaders obviously believe that their regime is sufficiently stabilized and their terror sufficiently refined that they need have less fear of the competition between family and nation for the individual's loyalty. Where the family heads are themselves completely integrated into the Soviet scheme, family and national loyalties tend to become parallel. The family promotes, rather than contests, national loyalty. The authority of parents acts as a transmission belt for the authority of the state. "Under Soviet conditions the father is the social educator. He has to prepare good Soviet citizens: that is his duty, that is also his pride."

Soviet family policy is less a mark of confidence in the loyalty of fathers than of confidence in the state's police power and a device to fulfil the state-defined need for increased population. The strains between a strong family and minute control of daily life are always resolved against the family and in favor of the state. The first duty of the Soviet citizen, he is told by propaganda and police example, is to the state. The family, like all other aspects of totalitarian society, is a captive of the state. It is, in this sense, an *ersatz,* a substitute for the free family life of democratic societies.

The whole state—the entire citizen mass—takes on some characteristics of the primary group. All are comrades, and there are no secrets among them. All are enjoined to think of themselves as sharing a common cause. All are led to believe that membership in the national group, whether as comrades or as bearers of the pure blood, transcends the importance of other roles. All are continuously reminded that they are protected and loved by an all-powerful parent.

Still another totalitarian *ersatz* for the primary group more nearly approximates the genuine. Under the necessity of organizing the whole of life, totalitarian governments must divide and subdivide the population into groups of operational efficiency. A squadron of Nazi youth, a Communist cell, members of collective farms, workers in a shop, soldiers in an army platoon—all develop patterns of mutual obligation, informal rules, and the intimacy and good fellowship that are characteristic of face-to-face groups. They learn what comradeship means. They deal at first hand with issues only imperfectly understood from a distance. They share together in victory and defeat.

But they differ profoundly from the primary groups in democratic nations. Most importantly, they are controlled in every way by the state. In democracies, freedom of movement into and away from primary groups is often difficult because of informal social pressures. The movement is far more restricted, frequently impossible, in totalitarian states because participation is enforced by government action. Similarly, group goals and group activities in fulfilment of those goals are dictated not by the members themselves but by the state.

The same manipulation extends to the larger organizations that proliferate in totalitarian nations. In the Soviet Union are found political assemblies at every level, down to the smallest village, in organized collective farms, producers' co-operatives, Communist youth clubs, sports and defense groups, and technical, scientific, and cultural societies of all sorts. In almost every case the organization is vast and based upon great numbers of relatively small discussion and action groups, each selecting delegates from its own membership to councils at higher levels. In Lenin's terms the Communist party is the "motive power" of the whole apparatus. "Every non-Party organization is a transmission belt linking up the Party with the working population as a whole."

Participation by the masses, as a characteristic of totalitarian social organization, is made possible only by the activation of great, complex group organizations. Their ritual and the sense of action and independence they give their members account in large part for the total loyalty that totalitarian governments receive from their citizens. Yet they are also devices par excellence for control from the top.

Even the manifestations of "democracy" allowed within the groups have their manipulative purposes. In the Soviet Union, for example, there exist on a huge scale group competitions in industry and, within particular groups, considerable leeway for participation in establishing production methods and for criticism of work programs and work supervisors. Such a program neatly capitalizes upon the importance of group morale for high productivity. Simultaneously, it shows on the part of the Russian rulers a keen sensitivity to the value of catharsis: the availability of work supervisors as immediate objects for aggression serves as one means of easing larger discontents and, by no means incidentally, of further increasing work productivity.

Some of this same manipulation of industrial and other groups can be found in democratic countries. But the manipulators are rarely the government. They are industrial, regional, and labor leaders, themselves competing with one another and struggling for control of the government. The difference is not that manipulation of groups is practiced in totalitarian countries and not in democratic ones. The difference is that in totalitarian nations the rulers are monopolists of social manipulation on a scale unknown in democracies.

As in democratic nations, the allegiance paid to smaller groups in totalitarian states is expressed as allegiance to the state. *Ersatz* groups kept alive over time may appear as "natural" as groups evolved without deliberate planning. Manipulated groups, as long as the controllers retain control, can produce loyalty to the state just as democratic groups do. There are, nevertheless, some loyalties that no state apparatus can control. They serve as a refuge from politics and a defense against the state; and they increase in number and potency as the totalitarian state passes beyond the militant period of its inception. The totalitarian substitute for spontaneous human groups is not a long-lasting product. The *ersatz* can be maintained and made palatable only as long as crisis can be made continuous.

We do not know the exact limits of totalitarian power. But we do know that "even . . . terror is not omnipotent to destroy all bonds of organization among its victims." The malleability of human beings is great, yet not great enough to divest them of their human qualities.

A central point is the ruggedness of the small group. Industrialists in America have learned that the ten o'clock coffee-hour group, if disturbed in the office or the factory, will simply move to the washrooms. At a far remove from this homely example, yet still a consequence of small-group bonds, the most vigilant and ruthless police systems have not been able to stamp out clandestine revolutionary cadres, sometimes linked only by single contacts, the group gaining greater strength from the very violence of its oppression. The war brought to light such opposition movements in both Nazi Germany and the Soviet Union.

Opposition is less likely than compromise: living with the system without liking it. Thus the "internal emigration" in the Soviet Union: people who search for jobs of no political consequence and with minimum political supervision. Thus the primary groups may express their power, against the dictates of the state, through friendship and family affection or pity and compassion or distaste for spies and informers—all human qualities that the greatest oppression and fear cannot completely extirpate. The unconvinced may also show themselves as corrupters: people defending themselves "against the Soviet system's high demands for performance by building personal cliques, by favoritism, by cultivating cronies." In some cases this takes the form of outright antistate activity: the theft of state property or the juggling of production statistics. In Nazi Germany, even during the war, the relations between the rulers and the ruled were mediated by "an ever-increasing number of parasites trading in pull and vice."

Refuge from the state is thus possible even under a harsh totalitarianism. The more completely the state controls the society, the more difficult it is to withhold allegiance and to express opposition. But even in the most extreme expression of totalitarianism—the concentration camp—opposition is still possible. Bruno Bettelheim has written most persuasively concerning the great difficulty of living under a dictatorship and maintaining opposition to it. Yet Dr. Bettelheim's own career is a striking exception to his very point. He preserved his own personality and his opposition to totalitarianism in the Dachau and Buchenwald concentration camps. He did this by utilizing his old professional skills, to observe and to analyze what was happening to other prisoners. This was *private* behavior, achieved without immediate group sustenance of any sort. Bettelheim's reference groups were to the world he had known before and to the world he hoped again to know. Thus, even in isolation, independence and autonomy are possible.

A Jew, whatever he did, was, by definition, an enemy of the state in Nazi Germany. For non-Jews, expressions of patriotism were rewarded; and therefore non-Jews had less reason to follow Dr. Bettelheim's example. Nevertheless, the escape from politics by turning inward is also available to others. There is a withdrawal into the self, minimal support coming from others only through the most indirect means, the individual concealing his true attitudes by playing the state-demanded role. Sometimes he may even overplay this role. American railroad workers have demonstrated how the literal obedience of extravagant rules can become a subtle sabotage; and the same phenomenon is apparently not unknown in the Soviet Union.

Not all these forces show themselves publicly; and they have peculiar effects. For though they reveal opposition to the totalitarian state, they may be positive aids to the strength of totalitarianism. The very defenses that people have against the system make it possible for them to live with it. The more successful the defenses, the more difficult it may be to break openly or to conspire with others to that end.

The inertia that generally makes disloyalty difficult in democratic states operates equally under totalitarianism. The stigma of the traitor is a most difficult one to contemplate, and many rationalizations are available for compliance. One can bury one's self in work or play and plead ignorance of political ills. The citizen of Nazi Germany and Russia, no less than the citizen of the United States and Great Britain, buys life-satisfactions by political compliance. Under a regime of violence he buys the greatest of all satisfactions—life itself.

There are many examples of these kinds of action. The Italian dictatorship was established just as the brilliant physicist, Enrico Fermi, began his research career at the University of Rome. Living in Mussolini's Italy, Fermi conducted the historic experiments with slow neutrons that later earned him the Nobel Prize. Living in Mussolini's Italy, he married, had children, and engaged in a full and undisturbed family life. Living in Mussolini's Italy, he made lifelong friends, companions with whom he worked and skied, argued and joked.

Fermi and his wife expressed a distaste for fascism from its earliest days. When they thought of it, they did not like Mussolini's regime—but they thought of it relatively infrequently. From time to time they discussed emigration. Mrs. Fermi was shocked that their children were taught to look upon Mussolini as a deity, as if he were an equal of Christ; she attempted to undo what was done in the schools. But she, with almost all others, followed the Queen's example and exchanged her gold wedding ring for a steel one in a dramatic ceremony designed to supply the regime with psychic, as well as mineral, resources. She had misgivings, but she felt duly patriotic.

There were even fewer misgivings over another event. At the age of twenty-seven, Enrico Fermi was chosen a member of Mussolini's newly founded Royal Academy of Italy, established to rival the British Royal Academy in prestige and to demonstrate to the world the intellectual greatness of the Fascist state. Fermi thought the elaborate uniform was silly, and he was embarrassed by the title "Excellency." But he accepted membership in the academy, and he found satisfaction in so doing:

> Not that [Enrico] cared for honors. . . . All he wanted was to live in peace and to work. But along with membership in the new academy went a handsome salary that would help him to live in peace: it was one and a half times as large as that of the university and could be combined with it.

Nobody's imagination can be stretched far enough to consider the Fermis as Fascists. They did not like fascism. When they came to the United States, they became exemplary citizens. Yet for fifteen years they lived in Mussolini's Italy and liked it. More precisely, they liked the life they were allowed to live, a life relatively untouched by politics and centered on work, family, and friends. They felt no tradition of participation in politics. They were content to be left alone. "The scholars' ivory tower . . . aloof from politics, was considered as worthy as, if not worthier than, the courageous but ineffectual acts of rebellion of some members of the intelligentsia.

Despite fascism, life in Rome had been pleasant for us, and we had stayed."

The Fermis left Italy in 1938 only when anti-Semitic laws were promulgated. Enrico and the children were Catholics. Mrs. Fermi was from a non-observing Jewish family. It is possible that the discriminatory laws would not have touched the Fermis at all. But "there is a limit to what one is willing to tolerate," and the family left Italy as soon thereafter as it was possible.

Eminent scientists are not the only ones who escape the impact of totalitarianism. At the opposite end of the scale of prestige, the "little" men—bakers, mechanics, mailmen—can sometimes insulate themselves from a good deal of politics, at least the politics that is distasteful. (The distaste frequently becomes apparent; but then it is too late to do anything about it.) All those who live uneasily in the regime can find some things that are good. One can solace one's conscience by acts of kindness and decency toward the nation's political victims, as when a Nazi police officer allowed a Jew to escape arrest. And despite the strenuous efforts of the rulers to monopolize all acceptable definitions of nation and national loyalty, some citizens can secretly justify compliance by distinguishing the state (or government) in power from the more enduring nation. The Fermis despised Mussolini but loved Italy and felt deeply that they were Italians. The old-line officials of the German foreign office who retained their positions under Hitler had no illusions concerning what they worked for. "The idea of the immortality of the Third Reich evoked only a smile." "The Communists be damned," said a Russian partisan, "Mother Russia must be saved from the Huns."

So it is that opposition by even the disaffected is difficult. Terror always stands in the way of outright opposition; but, terror aside, when and under what circumstances is opposition justified? And, if justified, when is it possible? Pastor Niemöller finally did oppose Hitler, and with heroism. A statement attributed to him expresses the dilemma of all the unconvinced. When the Nazis attacked the Communists, he said that he was a little uneasy, but, after all, he was not a Communist. So he did nothing. Then the Nazis attacked Socialists, and he was a little uneasier, but he was not a Socialist, and he still did nothing. Then the Nazis attacked the schools, the press, and the Jews, and he was much uneasier; but still he did nothing. "And then they attacked the Church, and he was a Churchman, and he did something—but then it was too late."

The compromises of the unconvinced are probably not relevant for the great majority of the totalitarian population. A relatively small number must be bludgeoned or bullied; another small group remains implacably opposed and is kept silent only by the threat of violence; still a third group compromises uneasily. But the mass of people are loyal to the state because they come to like it. They like it because they come to believe that the dictatorship is good, good for them and their nation. They do not suffer under dictatorship. They do not think of their nation as a dictatorship. They find genuine joys in inexpensive holidays, in following the all-powerful leader, in advancing the welfare of themselves and their families, in political participation for the greater glory of themselves and their nation.

The strength of totalitarian loyalties is thus great. It is great partly because of the failure of totalitarian states to be total: the state cannot, and need not, efface the vitality of family, work, and friendship groups. From this perspective, the less total the state becomes, the more likely it is to build strong and lasting national loyalty. The state is at the same time engaged in bringing direct benevolences to the people; it is loving and dutiful, rewarding the worthy, caring for the needy. The more benevolent the totalitarianism, the more likely it is to build strong loyalties. The state finally directs large segments of life, extirpates opposition, and terrifies the living with the example of the mutilated dead. The more total the totalitarianism, the more obedient the people; and, in the view of the leaders, obedience can be equated with loyalty.

These views of totalitarianism appear to be flatly contradictory. But they are all true. Totalitarianism can exhibit, according to its purposes, a single facet at a given time; or it can terrorize one group while doting upon another. For most population groups, it presents love and terror simultaneously. Totalitarian governments are like the Egyptian king, celebrated in an ancient document: "Exulting is he, a smasher of foreheads, so that none can stand near him. . . . He is a master of graciousness, rich in sweetness, and he conquers by love."

PART III
The Loyalty of Disloyalty

7 Making Un-Americans: A Pathology of Disloyalty

The room was long and narrow, a mess-hall with the tables pushed to the walls and wooden benches lined up facing the speaker. Unshaded light bulbs hanging down the center of the room cast long shadows over the crowd of some two hundred people. Most of them were men, all of them were Americans of Japanese ancestry. This was the Manzanar Relocation Center near the sand-filled town of Independence, California, in August, 1942. The speaker was urging those in the center to protest against camp conditions: bad food, jerry-built barracks into which the powder-fine Inyo dust blew freely, low wages, lack of work opportunities. He spoke slowly but with the deepest passion. He concluded as follows:

I am one of the few Japanese Americans who served in the American Army during the first World War. I was wounded fighting for the United States. I draw compensation for my wounds from the United States government while rotting in a United States concentration camp.

The speaker ripped open his shirt and jabbed with his thumb at scars on his chest:

> These are the scars I have, keepsakes of my army service for this country. It is no longer my country. I am now a hundred per cent Japanese. I spit on these scars of the United States.

Deliberately he spat on himself and then sat down.

More than six thousand American citizens during World War II formally declared that they were not loyal to the United States. These "disloyal" citizens were Japanese in ancestry. Theirs was a frankly pathological situation, one far removed from the experience of most people in most parts of the world. Yet pathology in society, as in physiology, is frequently instructive. It illuminates, sometimes by bitter caricature, what we call the "normal."

Japanese Americans were an unpopular group on the West Coast even before the war. They faced discrimination in finding jobs and homes, and they were believed by many to be unfair business competitors. Though second-generation Japanese were gradually winning wider acceptance, the war with Japan rekindled old animosities and made the entire group the object of widespread distrust. American citizens of Japanese ancestry were linked in the public's view with Japanese alien enemies, with the attackers of Pearl Harbor, and with those battling against Americans in South Pacific jungles. It was widely (and falsely) stated that the resident Japanese population had committed sabotage at Pearl Harbor and that they constituted a disciplined fifth column on the West Coast.

The public and political outcry against Japanese Americans was soon translated into an official policy of evacuation. All resident Japanese—even those with as little as one-sixteenth Japanese blood, even those unaware of their Japanese ancestry—were ordered to leave their homes and businesses. The forced movements were executed with remarkable speed and precision. Procedures established to protect evacuees from the forced sale of their property were relatively ineffective, and the evacuation meant financial disaster for virtually every Japanese American family.

Most evacuees were first moved to hastily constructed, temporary assembly centers. Here they suffered the first shock of barbed-wire fences, roving searchlights at night, armed guards, mess-hall feeding, and the crowding of entire families into a single room. There were, especially in the early days, inevitable shortages of food, tools, medical supplies, and other necessary equipment. At one center accumulated grievances led to a savage riot.

Evacuees were later sent to the more permanent relocation centers. Self-governing cities with adequate educational, housing, and work facilities were promised them by officials of the War Relocation Authority, the civilian agency established to supervise the relocation. But, even with the best of intentions, it was impossible to create democratic communities behind barbed wire.

The majority of the ten relocation camps were constructed in the semi-arid regions of the West. Physical facilities were inadequate from first to last. The idea of creating profitable enterprises proved unworkable. Public sentiment was adverse. And it soon became a bleak fact that the centers were costly wartime experiments. They were an unprofitable venture, and no labor could make them otherwise. So one of the highest hopes of the evacuees—that of some financial restitution—was frustrated. Salary schedules ranged from $19.00 a month for professional men to $12.00 for most others. These were powerful forces contributing to social disintegration.

There were others. American Japanese were themselves divided by wide gaps in education, occupation, and income; by differences in the extent to which they adhered to Old World cultural patterns; by their varying knowledge of, and affection for, the Japanese homeland. Evacuation tossed these diverse people indiscriminately into a closed community. Conflict, open or covert, ranged over a wide group of issues, from what kind of food should be served in mess-halls to what kind of government should be established in the communities.

In the very nature of the situation and despite the efforts of administrators, the committees became more "Japanesey" and less American. Power flowed to the elders. At the same time, young and old were forced to subordinate their own differences and to make common cause against the administration. The hostility generated by intra-group conflict was turned outward and expressed against administrative officers and their programs.

Frustration, fear, and bitterness aroused by camp conditions were aggravated by the hostility outside. The governor of California warned other states about the dangers of Japanese Americans, and the district attorney of Los Angeles reported that they might be slaughtered wholesale if they reappeared on the West Coast. American Legion posts held forth on the dangerous—and mythical—excessive birth rate of Japanese Americans, and the Native Sons and Daughters of the Golden West passed resolutions urging separation of the sexes in the camps in order to prevent reproduction at the taxpayers' expense. Court cases were initiated to deprive evacuees of their American citizenship. Congressional committees sought to uncover subversiveness in the centers. California groups periodically claimed that evacuees were being "coddled" in their barrack cities.

There were some opposing forces. Many Americans viewed the evacuation as a sore mistake and supported the non-repressive policies of the War Relocation Authority. Churches, educational institutions, and groups concerned with civil liberties provided powerful sustaining props for the morale and hopes of many evacuees. Officials of the War Relocation Authority encouraged these expressions of friendship.

But for very large numbers their situation was grievous, their future bleak. They had been singled out on a racial basis and had suffered discriminations which seemed to abrogate all tenets of Americanism. They had been moved from their homes and businesses. They had suffered great economic losses. They had lived for more than a year in physically uncomfortable and socially abnormal communities. They were attacked as disloyal. They were threatened with deportation and the loss of citizenship. They were a dispirited, a demoralized, and a rejected group.

This was the situation of Japanese Americans when, in January, 1943, it became mandatory to declare themselves loyal—or disloyal—to the United States.

By the winter of 1942, War Relocation Authority officials had given up the scheme of providing war-duration communities within the relocation areas. These government officials were alarmed by the deplorable social conditions in the camps, and they feared evacuees might become a permanently institutionalized group. They were also impressed by the growing good will of church and other groups and by the great demand for labor in wartime America. They concluded that the best plan was to empty the centers as rapidly as possible.

They believed that the policy adopted by the War Department soon after Pearl Harbor of not utilizing Japanese Americans in the armed services was an unjustified aspersion on the minority group and a grave deterrent to the group's acceptance by the people of America. War Relocation Authority officials were therefore jubilant when the War Department announced in January, 1943, that it would accept volunteers for an all-Nisei* combat team. In order to facilitate this call for volunteers, to "clear" others for leaving the centers, and to prepare for the probable reinstitution of regular draft procedures, a general registration of all adults within the relocation centers was ordered.

For citizens of seventeen and over the crucial question of the registration questionnaire was: "Will you swear unqualified allegiance to the United States of America . . . and forswear any form of allegiance or obedience to the Japanese emperor?" Registration created a crisis at each of the ten relocation centers. When the program was over, almost thirty-one thousand Japanese American citizens had answered "Yes" to the loyalty question. More than six thousand answered "No," and three thousand others qualified their answers, or refused to answer, or refused to register at all. What accounts for the declarations of disloyalty?

A substantial group declared themselves disloyal as a protest against their wartime treatment. The bitterness of this protest was caught during the registration interviews. Some people cried as they answered "No"; others tore up their birth certificates; still others wrote explanations on the registration form, such as "No—but if not for evacuation—Yes." Some months later the meaning of the "No" answers became clearer, when the War Relocation Authority accorded interviews to the "dis-

* Nisei: second-generation Japanese Americans, citizens of the United States.

loyal" (non-affirmative) respondents and gave them an opportunity to explain and, in some cases, to change their answers. Those persisting in disloyal answers were scheduled for "segregation" in a special center; all others became eligible to leave the centers.

Verbatim reports taken at segregation hearings record the vehemence and emotion of the protest. A young Nisei at Manzanar spoke both for himself and his wife:

> We are not dual citizens. But in the first place if we are citizens, how come we are in these camps? . . . I answer "no" because of resentment and because of how they treated us. When they asked us to come here, they told us they would pay us union wages. . . . How can I have faith in this country? I lost all my ideals about this country. . . . I went up to Idaho on furlough [temporary farm work]. We were told that would be a proof of our loyalty. We went to help the farmers. We went in to eat. They kicked us out of there. I was actually kicked out of a cafe!

Another young man, whose father fought in the American army during World War I, testified:

> NISEI: We have citizenship and still we are in camps. We are treated just like aliens. So what's the use of talking about citizenship and being loyal citizens.
>
> HEARING OFFICER: But that's what this hearing is for, so that you can prove that you are a loyal citizen and help free yourself of restrictions.
>
> NISEI: If we say "yes," can we go back to California?
>
> HEARING OFFICER: We can't promise anything like that. That is strictly up to the Army. . . .
>
> NISEI: If "loyal" citizens can't go where they want to it's discrimination. That's why we said "no" in the first place. . . .
>
> HEARING OFFICER: Don't you think you should consider what this question means? It is a loyalty question and if you say "no" to it you are saying that you are not loyal.

NISEI: . . . You people say that a Jap's a Jap. . . . You've ruined our future. We had something to look forward to; now it is all gone.

In some cases disloyalty declarations were a protest against loss of property as well as civil rights, as a twenty-seven-year-old Nisei explained:

NISEI: . . . We'll have to start all over again. We were farming. We sold everything very cheap. We're cleaned out as far as this country is concerned. I have some property in Japan. If I have to start over, I think it would be better to do so where I have a little something.

HEARING OFFICER: Does this mean that you're loyal to Japan rather than to the United States?

NISEI: The only way I can say is that my loyalty is now more to Japan than to the United States. That's the way my conscience tells me to say. Before evacuation it was different. We were making a pretty good living. I was just beginning to get started. Then this thing came and took our property. It didn't seem fair. A country that wants you or wants your loyalty doesn't treat you this way.

This pattern of response was repeated at each center many times with many variations. To large numbers of evacuees a declaration of national loyalty meant acquiescence in the loss of civil rights and property and acceptance of what was believed to be unjust persecution, discrimination, and second-class citizenship. A declaration of disloyalty, on the other hand, was a protest, a demand for equal status, an expression of repugnance for what America had done in the past and offered in the future.

In some cases a husband or a wife refused to affirm loyalty if married to an alien or to a citizen who answered "No." During the registration, a young woman at Tule Lake said:

I am loyal to this country, it's the only one I know, but my husband is an alien and I want to be where he is. The only place we know is Sacramento and if we can't go there we might as well go to Japan.

Regard for the welfare of parents was an even more important factor. Before stating unqualified allegiance to the United States, the young people among the citizen group demanded that their alien parents be allowed to return to the West Coast, that compensation be made for economic losses, or, at the very least, that the government promise to shelter the older group for the duration of the war. Officials could make none of these pledges.

Many evacuees believed that the young men who answered "Yes" to the loyalty question would soon be drafted if they did not volunteer. If they were killed, they asked, who would care for their impoverished and unacculturated parents? In a number of cases the older people had decided to return to Japan. What reception would they receive if their sons fought against the mother-country? The bitterness of some parents, whose entire lives seemed irreparably smashed by evacuation, was very deep. How could the younger people be loyal to, or fight for, the country that had ruined their parents?

These were hard, sometimes unanswerable, questions. Japanese family ties are traditionally strong, and the parents' influence was increased as the result of relocation-center living and the youthfulness of the citizen group. Pressures, in many cases, were strongly applied. Some parents gave "glowing accounts . . . of the future that would lie ahead of the Nisei in Japan or Manchuria and other conquered territories in the Far East." And they argued that it was foolish to believe that America held any decent future.

Many facets of the problem were typified in a single case of a twenty-two-year-old unmarried man at Manzanar. He believed that since the war was against Japan, the American people were "taught to hate us." His first idea after Pearl Harbor was "to help this country," the United States. Later he "wanted to be neutral." Since he was now forced to a decision, he had to say "No."

Before evacuation, this young man had worked on his family's farm, and he did not believe that the United States would take repressive action against American citizens of Japanese ancestry. His family had been evacuated after crops had been planted, and they had suffered heavy losses. Their effort to leave the center to take up farming in Utah had been unsuccessful. Now, after being "kicked around and treated like persons without any minds," it was "too late." His plans for the future were not definite. He did not know, and he was "not interested" in, Japan. His final decision was weighted heavily by the duty he felt toward his father:

> My dad is 58 years old now. He has been here 30 years at least. He came to this country with nothing but a bed roll. He worked on the railroads and he worked in the sugar beet fields. If I told you the hardships he had you wouldn't believe me. I owe a lot to my father. . . . All through his life he was working for me. During these last years he was happy because he thought he was coming to the place where his son would have a good life. I am the only son. I have to carry on the family name. . . . My mind is made up. I know my father is planning to return to Japan. I know he expects me to say "no" so there will be no possibility that the family will be separated. There isn't much I can do for my father anymore; I can't work for him the way I used to. But I can at least quiet his mind on this.

Thus a second definition of national loyalty and disloyalty was constructed. Loyalty to nation meant disloyalty to family. It meant separation of family members and the addition of new burdens upon parents who were already broken by the economic, psychological, and moral effects of evacuation. National disloyalty, on the other hand, meant loyalty to family: the continued cohesiveness of the family group, fulfilment of the obligation to support aged parents, capitulation in the face of insistent parental demands, the contribution of at least one comfort to parents' lives.

During the registration crisis it was widely rumored that all those who answered "Yes" to the loyalty question would be forced to leave the centers; those who answered "No" would be allowed to remain in camp until the war was over. Why residents should object to leaving the physically uncomfortable and socially abnormal communities is at first difficult to understand. But they had many cogent reasons.

They had a near-pathological fear of meeting violence on the outside, a fear that was confirmed by almost every edition of West Coast newspapers. They were impoverished. Jobs in which they were most skilled, such as irrigated farming, were practically non-existent. Available jobs were largely for laborers or household help, and these were degrading to people previously self-employed. There were no culturally congenial communities for older persons to join. Language barriers existed. Difficulties in meeting wartime rationing and food shortages were widely exaggerated.

On the other hand, for all their gross unattractiveness, the relocation centers offered shelter, safety, food, friends, and cultural compatibility. They offered institutional answers to personal problems. They offered a social structure in which individuals could achieve status and respectability, in many cases as champions of their own group opposing governmental policies.

The rewards of continued residence within a center seemed

to many far more important than the penalty of being "disloyal." Many of those who would be most offended by the stigma had already left the centers. Those citizens remaining were, on the whole, young, inexperienced, tied to parents, or bitterly disillusioned. At Manzanar, a twenty-year-old unmarried girl put the issue of security in a very brief form:

> Father is dead. Sister can't talk and mother is all alone. We can't go out. So we have all planned to go to Tule Lake [the segregation center for the "disloyal"]. We have close relatives we can depend on in Tule Lake.

For young men, the concern for security was related not only to their concern for their parents but also to their disinclination to be drafted at a later date by a discriminatory government. A young man of twenty-two, oldest of seven children, exchanged the following views with the segregation hearing board:

> NISEI: . . . I have a big responsibility. I can't go out on relocation. . . . If the war goes on . . . we figure that the place will be closed down. . . . And what about the draft? If I and my brother get killed what happens to my family? My brother and I are the only ones old enough to help support the family.
>
> HEARING OFFICER: Lots of mothers are losing sons.
>
> NISEI: Yes, but they put us in here and then they expect us to fight for this country. It's one thing for a son to go off to war when the father still has his job and the family still has its possessions; it's another thing to expect it after people have been through what we have and have lost everything.

And so a third definition of national loyalty was constructed. Loyalty meant the threat of being forcibly moved from relocation centers, the necessity of facing an uncertain, immediate future without economic resources and under threats of social ostracism, if not actual physical violence. Disloyalty meant the comparative security of relocation-center life and escape from the harsh realities of existence on the outside.

In February, 1943, the Allied offensive in the South Pacific was barely under way. Earlier successes of the Japanese forces plus the indignities of evacuation had heightened the older evacuees' emotional ties with the homeland. Many of them had come to the wishful conclusion that Japan would win the war. This was one reason for parental pressures to answer "No." Relatively few of the younger citizens had any real conviction of Japanese victory. But some were persuaded that a "No" answer was a hedge against discrimination and a positive recommendation for preferred position, should Japan win. The meanness of the foreseeable future in America made such a view especially attractive.

A number of citizens who had been educated in Japan and who knew the Japanese language expressed a fanatical devotion to the Japanese political system and a fanatical hatred of the United States. They were Japanese in culture, and they professed a veneration of the emperor. They pointed to the evacuation as a sample of what democracy produced and derided those who believed that America would ever offer a decent life for Orientals. Eventually, they organized themselves to impress their views, sometimes with violence, on those who maintained loyalty to the United States.

This was a fourth definition of disloyalty: an expression of preference for Japanese life-ways and a preparation for living in Japan in the event of Japanese victory. On the surface, this comes close to what people usually mean by "disloyalty" to the United States: it seems to express a conviction, a choice of one political system over another. In fact, it was not possible to separate those who answered "No" for reasons of "conviction" from those who did so as a means of protest or to maintain family units or to attain security. The reasons were hopelessly intertwined, and all of them—or any combination—could go into a single "No" response. Thus parental pressure could be more easily exerted because of the citizens' outrage over evacuation; thus the Japanese political system appeared more attractive if a young Nisei feared to leave the institutional comforts of center life. Disloyalty as conviction certainly existed; but conviction was the result of what had happened to an individual, just as it in turn colored how that individual evaluated his situation.

If the Japanese Americans had not been so bluntly faced with making a choice, few, if any, would ever have openly declared themselves not loyal to the United States. How the question was asked is also important. Sheer administrative confusion was one reason that led many evacuees to responses of disloyalty.

Male citizens were the only group faced with the issue of army service. But the War Relocation Authority leave program applied to all persons in the center, and the leave registration forms for female citizens and for aliens of both sexes also contained a loyalty question. In its original form, this question was like the one asked male citizens: would they "swear unqualified allegiance" to the United States and "forswear any form of allegiance or obedience" to the Japanese emperor?

Aliens found it almost impossible to answer "Yes" to such a question. They were barred by law from becoming naturalized. The war had made them "enemies," and their only legal defense against this country was by appeal to Japan through a neutral government. War Relocation Authority officials soon realized that the question was unfair and that it invited from the aliens either a "No" answer or a refusal to answer. So the question was changed. Aliens were asked if they would "swear to abide by the laws of the United States and take no action which would . . . interfere with the war effort." In this form the question was answered affirmatively by almost all the alien group.

But the original question had important repercussions among the citizen group. At the Tule Lake center, original opposition to registration took the form of refusing to register at all, and almost two thousand aliens persisted in this refusal even when the new question was used. At all centers the aliens were led directly to the issue of rejecting plans for any future in the United States and to the consideration of repatriation. Parents were thus faced with cutting all ties with the United States at the precise moment that their sons and daughters were asked to declare their "unqualified allegiance." This led directly to many disloyal responses.

The combining of the registration with a program soliciting army volunteers and the wording of the questionnaire itself had a similar effect. Immediately preceding the loyalty question for male citizens was one that asked: "Are you willing to serve in the armed forces of the United States in combat duty, wherever ordered?" To answer "No" to this while answering "Yes" to the question on loyalty seemed a dangerous inconsistency. In at least one center, registration officers required consistency in the two answers. Yet to answer "Yes" to both questions seemed tantamount to volunteering. And by far the largest number who wished to declare themselves loyal did not wish to volunteer.

What the combination of questions did not provide is precisely what many Nisei desired: to answer "Yes" to the loyalty question but to express a disinclination to serve in a segregated unit or to serve unless drafted or to serve unless full citizenship status was restored. To many, the failure to provide for an expression of these qualified attitudes made the whole registration an underhanded device to compromise their future status in America. They also resented being asked if they would "forswear" allegiance to Japan, because this implied that they actually held such allegiance. At one center, registrants were allowed to answer the armed service question "Yes, if drafted," although this was not consistent with War Department instructions. At other centers, however, many registrants believed they were being cruelly asked to answer unanswerable questions.

There were striking differences among the ten relocation centers in the proportion of Japanese Americans who declared themselves disloyal to the United States. At the Manzanar center in California, 52 per cent of the adult male citizens answered "No" to the loyalty question, qualified their response, refused to answer, or refused to register at all; at the Minidoka center in Idaho, these groups constituted 8 per cent of the male citizen group. At the Tule Lake and Gila centers in California and the Jerome center in Arkansas, at least one out of three male Nisei refused to declare themselves loyal. At the Granada center in Colorado, the ratio was one to fifteen.

These differences in loyalty responses can be explained only by differences in the social situation of the various centers, including the fact that the administration of registration varied greatly from one center to another.

At Manzanar, where the percentage of non-affirmative answers among male citizens was highest, community conditions were particularly bad. Manzanar had originally been an assembly center under military control, operated by a generally unfriendly staff drawn from personnel of the Works Progress Administration. Its physical accommodations were substandard. Residents of the nearest town—Independence, California—demonstrated great hostility toward evacuees. The community itself was torn by factional splits, and gang warfare was intermittent. With the help of a stool-pigeon system, a number of arrests were made by the F.B.I. Those removed from the center as "troublemakers" were regarded as heroes by many evacuees. The administrative personnel was badly splintered, some members refusing to "fraternize" with the evacuee residents. The camp directorship had changed four times within a year. Just two months before the registration, military police units patrolling the camp periphery had been called into the center to quiet a disturbance. A riot developed, inexperienced soldiers fired into the crowd, and nine evacuees were wounded, two fatally.

In this disorganized community, registration was conducted without adequate explanation. It was announced suddenly and carried through hastily. Its multiple purposes were not clear, the questions of evacuees were unanswered because officials had not anticipated them, and wild rumors spread through the colony. No concerted effort was made to gain the co-operation of evacuee leaders. The group effort that finally emerged was the result of fear and frustration and was largely turned against the government's program.

In contrast, conditions at the Minidoka camp, where "No" responses were few, were far less grim. Barracks were more firmly constructed. The sentiment of near-by communities was relatively friendly. Center administrators were generally on good terms with evacuees, and established procedures encouraged discussions of policy between appointed personnel and evacuee leaders. When the registration policy was announced, a series of meetings was immediately scheduled at which the registration was explained. Five full days of consultation preceded the registration. Evacuee leaders helped to answer questions and urged male citizens to volunteer for army service. Special recruiting meetings were held. Volunteers were told (untruthfully, as later events proved) that their parents would be cared for "as long as they wish to remain in this center." A number of alien enemy leaders publicly urged the young men to enlist.

At every center face-to-face groups and group leaders were of first importance in influencing the responses of individuals and in establishing reaction patterns for each center as a whole. The general solidarity of family groups has already been noted. Thomas and Nishimoto have graphically demonstrated the existence at Tule Lake of "clearly defined areas of 'loyalty' and 'disloyalty' " according to block residence within the center—a pattern that also developed at other centers. This relationship may have been influenced, in part, by the common pre-evacuation place of residence of those in certain center areas. It was largely the result of family solidarity, of block leadership, and of the common attitudes that emerged from continuous face-to-face relations.

Center residence was the major factor accounting for the striking differences in response to the loyalty question. Where residents defined the registration as threatening and unfair, their reaction was "disloyal." Where they defined it as a possible entrée to better things and a challenge to their Americanism, their responses were "loyal." Three points need emphasis. First, the great differences between one center and another in the "disloyalty" rate illustrate how differences in life-situation influenced loyalty decisions. Second, "life-situation" must be understood as including the way people felt about their circumstances as well as the way an outsider would have described them. W. I. Thomas' aphorism was clearly demonstrated: "If men define situations as real, they are real in their consequences." Third, face-to-face relationships, in this case family and block groups, were of first importance in influencing the decision to declare loyalty or disloyalty.

The center-by-center differences in loyalty responses were so great that they overshadowed other influences. Yet social and economic factors were also operative. Evacuees who had successfully adjusted themselves to American ways and who before evacuation had been accepted upon relatively friendly terms by the larger community were more likely to retain their loyalty to the United States than those who had not acquired American habits and who felt themselves to be objects of hostility. These relationships have been statistically demonstrated. Americans of Japanese ancestry were more likely to answer "No" to the loyalty question if:

They had been educated in Japan (rather than in the United States)

They were members of, or expressed preference for, the Buddhist church (rather than for Christianity or for no church at all)

Their pre-evacuation residence was in an area of relatively unfriendly relations between Japanese and Caucasians, as in California (rather than in "friendly" areas, i.e., the Pacific Northwest)

Their previous occupations involved little contact with non-Japanese groups, as was generally the case with those who worked in rural, agricultural areas (in contrast to city residents, whose work brought them in frequent contact with non-Japanese)

These relationships were revealed by confining attention to a single center and by comparing evacuees according to religious preference, prior residence and occupation, and education. In almost every case the differentials were striking. At one center, to take a single extreme example, among non-Buddhist, non-agricultural males, persons educated in Japan were eleven times more likely to be "disloyal" than persons educated in the United States.

Other variables, not amenable to statistical demonstration, were also probably important. Disloyalty declarations were relatively fewer (one can hypothesize) among those who had received longer education in the United States, those less facile in the Japanese language, those who lost least economically (proportionate to total stake rather than in absolute dollars) as the result of evacuation, and those who preserved at least one strong tie with a non-Japanese friend on the "outside" during the evacuation experience.

Two sorts of reaction to the loyalty registration were contrary to the central tendency that made those least Americanized most likely to answer "No" to the loyalty question (other things, such as center residence, being equal). One was the loyal reaction of the poorly Americanized; the other the disloyal response of those who seemed most American in speech and action.

One type of loyal response from the poorly acculturated was the result of submissiveness. Obedience to authority is a characteristic of Japanese culture, and authority during the registration asked for and expected "Yes" answers. Some rural evacuees, Japanese in behavior patterns and possessing little political awareness, reacted characteristically to this expectation of authority. They were especially likely to do so if instructed by their parents; and parents of the earlier wave of migration to this country (before 1900) were themselves relatively sensitive to authority and relatively immune to the newer Japanese nationalism. The number so influenced was probably very small. They illustrate how "loyalty" to America resulted from adherence to non-American cultural traits.

In some cases, less Americanized, Japanese-educated persons turned with enthusiasm to declarations of loyalty and to voluntary enlistment. Some of these individuals had found their experiences in Japan distasteful. Some saw no financial opportunity in Japan, and others were repelled by the Japanese political-military system. Yet, because of language difficulties and other cultural characteristics, they were not fully accepted by the more Americanized Nisei, to say nothing of the larger American community. Conscious of the disdain of those who shared their social and economic position and who had declared themselves disloyal, they were at the same time driven by the demons of distrust apparent among those they sought to join. They felt compelled to demonstrate extraordinary allegiance toward the United States.

Their action was a counterpart of the actions of other marginal men. Like the renegade described by Simmel, they were motivated by the hatred of former friends and the distrust of new ones. Like recent religious converts, they were more zealous than the bishop. Like the Jewish self-hatred described by Lewin, like the rejection of old friends by those climbing the social ladder, they conformed and overconformed to the demands of the new group with which they aligned themselves.

All Japanese Americans who declared themselves loyal suffered to some degree from these compulsions. All could be linked with the Japanese enemy by those who identified race with allegiance. This accounts in some measure for the self-conscious protestations of loyalty and the lofty verbalisms of those who declared themselves loyal and perhaps also, in part, for the extraordinary war record of Japanese Americans in the armed services. As one soldier put it, "We fight two battles; one against the Axis enemy, one against the enemy of intolerance at home."

The second response, contrary to the general positive relationship between acculturation and loyalty, is the obverse of the one just discussed: disloyalty where, on outward counts, one would expect loyalty. Here we find those most attached and most adjusted to American ways declaring themselves disloyal because they deeply felt that the evacuation was an affront to

America as they conceived it should be. They were disloyal Americans because of their Americanism.

Loyalty is both attitude and act. Loyalty, as attitude, given the usual compartmentalization of life, has few bounds; one can preserve loyalty to diverse groups and easily reconcile any contradictions that exist. But loyalty as behavior is another matter. Behavior can be seen; one cannot behave in two contradictory ways at the same time; and (though this aspect of the matter was not illustrated during the registration) action, unlike attitude, has the tendency to demand an individual's total resources of time and energy. The ill-fortune of Japanese Americans was that they were forced to a declaration of loyalty as behavior under circumstances of extreme deprivation and in full view of an audience that excluded no significant group and that included government officials.

The declaration thus forced upon the evacuee citizens was one few Americans are ever asked to make. Their behavior, defined as "disloyal," was, furthermore, no more than an answer to a question, the sort of behavior not often considered relevant to national allegiance. The "disloyalty" demonstrated was only a temporary response to a situation, and, unlike other such responses, it was not dangerous to the nation's security. As soon as the deprivational pressures became less burdensome, many of those who had answered "no" wished to change their views.

These unusual circumstances of the Japanese Americans do not efface the basic similarities between their declarations and other acts of disloyalty. Such acts, too, often occur under extreme pressure, are often responses to immediate situations, and are often subject to second thoughts. Other persons also believe their disloyal conduct is unfairly forced upon them and unfairly judged by others.

The wartime experience of Japanese Americans was an oddity. Caution must be exercised in drawing general conclusions from that experience. This social pathology, nevertheless, has important lessons to teach. Evacuees gave declarations of disloyalty for the same reasons that other people in other situations take sides in a more serious way against their nation. The registration crisis laid bare the social processes that produce disloyalty, processes that in other cases are hidden.

Above all, the experience of Japanese Americans demonstrates how loyalty is influenced by life-situation. Declarations of loyalty and disloyalty were concrete responses to concrete situations. Disloyalty grew from estimates of past experience, current plight, and what the future might hold.

The Japanese Americans of Hawaii, when asked to volunteer for army service, responded in great numbers: one out of every three male citizens between the ages of eighteen and thirty-eight offered his services, 9,507 in all. On the mainland, 1,208 volunteered from the centers, approximately one out of fourteen of those eligible. In Hawaii, no evacuation took place; in the United States, Japanese Americans were asked to volunteer from barbed-wire inclosures.

Within the relocation centers the variety of conditions also produced great variation in disloyal responses. Male citizens at Manzanar were seven times more likely to declare themselves disloyal than those at Granada. The differences among centers were more important than all other influences determining loyalty or disloyalty. The accident of being in one center rather than in another led many to declare their lack of allegiance.

Deprivation, scorn, isolation, and persecution erode national loyalty and produce national disloyalty. This is the meaning of the Hawaii-mainland comparison. The greater the deprivation felt, the greater the erosion of loyalty. This is the meaning of the center-by-center differences.

This evidence minimizes the distinction between "practical"

and "ideological" reasons for disloyalty. Instead of being "irrelevant," the practical considerations of social situation are of prime importance.

Out of life-situation are formed the indirect ties between individual and nation that are the principal ingredient of democratic national loyalty. To believe that loyalty, or disloyalty, is the result of some sort of pure "conviction" is to believe falsely that only the direct nation-person tie is important. This is not so in any nation, particularly not so in a democracy. Conviction, or ideology, whatever its strength as an influence of action, is related to one's circumstances. Ideology and objective situation profoundly influence each other. The chain is endless. Situation contributes to the acceptance or rejection of ideal; ideal in turn provides an interpretation of situation.

The interaction between deprivations and disloyalty is not a simple one. Those Japanese Americans who had been accepted by the larger community before the war, who had been educated in the United States and had become culturally assimilated, were more likely to retain their loyalty under stress than those who had lived their lives in cultural islands under the prewar pressures of an unfriendly larger community. But some of the well-integrated used disloyalty as protest, and some of the rejected used loyalty as a passport to acceptance.

Disloyalty is compounded out of more than deficiencies of food and shelter. Indeed, there is almost no limit to the sacrifices that men will make and still remain loyal to a cause. Royce held it an "obvious truth of human nature, that loyalty is never raised to its highest levels without . . . grief." The history of the early Christian church gives perhaps the best example of this phenomenon; and striking contemporary illustrations can be found in the experience of Russian partisans, German SS troops, and American Rangers.

When are the fierce loyalties generated within the deprived

groups turned against the nation? When are they linked to the nation's cause? The group's own definitions of the right and proper and the extent to which its own ideology is linked with the nation's are of first importance. The experience of Japanese Americans indicates that deprivation leads to national disloyalty when the deprived believe themselves to be despised, when they have no hope of future reward, when they are confronted with alternative attachments that promise fewer evils. Suffering *on behalf of* nation cements national loyalty; suffering *as the result of* national policies destroys it. Outsiders, including government officials, can influence acceptance of one definition or the other; the crucial definition comes from the sufferers themselves.

More accurately, it comes largely from their face-to-face groups. Loyalty to nation is shaped by loyalty to other groups and other ideas. When state policies promote the welfare of smaller groups with which a person identifies himself—and the family is the prototype—national loyalty is likely to be strong. When state policies conflict with the welfare of primary groups and choices have to be made, the stage is set for crisis, and national disloyalty is more likely to result.

There are strong suggestions that a far greater number of Japanese Americans would have declared themselves disloyal to America if they had been able to visualize a viable existence for themselves in Japan. The issue of changing national loyalties, in other terms, becomes important only when there exists an attractive alternative to current loyalty. Without alternatives, deficiencies in the current situation do not lead to a new national loyalty but produce withdrawal or obstructionism or the urge to reform. And where obstructionism leads to severe penalty and reform agitation promises no results, a state of helplessness and indecision ensues.

All this was illustrated during and after the registration.

There were protests, mass meetings, riots. And there was sore dilemma. On one side, Japanese Americans were pushed toward declarations of disloyalty as a consequence of their past treatment and current low status, of family pressures, and of the personal security in the relocation centers offered them as a reward for such a declaration. On the other side, they were pulled to declarations of loyalty by their American experience and values and, more pertinently here, by the absence of an alternative: they had few positive ties with Japan. Their final indecision was illustrated by those who declared that they wanted to be loyal to both the United States and Japan, by those who said they wished neither nation to win the war, by those who wished to declare themselves "neutral," and by those who vacillated wildly between statements of devotion and hatred.

The Japanese American case also illuminates the wide range of ambiguities contained in the concept of national loyalty. To some people the issue of loyalty pivots on specific policies of the government; to others, considerations of program are subordinate to a concern for ideology, for leaders, for systems of government. During the registration some evacuees regarded the fact of evacuation itself as the crucial point of judgment: program and nation were equated, and nation was damned. The United States was rejected in favor of family solidarity, security, or an uncertain future in Japan. Others distinguished program from principle and from system. Many regarded evacuation as an aberration of the democratic norm and preserved faith in a later return to it. These people answered "Yes." Others, while making the same distinction, came to the opposite decision. They regarded evacuation as a palpable distortion of democratic principles and declared their disloyalty to America as an expression of their commitment to those principles or as a protest against the discrepancy between program and principles.

Disloyalty declarations were rarely simple expressions of rejection. They were also expressions of preference, acts of positive identification with ideal, block group, family. In each case, nation was rejected because, under the circumstances, another loyalty became primary.

Japanese Americans were not unique in believing that their declarations of disloyalty had little to do with the "real" problem of national allegiance. The "real" problem to them was their own security, the obligations they owed their parents, the expectations of their friends and neighbors. What sense of evil or betrayal they may have felt as the result of subordinating the demands of nation was overshadowed by the imperative of maintaining faith with persons closest to them, with ideas meaningful to them.

And so it is with virtually all acts of national disloyalty. Other groups, other causes, other nations become dominant. The most blatant traitor does not look upon himself as such. He regards his acts as an expression of loyalty to, not disloyalty against. Brutus aided in the assassination "not that I loved Caesar less, but that I loved Rome more." There are few Iagos who glory in villainy. "No man at bottom means injustice," Carlyle wrote. "It is always for some distorted image of a right that he contends."

8 The Achievement of Treason

Where content is overburdened by discontent, old loyalties weaken and new loyalties grow. One difficulty in making predictions about the strength or weakness of national loyalty is in defining what constitutes human satisfaction. The Platonic emphasis on temperance and justice—that each person and each class must find an appropriate station in life and desire no other—stands in contrast to "life, liberty, and the pursuit of happiness" and to the French revolutionary's "natural right" to social mobility and political regicide. "Wine, women, and song" competes as a definition of the desirable with "blood, toil, tears, and sweat." The last phrase is a valuable reminder of the manner in which modern psychology has deepened our understanding of satisfaction. Some people enjoy unhappiness, others suffer from privilege in an underprivileged world, still others find their highest joy in self-sacrifice. "Why do I long for Communism?" Gide asked. "Because I believe it to be equitable and because I suffer on account of the injustices which I feel more strongly than ever when it is I myself who am favored. . . . the happiness of man does not consist in liberty but in the acceptance of a duty."

Individual differences aside, the controlling variations in the definition of human satisfactions are variations in social definition. What is heaven to a Hottentot, or even a Russian, may be hell to an American. Within a nation, definitions of the desirable and the undesirable vary with age, class, occupation, and ethnic group, among many other factors. Loyalty flows to those groups and institutions that supply the individual with psychic and material comfort. So long as he is content, other objects of loyalty are not likely to attract him. When he is ignorant of, or rejected by, alternate focal points of loyalty, he is similarly inert, no matter how great his current discontent. Loyalties are essential to men; but their focus is by no means fixed.

The specific paths to national disloyalty are numerous. The Japanese case study illustrated how a deprived people, in this instance those directly deprived by the nation, placed other loyalties above national loyalty. The crucial factor was the strength of other loyalties asserting themselves over loyalty to nation in a crisis situation.

Disloyalty is also achieved under more generalized conditions of dissatisfaction, when the weakness, rather than the strength, of smaller loyalties is controlling. Marx called this illness of modern life *alienation;* others have described the same social facts as *anomie* and as the quality of *social massness.* Avoiding differences in the technical meaning of these concepts, all refer to the quality of modern society that denies people enjoyment or even understanding of life.

This is the state in which individuals feel no sense of "belonging" to their community or nation. Personal contacts are neither stable nor satisfactory. An individual works with one group, lives with another, plays with a third, and worships, if he worships at all, with still a fourth. In no group and in no combination of groups does he feel completely at one with his fellows.

In work, for example, he collaborates primarily with a machine rather than with fellow-workers. No individual contributes to the final product any part of his personality and skill that can later be identified with pride or satisfaction. Alienation thus extends both to fellow-workers and to work products. Family life is similarly perverted. An individual is a father, mother, son, or daughter for only a bare fraction of a day. Cramped city quarters reduce the home to a site for eating and sleeping. Young members of the family play in the street or in the bureaucratized YMCA or with bureaucratized Boy Scouts. Aged members are cared for by the bureaucratized state.

The segmentation of life is accompanied by the segmentation of beliefs. Religion is marked by sporadic church attendance but not by faith. Political participation declines because political issues surpass the common man's understanding. Cultural leaders find no followers because there is no single culture; there are only competing and overlapping ways of life. Each person must decide whether to adhere to old beliefs, if he can identify them, or accept new beliefs, or attempt to live without beliefs.

Many observers see modern culture as predominantly one that produces alienation. This is certainly an exaggerated view (see chap. 14), but there is abundant evidence that large numbers of people find themselves at some point in their lives in an alienated state. The German middle classes, ruined by inflation during the interwar period, exemplified such a situation. The unemployed in the United States during the middle 1930's also displayed many signs of alienation, including the weakening of family, church, and friendship ties, the loss of self-respect, and the loss of faith in democratic institutions. Young people, when the stable relationships in school and with parents have not yet been replaced by the new stability of job and their own family, also approach the edge of personal alienation and the political attributes of massness.

These political attributes include most crucially the willingness to seek new causes, to join new leaders. The alienated person is the isolated person. He looks for new loyalties. He is the potentially disloyal citizen.

The path to disloyalty via alienation is, on its face, the exact opposite of the path to disloyalty via the choice of placing other group loyalties over the nation. Yet these opposites are, in fact, only the same social process viewed at different times. In one case, disloyalty is achieved because strong, non-national group bonds already exist; in the other case, disloyalty results from seeking group bonds to replace the emptiness of alienated life. Disloyalty through alienation is the successful search for satisfactory group relations.

As all such descriptions do, this sketch of two paths to disloyalty fails to catch the subtleties of particular situations and to make clear how complex the process of achieving disloyalty really is. Among other things, the disloyal person in almost every circumstance will justify his action in terms of some larger ideal. The ideal may indeed be the controlling factor: influences on human action are numerous and the moral injunction is, in operation, not different from the pressures of face-to-face companions in an unhappy social situation. If you were to search for the perfect revolutionist, Crane Brinton tells us, "you will do well to consider . . . the idealist."

Justifications of those who are disloyal because of group ties are often similar to justifications of those disloyal because of alienation. The conscientious objector, a firm member of a church group, opposes army service on the grounds that all men have an innate dignity and that killing is against God's law. The plotting revolutionary, at odds with most of society, avows the same sentiments for the same dignity of the same men.

Yet there are genuine differences in the goals which the disloyal seek. At one extreme is the person who rejects some part of his society, though accepting it as a whole. The conscientious objector again is a prime example: he seeks justice and the better life within his nation; and he accepts punishment by the nation, hoping by his fortitude to dispel the charge of cowardice and to inspire others to pacifism. He honestly believes himself to be a good citizen. At the other extreme is the saboteur or revolutionary. He seeks justice by creating another world, and he derives joy, even if persecuted, by participating in the creation of that world. The draft dodger represents an intermediate type. He accepts his nation, acknowledges his obligation to it, and seeks not justice but his own comfort. While the others believe passionately in their cause, the draft dodger is burdened with guilt. He will often try to justify himself in terms that are used by the conscientious objector; and he may find himself pushed into the revolutionary's role as a consequence of his burden of conscience and the hostility he meets.

Though objector, draft dodger, and saboteur all engage in disloyal acts, society recognizes differences among them. The objector is respected, and accommodations are made to his protest; he is punished reluctantly. The draft dodger is derided and shamed. He is detested, and, if he cannot be rehabilitated, his punishment is harsh. The saboteur or revolutionary is feared and therefore is hated. He is punished with vengeance.

The objector's loyalty to the nation is weaker because, typically, his church loyalty is stronger. The saboteur is the product of alienation. His loyalty to nation is weak because he has no loyalties related to his nation; rather his allegiances are to groups and ideals rejected by nation. And this typifies the different kinds of disloyalty produced by strong non-national loyalties, on the one hand, and alienation, on the other. The former weaken the state but rarely destroy it outright. The alienated, on the other hand, are more easily recruited into programs of revolution. They have least to lose and most to gain with a complete change of rulers.

Yet this contrast cannot be pushed too far. Under extreme circumstances—when, for example, an enemy army occupies a nation—ready collaborators are found among both groups. For those with strong non-national loyalties, collaboration with the enemy is the result of the attempt to save what is thought most precious. If the enemy destroys a man's home and business, he is likely to join the partisan band; but if he is allowed to work to save home and business, he is more likely to work for the enemy. The alienated person can also be recruited on either side. Having neither home nor business to guard, he may be less fearful of fighting to the end; or he may become a collaborator because the enemy promises him a better life.

Each of the principal modes of achieving disloyalty to nation can be illustrated by examples that arise out of the prosaic day-to-day business of life. Here the most frequent loyalty choices are made. Though the national interest may be ignored and though the result may be harmful, even dangerous, to the national welfare, the result is not overtly disloyal action. At least it is not so judged by society, and here, as elsewhere, the definition of the event is what makes it real. What such actions reveal, therefore, is not disloyalty as such. They are cases on the fringe of disloyalty.

Where non-national loyalties are strong, the social mechanisms are very similar to those described in the previous chapter. Only one new example need be given.

The conscious evasion of national price-fixing laws by American butchers during World War II was apparent to all. Agreement has not been reached upon the statistics. Estimates of the extent of lawbreaking range from 25 to more than 90 per cent of the independent owners of butcher-shops. Their denial of the wartime law was not through ignorance. They did what they did in full knowledge. Their secret was an open one, their attitude self-righteous. Their justifications, where given, were short and pointed. They spoke, above all, of the stupidity, the inflexibility, of bureaucratic rule. And they pointed to responsibilities that loomed more important in their eyes than responsibility to governmental orders.

First was a responsibility to client. Obedience to regulations would mean no meat for customers. Customers were important civilian soldiers. They needed food to win the war.

Second was a responsibility to family. If regulations were obeyed, profits would be drastically reduced or become nonexistent, and families would suffer. Compliance with regulations was an immediate threat to family; non-compliance was a tenuous, an unreal, threat to nation. Family was put first.

Third was a responsibility to business career. The independent butcher fights a hard battle against the supermarket. The latter's advantages in mass purchasing and assembly-line dispensing are overcome only by the independent's skill in trading pennies for quality at the stockyard or the wholesaler; in providing storage with minimum wastage; in making the customer believe she is getting what she wants when those wants may be impossible at going rates. The clue to the whole enterprise is personal service: when service is no longer available, cheaper cuts are around the corner. And here, as in many other endeavors, it is far easier to keep an old customer than to get a new one or to recapture the old one, once new buying habits have been established.

To many independents, OPA regulations meant the destruction of a carefully cultivated market. It meant losing the hard way to chain competitors. It meant closing shop and seeking new and uncertain careers. It meant the loss of independence. It meant severe deprivations for families. These were hard choices. The alternative of non-compliance was easy, the penalties for lawbreaking unimportant in comparison with the penalties of law compliance.

Outside the area of meat rationing, butchers, in common with other Americans, contributed in full measure to the nation's war effort. Their failure to obey OPA regulations was contrary to legislation enacted as a needed wartime measure. It was sanctioned by a large segment of public opinion and by the most relevant opinions, represented in the black-market slaughterer, the black-market customer, and colleagues in the retail business. All collaborated with, and protected, one another. Violation of OPA rules may not be regarded as disloyalty, but such violations clearly define the stuff out of which disloyalty is made.

The case of the butchers involves the nation being placed second to strong, existing loyalties to business, career, and family. Turn now to the case where alienation—the lack of existing loyalties—is controlling.

Richard Wright has sensitively documented his conversion to the Communist cause. As a young man in Chicago, he could find no place for himself, no friends, no appreciation for his writing. In his misery he was impressed by efforts in the Soviet Union to encourage the cultural development of diverse ethnic and racial groups. Communism seemed to promise the Negroes "a home, a functioning value and role." "How different this was from the way in which Negroes were sneered at in America."

He drifted into contact with left-wing groups and finally became a member of the John Reed (Communist) Club. There he found tasks to perform and appreciation for his work: "Here, then, was something that I could do, reveal, say. . . . I would tell Communists how common people felt, and I would tell common people of the self-sacrifice of Communists who strove for unity among them." In the Communist group, Wright also found friendship. "I was meeting men and women whom I should know for decades to come, who were to form the first sustained relationships in my life."

The John Reed Club gave Wright all that he most needed. He was a Negro affronted by white assumptions of superiority, a writer desperately in search of a market, a human being longing for human affection. Through his contact with Communists, he acquired the status of an equal, the respect due to a man of talent, an outlet for that talent in writing for the Communist cause, and, perhaps more than anything else, the warm friendships for which he felt so profound a need.

Alienation is not confined to the poor or to members of minority races. And the processes by which the nation is made subordinate to the satisfaction of other needs is repeated for the rich and powerful as well as for the poor and weak.

The abdication of Edward VIII from the British throne makes these points clear. The patriotism of the present Duke of Windsor cannot be doubted. As he himself observed, his marriage to Mrs. Simpson need not have eventuated in abdication if he had wished openly to defy the cabinet. But this would have impaired the prestige of the throne, a risk the king, in patriotic duty, did not wish to take. These and other extenuating issues aside, it remains true that his marriage and consequent abdication constituted a clear case in which the nation became subordinate to other desires, to the need of an alienated king for the joys of marriage and family.

Before his marriage, Edward was caught in a situation which he found disturbing and distasteful. Despite the fact that he had been "bred in the constitutional tradition by [his] Father," he chafed at the restrictions under which he labored. As prince and as monarch, his life "appeared to form a disconnected pattern—duty without decision, service without responsibility, pomp without power." To difficulties with his job were added dissatisfaction over lack of family. He was determined not to contract "a loveless marriage" of state convenience; he had seen "too many unhappy unions of this kind to wish to risk one" himself. He yearned for a wife "dictated not by considerations of State but by [his] own heart."

Edward envied the content of his parents and brothers. His own life was "pervaded . . . by a sense of incompleteness and inner discontent." He saw that both his father, the king before him, and his brother, the king after him, "were devoted family men, a quality that goes a long way for a king and in a constitutional monarchy." He described the Christmas gathering before his father's death: "In this closely knit fabric of family ties I felt detached and lonely. My brothers were secure in their private lives; whereas I was caught up in an inner conflict and would have no peace of mind until I had resolved it."

When crisis came, the point on which Edward's choice pivoted was clear-cut: abdication and the bride of his choice or retention of throne without "the woman I love." The decision was made easier by his knowledge that his brother would fulfil the duties of constitutional monarch and by his own ambivalent attitudes toward "pomp without power."

Allegiance to nation was not compromised. But clearly, even for the king, national duty was subordinated to the moving demands for love, home, and family. "If it had been hard to give up the Throne, it had been even harder to give up Great Britain. I knew now that I was irretrievably on my own. The drawbridges were going up behind me. But of one thing I was certain; so far as I was concerned love had triumphed over the exigencies of politics."

Whoever the persons involved—whether American butchers, Negro authors, or Edward VIII, King, Defender of the Faith, Emperor of India—action that elevates other values over national duty depends upon the equilibrium of life-satisfactions and dissatisfactions. Traitors and revolutionaries are not different species of man. The cases discussed do not involve overt cases of disloyalty. But the processes they reveal are repeated in every traitorous act.

A familiar Civil War example best illustrates how allegiance to smaller groups and institutions produces overt national disloyalty. Robert E. Lee, a distinguished career soldier of the United States and a former superintendent of West Point, was offered field command of the Union armies when secession was threatened by the southern states. He had no hesitation in declining the offer. From the first rumblings of southern discontent and the first threats of war between North and South, Lee's course was established. He believed secession an error, and he expressed his fervent hope that the Union would be preserved:

> I wish to live under no other government, and there is no sacrifice I am not ready to make for the preservation of the Union save that of honour. . . . I wish for no other flag than the "Star Spangled Banner" and no other air than "Hail Columbia."

Despite all this, Lee believed that his "loyalty to Virginia ought to take precedence over that which is due the Federal Government." He would serve the Union only if Virginia did not secede. Secession was "nothing but revolution" and no constitutional right; and there were not sufficient causes for revolution in the situation as it existed. He was nevertheless prepared to "follow my native state with my sword, and if need be with my life." He gave his most complete explanation of his action in a letter to his sister:

> The whole south is in a state of revolution into which Virginia, after a long struggle, has been drawn; and, though I recognize no necessity for this state of things, and would have . . . pleaded to the end for a redress of grievances, real or supposed, yet in my own person I had to meet the question whether I should take part against my native state.
>
> With all my devotion to the Union and the feeling of loyalty and duty of an American citizen, *I have not been able to make up my mind to raise my hand against my relatives, my children, my home.*

Lee represents par excellence the case of strong conflicting loyalties, the choice of other loyalties over nation. A century and an ocean removed from Lee—and perhaps equally distant in terms of popular esteem—stands William Joyce, who illustrates national disloyalty resulting not from strong ties of other allegiances but from alienation.

Of Irish ancestry, Joyce as a youth supported the British in the savage struggle against Irish independence. When his family was forced to leave Ireland after Home Rule was granted, he found himself "exiled from his real motherland, Ireland . . . and confined in England, for love of which he had betrayed Ireland, and which showed no gratitude for that sacrifice."

Joyce's life was a succession of unfulfilled ambitions. His application for a position in the British army officers' corps was rejected because of doubts over his citizenship and the suitability of his social background. A university graduate with first-class honors, it was "inconceivable that he could have arrived at any position of distinction in the academic world." Interested in politics, he was acceptable to the Conservative party of his choice only in minor capacities. He broke with his parents, and he was married outside the Catholic church. His first marriage was a failure. He nowhere found acceptance on the terms that he desired.

A police officer said Joyce was the sort that "did not seem to fit in anywhere." His parents traced his difficulty to the fact that he was "too brilliant." He failed to achieve eminence, Rebecca West tells us, "because of his personal limitations, the clownish extravagance which left him, even after he had played a uniquely sinister part in history, with the comic nickname of Lord Haw-Haw, the odd vulgarity which made it almost impossible to believe, looking at him or listening to him, that he was a University graduate or the child of people with a position in a community." If Joyce had lived "innocent as snow he would still have looked dubious and at that comically dubious."

Joyce's life was typified by an incident which occurred after he had joined the British Fascists. He was the guest of an army man who kept a stable of horses, and after showing his skill with less valuable animals, he was allowed to ride a difficult thoroughbred. The host's elderly father, who was deaf, stood among the other guests and watched. " 'How marvelously Mr. Joyce rides!' a lady bawled into his ear. 'Yes!' he bawled back. 'But not like a gentleman.' "

With aspirations that could not be satisfied within the main stream of British life, Joyce was forced to society's edges in order to gain what he wanted. Opportunity was available in the British Union of Fascists. He was initially successful and became, in short time, first deputy leader of the movement. Here he found a sort of social status, public attention, and opportunity for travel abroad. "The life of the political conspirator [offered] the man of restricted capacity but imaginative energy excitements and satisfactions which he could never derive from overt activities."

Ever the discontented, Joyce found no firm place even among the Fascists. He recoiled from the snobbishness of his leader, Sir Oswald Mosley, who would not accept him as a social equal, and he quarreled with Mosley over matters of tactics, policy, and pay. He left the movement under the accusation that he had misappropriated funds for his own use. Shortly thereafter he founded his own Fascist organization. And in September, 1939, Joyce appeared in Berlin, beginning his broadcasts for the Nazis exactly fifteen days after the outbreak of war. Miss West speculates that he left London believing that if he won his gamble, "he would return to it as the right hand of its conquerors." He returned instead to the gallows, the ultimate alienation.

The alienated person need not be disloyal. He may become indifferent or withdrawn. He may alter his expectations for life. He may become sick or turn to hoboism. He may conform completely because he has no other alternative. He may follow other courses of deviance.

He is most likely to turn to disloyalty if he can find a face-to-face group to support and promote the expression of his discontents. Such groups act as connecting links between dissatisfactions with old ways of life that erode old national loyalties and satisfactions with a new mode of living that builds new national loyalties.

In many cases it is not important which group one joins. Almost any will serve, as long as it is composed of others who also suffer the pangs of social malcontent. "When a person is ready to become a radical," an ex-Communist explained, "it is just an accident whether he becomes a Stalinist or Trotskyist. . . . The first people he has contact with he joins." And another organizer of a radical party said the organization "that gets to [the prospective member] first will recruit him."

No political discontent need exist. Persons can drift into radical groups out of sheer boredom or loneliness, as the result of anxiety over their position in life, as a revolt against parental authority, in consequence of a love affair, or for an infinite number of other reasons. The very existence of the group can create political protest from more generalized dissatisfactions. The finding of friends who are revolutionaries may be enough to create revolutionaries out of the politically apathetic. This is especially so in the urban situation—where loneliness is all the more painful because of the crowd.

The case of Richard Wright illustrates this mechanism. It is the basis of virtually all Communist recruitment, which is pursued through cell organizations, groups whose members meet intimately over long periods of time. The large, intricately built, and successful spy ring in Canada, established to deliver military secrets to Russia, was based on what were called "Marxist study groups." Members were recruited for purposes of discussion. Strong friendship ties were forged. Only after a long period of primary group indoctrination were members requested, sometimes only casually, to undertake espionage. Friendships were the first steps to treason.

And the power of friends also expresses itself in the reverse situation: it can lead to disloyalty to the disloyal. This is clear in the case of the physicist Klaus Fuchs. After supplying information about American and British nuclear weapons to the Soviet Union, he stopped of his own volition because "he . . . was very worried about the effect of his behavior upon the friendships which he had contracted at [the scientific laboratories at] Harwell." While continuing to believe in communism, Fuchs had come to disapprove of "many actions of the Russians." Once interrogated by security officers, he knew he had to leave his secret work. But he could not leave under suspicion, and he therefore confessed:

> . . . It became clear that in leaving Harwell in these circumstances [of being questioned by security officers] I would deal a great blow to Harwell and all the work I had loved and also leave suspicions against friends whom I had loved and people who thought I was their friend. . . . All I can do now is to try and repair the damage I have done. The first thing is to make sure that Harwell will suffer as little as possible.

Fuchs confessed because he felt guilty over being disloyal to his professional colleagues and friends, not to Great Britain.

Once imbedded in a face-to-face group whose aims are disloyal, once acknowledging rejection of, and rejection by, the larger society, the individual can admit no limitation upon his allegiance to the other members of the group and to its cause. He becomes firmly socialized within the disloyal group, and he achieves satisfactions from the group to which his discontents have brought him. He escapes the censure of the larger society in the appreciation he receives from his deviant associates.

This constitutes a social and personal paradox of the greatest importance. The larger social disorganization produces small deviant groups which are tightly organized. Personal disorganization in the larger society leads to the most complete kind of personal integration and satisfaction within the marginal groups.

Nor is this difficult to understand. Members of such groups become both "insulated and absorbed." They are able in a group to deal with the pressures and penalties imposed upon deviants by the larger society. In partnership, they express their alienation; at the same time they fulfil their emotional needs for conformity. The deviant group generates and maintains a claim that its goals are the legitimate goals of the larger society. This claim is often made "by turning the tables on the wider society and declaring the latter's value-orientations to be illegitimate in its own terms."

The despised and rejected have no life apart from the despised and rejected. If segments of their daily round of activity must take them outside their own group, these aspects of life are viewed as peripheral, either as temporary stopgaps until the cause triumphs or as necessary expedients in the service of the group and its ultimate victory. No friendships are formed, no pleasures are realized, outside the group. Friends, work, family—all must be incorporated into political activity. If this is not accomplished, the individual will suffer severe cross-pressures, other loyalties conflicting with his political allegiance. Such conflicts are intolerable. The person who becomes involved in such a group is like a resident of a totalitarian state: his whole life is politics.

The most grotesque acts are accepted as a matter of course and the most flagrant dishonesties are regarded as marks of virtue if they contribute to the group and its cause. Both Marx and Lenin made this point explicit. It is acted out in many ways and many places. To take but one example: almost all the members of a revolutionary group in Chicago during the depression found their source of income in work for federal relief agencies. They voted to contribute the largest fraction of their government payments to their program for overthrowing that government. This was natural and convenient. It was not even a cause of merriment, let alone of conscience or ill-ease.

To prosper in membership, the cause needs to be differentiated from other causes. It also needs to have objectives, however grandiose in scope, which the members can hope to achieve. Even in the face of the greatest adversity, participation with familiars in a task that consumes one's whole life and energies is an important source of human satisfaction, a resolver of doubts, and a means to deny frailty and inadequacy. "Work is a potent drug; to make oneself feel that one is doing a useful job anonymously and wholeheartedly is the most effective way of bribing one's conscience."

Hatred and calumny from outside the group are a mark of credit. Oppression strengthens rather than weakens the resolve of the hard core. As the group rejects portions of the larger society, it tends to reject all of it. And its members must increasingly depend upon their own circle of the like-minded.

Men under these circumstances despise even comfort. They cannot turn back. Sacrifice becomes pleasure. Ignazio Silone has written of the extreme conditions under which Communists were forced to live in Italy, once the Italian state had fallen under the control of Mussolini's Fascists. He had to adapt himself "to living like a foreigner in [his] own country." He changed his name, abandoned his family and former friends.

> The Party became family, school, church, barracks; the world that lay beyond it was to be destroyed and built anew. . . . Every sacrifice was welcomed as a personal contribution to the "price of collective redemption"; and it should be emphasized that the links which bound us to the Party grew steadily firmer, not in spite of the dangers and sacrifices involved, but because of them.

This explanation of how the alienated find integration and joy in disloyal groups is also the explanation of why it is so difficult to "break" with the radical group, a difficulty that is documented in virtually every ex-Communist memoir.

Since a person's entire personal relationships are centered in politics, breaking involves no simple shift in political beliefs. Rather it means the destruction of one's entire perspective of society, the smashing of a whole way of life. It means losing all the emotional gains derived from submerging one's life in the cause. It means losing friends and in many cases also losing wife or husband. It means the possibility of physical reprisal and the threat of finding one's self unemployed and unemployable. It means a return to emptiness, to alienation.

"I knew in my heart," Wright thought after being expelled from the Communist party, "that I should never be able to write that way again, should never be able to feel with that simple sharpness about life, should never again express such passionate hope, should never again make so total a commitment of faith." Wright left without wishing to. For those who leave voluntarily, the act appears to be one of renouncing all that is real and good in life. They must face life without "a holy cause"; and this explains why ex-Communists frequently find new causes in religion or in superpatriotism. If they find no new cause, they have great difficulty in giving meaning to their lives. "An individual existence, even when purposeful, seems . . . trivial, futile, and sinful."

Those who quit such groups frequently do so with great feelings of guilt. In very many cases they cannot do it alone. They need the sustenance of companions, so a typical pattern is for a group to leave together. "Since many of my friends had left or were leaving at the same time, it was easier for me." Or they build, while still in the disloyal group, new ties with spouses, colleagues, or friends who are outside the group. This then leads to their departure; the new affiliations are incompatible with the demands of the political group, which will take nothing less than everything.

When conformity to the deviant group is established, the basis for overt disloyalty has been laid. The formation of a corps of the like-minded is the crucial point. The group commitment grows as the group removes itself further and further from the larger society. The more deviant the group is, the more deviant it is likely to become. This is the pattern of the vicious circle. As the group separates itself from the larger society, so society reacts adversely; thus new justifications for even greater deviance are found by the group, and, in turn, new acts of repression by society are warranted.

The pressures of the larger society discourage some members of the disloyal group. They splinter away and try to find spheres of activity that are more acceptable to society, or they attempt to re-establish themselves within the larger community. For many this is impossible. And there tends to be a point of no turning back, especially when the established groups have openly expressed their rejection. When this happens, the reaction of the deviant is likely to be extreme, especially when he believes, as he almost invariably does, that society has treated him with injustice.

The vengeance of the rejected was expressed by Coriolanus, the Roman hero of legend who fought long and bravely for his city, won great victories, and was elected consul, only to be banished because of his unpopularity with the plebeian masses. Coriolanus fled to his most bitter enemy, and the enemy of Rome, to offer his services against his native city.

> And make my misery serve thy turn: so use it
> That my revengeful services may prove
> As benefits to thee; for I will fight
> Against my canker'd country with the spleen
> Of all the under fiends. . . .

Italian Americans have been pushed into support of fascism by the sting of being called "wops" and "dagos" by other Americans. A Japanese American boy refused to change his declaration of disloyalty to the United States, explaining: "You people are just not loyal to us; so that's the way we have to feel." The central figure of a contemporary novel does not openly commit treason against the United States until he learns with dismay that he has been indicted for treasonous acts by American authorities.

All this only repeats the experience of that prototype of all traitors—the brilliant and unscrupulous, the gentle and awful, the ambitious Alcibiades of fifth-century Greece. He led the armies of his native Athens to victories over the Spartans; and later the Spartan armies to victories over the Athenians; and still later the Persian armies to victory over both Spartans and Athenians. Before his first great acts of treason, Alcibiades was with Athenian forces in the field when word was brought that he had been condemned by his own state. Plutarch writes: "When . . . [Alcibiades] was told that the [Athenian] assembly had pronounced judgment of death against him, all he said was, 'I will make them feel that I am still alive!' "

9 Totalitarian Disloyalty

Totalitarian nations appear immune from the two principal causes of democratic national disloyalty. They protect themselves from the competition of lesser loyalties by attempting to destroy or capture them. At the same time, they use controlled alienation as a positive tool for binding the individual to the state, giving him a cause to embrace, a leader to follow, and *ersatz* primary groups to monopolize his time and energies. These policies can never be completely successful. To the extent that they do succeed, they produce their own disaffections and create an unstable social organization.

It can be argued that the totalitarian systems must destroy themselves. Industry and warfare, the foundation stones of modern states, depend upon a rational way of thinking and a scientific technology that appear completely at odds with the irrational, terroristic methods of the totalitarian rulers. Those rulers are therefore doomed. They have only two alternatives: to depress the level of their nation's culture, thus preventing the development of rational, skeptical individuals, or to exploit the science and the intelligence of their age. The first alternative makes their existence impossible because they are wholly dependent upon science and scientific habits of thought. The second alternative produces the very intelligence and capacities that foment discontent and revolution.

This argument is an old one. It was used by the English historian Gibbon, who concluded that Europe would never again be overrun by the barbarians because they had acquired Western culture. It was used by the French scientist Pasteur, who believed that advances in the sciences could not fail to educate and pacify mankind. It was used by the American economist Veblen, who argued that the rationality produced by rational work would display to the whole population the inadequacies of the imperial Germany he saw and of the fascism he foresaw.

The history of the last two centuries and the forecastable future do not hint that these factors are important destructive forces for totalitarian loyalties. Man can simultaneously be "a god in technology, an ape in life." Science and rationality give weapons to the oppressor as well as to the oppressed. They can be used equally to educate and to destroy, and they can make barbarians more effective in their barbarousness. In the very long run, the daily utilization of science may educate populations to the extent that they will not tolerate tyranny; but populations may also become permanently cowed and discouraged, or educated to enthusiastic support of the regime. If a discussion of the weaknesses of totalitarian loyalties is to have immediate relevance, it must concentrate on factors that are less subject to the uncertainties of long-term social drift.

Some totalitarian policies contribute simultaneously to the strengths and to the weaknesses of national loyalty. A policy of rapid collectivization of farms may cement the loyalty of industrial and military leaders while bringing peasants to sullen disobedience; another policy might have the opposite consequences. The sharpest insight is one that reveals both strengthening and weakening effects operating at the same time for the same individuals and the same groups. This is not a difficult concept in political analysis. It is a commonplace in almost every other sphere of life: in marriages, where affection for the husband's charm is matched by a horror of his household sloppiness; on the job, where resentments over the time clock are subordinated to satisfaction over the paycheck; in the church, where dislike of the minister is overcome by the spiritual and social satisfactions of Sunday attendance; in professional sports, where animosity toward owners and managers is erased by the satisfactions of playful work (or worklike play) and the plaudits of the crowd.

These simple examples illustrate the universality of ambivalent attitudes, and they demonstrate the larger point: that like and dislike, forces for loyalty and disloyalty, exist side by side within a single individual and a single group.

One facet of this phenomenon is illustrated by those who have fled from the Russian dictatorship but who, for all their hatred of the regime, still preserve affection for some of its aspects. The Soviet refugees uniformly excoriate the Soviet leadership, but they are by no means unanimous in criticizing the totalitarian system. Many look to authoritarian methods for altering the regime. Moreover, despite the fact that they may have fled the Soviet Union in fear of their lives, they not only cherish the Russian homeland but also speak with admiration of Soviet military and industrial achievements, of free schools, free medical services, and other welfare programs of the state. Similarly, anti-Nazi Germans found pride in Hitler's program of public housing, in his handling of economic crises, and in his restoration of the strength of the fatherland.

Soviet prisoners, unlike those in the United States, are largely political offenders; but, like prisoners everywhere, they frequently remain patriots. Zot Ivanovich Chepurnykh, a former vice-consul in New York, was interviewed just after he had been sentenced by a Soviet court to fifteen years in jail. The former vice-consul said:

> ". . . I'm a Communist from the ground up. In the village where I was born, no one thirty years ago had shoes or a bed or could call a doctor. The Soviet has given me everything. I was able to learn, to study, to enter the state service, to found a family, to become what I am."

His interviewer interrupted Chepurnykh to comment that he now had a fifteen-year jail sentence.

> "It was my own fault," he avowed. ". . . Moscow punishes severely, but can also show mercy."

The source of this story is somewhat suspect. Yet it is consistent with other analyses. Two scholars, after interviewing many Russian refugees, summarized the polarity of hatred and support that is characteristic of the disadvantaged citizens of all totalitarian states:

> Coupled with their helplessness in the face of a ruthlessly oppressive regime was their affection for their homeland, family, work, status, and the whole way of life to which they were accustomed. Confronted with these circumstances, they accommodated as best they could to those things they disliked, in order not to lose what little was left of that which they cherished.

Different population groups receive markedly different advantages and disadvantages under dictatorships. The individual's place in the economy and bureaucracy, his age, and his nationality will all color his total view. Yet even those who receive fewest advantages are in one way or another integrated into the society—propagandized and terrorized into political inertness; caught in a network of identification with homeland, job, and family; discounting sorrows as they are balanced against joys; seeking areas of life immune from interference, yet reacting positively to great leaders and great state programs; and, withal, comforted in the milieu of the only language, literature, customs, holidays, and countryside that they know.

To those looking in from the outside, life under totalitarianism seems intolerable. Yet the evidence available demonstrates that this is not at all the case for those inside looking out. This is even true for those who have no internal commitment to the regime and for those who actually dislike it. Here we find individuals who comply out of sheer fear—the reluctant totalitarian—as well as large groups who try to insulate themselves from the totalitarian demands—the unconvinced who must compromise. The last group, sometimes suffering, sometimes deriving incidental benefits from the regime, finds existence tolerable because its members succeed in sheltering themselves in non-political niches. The very existence of such niches is a mark of weakness for the totalitarian state. But in this case weakness leads paradoxically to at least short-term social strength.

Yet the obverse of this coin is of even greater consequence. If apparent weakness in the regime provides strength for loyalties, apparent strengths conceal great weaknesses. The monolith is a façade.

Those who gain the greatest advantages from the regime suffer with the rest of the population. Every career advancement, with its consequent accretion of wealth, power, and prestige, is matched by increased insecurity and tension. The higher an individual goes, the more carefully he is watched, the more susceptible he becomes to penalty for failure, to political purge, to becoming the scapegoat for others. Not even those in jobs of power and prestige are free from worry in a society characterized by suspicion and violence.

Worry is not the only weakening factor. In some cases competent people must be liquidated when the official line changes and they have been outspoken advocates of the abandoned policies. This robs the regime of needed talent. Talent unused is missed as much as talent killed: under the circumstances, caution, silence, and subservience are widely cultivated. And talent unused may become talent unusable. Those who do only what they are told develop a trained incapacity. Officeholders eventually lose initiative; they cannot meet novel problems that are not covered in manuals and directives. This has been noted in satellite countries as well as within the Soviet Union itself.

For most of the higher functionaries, joys probably overbalance dissatisfactions. Their loyalty is relatively firm. But this cannot be assumed without reservation. And for large groups only helplessness and terror enforce compliance and conceal disaffection. The disaffections are hidden because to express them means forced labor or death. Huge resentments build up. This is damaging to the personality and dangerous to the society. It dams up hostility for sudden expression on a day of reckoning. The strengths of the regime hide its weaknesses.

Totalitarian systems attempt to make themselves appealing to the intellect. Theories as old as Plato and Aristotle can be interpreted and misinterpreted to justify the idea that man can find true freedom only in fulfilment of rational laws that demand individual conformity. Marxism attracts many in this "objective" fashion. It looks at history as a process of ordered flow according to near-immutable laws. The individual elevates "personal aspirations into cosmic necessities." He does what he does because his role is dictated by history. Similar, if less compelling, dogma justified the role of individuals in both the Nazi and the Fascist states.

Yet totalitarianism—even that ostensibly based upon Marxism—is essentially anti-intellectual. Most of those who live under a dictatorship are attached to it by the fear of violence, the improvement of status, the serving of a cause. Even for the intellectual, the intellectual attractions are soon likely to wear thin, as they have for many Western converts to communism. The gap between the promise of the theory and the reality of the state grows wide, and cynicism replaces conviction. Cynicism itself can be a cement of totalitarianism, but it is a substitute for, and no manifestation of, sustained, rational belief.

Totalitarianism does not attract—in the end it repels—the intellect. Thomas the Cynic in Silone's *School for Dictators* advised the American politician, Mr. W., how fascism might be brought to America:

THOMAS THE CYNIC: . . . The only thing with which Fascism cannot be reconciled is clear ideas, and since these do not grow by themselves, like grass on the hillside, but are always the result of discussion between thinking persons, the only thing with which Fascism is incompatible is discussion. You must avoid discussion, Mr. W., like the devil holy water.

MR. W.: And if I am challenged to a discussion and invited to give my opinion on an important question?

THOMAS THE CYNIC: You will reply that no one can prevent you from fulfilling the mission entrusted to you by destiny.

MR. W.: And if they ask me what my mission is?

THOMAS THE CYNIC: You will reply that it is to save the country. "The country must and will be saved," you will say. "Nothing will prevent me from saving my country. No one can oppose destiny. That, brothers, is my mission."

MR. W.: And if they ask me details about my mission?

THOMAS THE CYNIC: You will reply, "My mission is to save the country. Destiny has entrusted me with that mission," and you can add that that is all you have to say to politicians, because your mission will be accomplished among the masses.

Such tactics may indeed move the mass of alienated individuals, the party capitalizing on the discontents of all groups by being all things to all men. But it does not wear well. And Lincoln's "You can't fool all of the people all of the time" explains why. Credence is not completely elastic. At some point the false honors, the non-existent victory, the need for new sacrifice in the face of an always evil enemy—all these ring hollow in the ears of the populace. Even Russian youth become bored with Soviet propaganda.

Furthermore, the tactic of the big lie runs counter to the long-term cultural trend. Medieval towns or Australian aborigines might exist at one time undisturbed, the populations content with misery and usufruction. But this was possible only because of isolation, because the people were unaware of alternatives. Such isolation is no longer possible. The most elaborate planning cannot insulate or isolate; it cannot succeed in enforcing ignorance over large population groups, whether attempted by the British in Africa or the Soviet masters in Russia. True facts when laid against false propaganda result in a pattern of disaffection. It is not accidental that those who have recently fled from Russia include many who perceived alternatives to the Russian way as the result of foreign service during the war and occupation.

The effectiveness of the propaganda weapon in the hands of dictators for inducing mass loyalty cannot be doubted. But propaganda alone does not make for love, for social stability, or for sustained loyalty. To the extent that propaganda is a lie, to the extent that it is used as a substitute for genuine life-satisfactions, to that extent are totalitarian loyalties weak. The anti-intellectualism of the totalitarian states produces an unstable loyalty.

An equally important weakness of totalitarian systems results from the quality of loyalty that is policed by violence without law. The functions of modern states are so extensive that responsibility for action must be widely devolved; and the exercise of terror that enforces action must also be delegated to others. This is an exceedingly difficult feat to accomplish without violating the monolithic structure of the state. The power of death in the hands of delegated leaders is the power to enforce complete obedience upon their subordinates.

This delegation results in a twofold weakening of a single national loyalty. On the one hand, it creates huge resentments against those leaders who have given the power of death to capricious secondary leaders. On the other hand, the latter tend to build their own hegemonies. Subordinates have little choice except to follow the person who directly wields the absolute weapon.

For this reason, among others, the ruthlessly totalitarian Nazi state was, in the view of some competent observers, no state at all but rather a series of competing power structures. Each structure—party, army, bureaucracy, and industrial group—was supreme in its own area, scheming to frustrate the others and, in the process, obstructing even the supreme leader himself. Another aspect of the same phenomenon was manifest in the struggle for power and personal following among the group around Hitler—Göring, Goebbels, Speer, Bormann, and others. This pattern has had its Soviet counterpart in the bloody warfare among Lenin's successors and, more recently, in the scramble for control, resulting in the execution of Beria, following the death of Stalin.

In the long run, therefore, terror destroys even some of the chief terrorists. This possibility of schism among the leaders, especially at the point where a successor to the chief must be chosen, is perhaps the weakest point in the totalitarian control apparatus. Even below this level the effects of terror are corrosive. Of all the reasons that lead people to flee from the Soviet Union, the most important one is that they fear arrest, or the previous arrest of themselves or members of their families has relegated them to a life of fear and second-class citizenship. Arrest leads to rejection of regime even when job and other life-conditions have been satisfactory.

All available evidence indicates that fears of the infinitesimal fraction of the population who have left the country are to some degree shared by all citizens. The arbitrary power of the secret police is hated, inside and outside the party, more than any other feature of the regime. Terror dries up joy and offsets many of the attractive features of life. For many people, at all levels of status and power, "the reliance on fear and repression as instruments of control has transformed the Soviet Union into a huge reformatory in which the primary difference between the forced labor camps and the rest of the Soviet Union is that inside the camps the regimen is much more brutal and humiliating."

Societies that rest heavily upon propaganda and force are subject to great internal strains. The totalitarian governments must cope with the disaffection of all those deprived of previous wealth, prestige, and power. Interviews with Russian refugees have revealed deep hatreds for the regime among all social groups adversely affected by state policies—intellectuals, farmers, businessmen, and others—and among their children and relatives.

This is, of course, to be expected. More significantly, workers resent government-defined pay scales, food allotments, living accommodations, and the piecework system; bureaucrats, scientists, and intellectuals have deep grievances growing out of insecurity and fear.

The situation of Soviet physicians provides a good example of the tensions that exist. In the Soviet Union the doctor is completely dependent upon the state, which educates him, finds a place for his work, and pays him. There exist no independent medical associations whatsoever, the prerevolutionary groups having been suppressed early in the Soviet regime. State directives emphasize that public welfare must take precedence over the individual. "The physician is viewed as the equivalent of the preventive maintenance and repair engineer whose main function is to keep up production by keeping the producers fit." Physicians must keep workers working. Their role is crucial because Soviet labor law provides stringent penalties if workers leave jobs without authorization, miss work, or are tardy. Any worker guilty of these acts escapes harsh penalty only by securing an official sick certificate.

The physician is caught between strong conflicting forces. On the one hand, the state insists that he be strict in granting sick certificates. Each dispensary is limited to a "quota" of illnesses it may recognize, and physicians are expected to compete with one another to reduce the amount of time lost through illness. On the other hand, the physician must be sensitive to his unique professional task of giving medical attention to the ills of individuals.

Balancing these factors is always an uneasy and unhappy task. Even for the genuinely ill, the physician must consider his available "quota" and the way his record looks to his superiors. He must always be alert for malingerers. He must face direct pleas for medical excuses for non-medical—but frequently moving—reasons. (One refugee doctor described a scene of some years past: "How do you think we felt when women came to us crying, begging, 'Comrade doctor, give me just one day off. I want to go to my mother's in the village and get some food for my children who are starving.' ") And he must walk a tight-rope over censure; though the system demands that he be strict, he must also guard against the ever present danger of being publicly denounced, or accused in court, if he is overstringent.

The physician's total role is probably one in which he protects individuals against the demands of the government. He thus contributes "to the stability and functioning of Soviet society." Yet his own position is fraught with strain. Fostering of career opportunities by the state promotes national loyalty. By the same token, interference with job performance promotes disaffection, which is all the greater when force is the sanction and when the state action has the effect of denying professionals the free use of their competence.

Even the highest functionaries are not immune from the strains of the social structure. The circulation of top officials may enlist the loyalty of those who are given rapid advancement, but it also undermines the faith of those who feel their positions are threatened. The more responsibility a person has, the more involved he is with the state, but the more he is the object of surveillance and suspicion. This is true of the party leaders, the administrative and economic bureaucracy, and the upper stratum of scientists, professional men, and cultural intelligentsia.

What is experienced by the elite is also felt by those at the bottom layers of the status pyramid. They may be less sensitive to the disadvantages of their position, but not only do they face interferences with their jobs and the threat of violence; they also face—especially in the Soviet Union—a grinding poverty. It is a poverty felt all the more keenly by many because they see the revolution settling down and because they witness growing disparities of income and power in a society ostensibly and ostentatiously dedicated to social equality.

The particular strain on loyalties as a consequence of the political control of work is also traced through the entire social structure. Virtually every memoir of expatriate Russians records this as an important factor in the decision to flee the Soviet Union. Victor Kravchenko wrote:

> Under our Soviet system every step required formal decisions by endless bureaus, each of them jealous of its rights and in mortal dread of taking initiative. Repeatedly petty difficulties tied us into knots which no one dared untie without instructions from Moscow. We lived and labored in a jungle of questionnaires, paper forms and reports in seven copies.

Kravchenko's experience has its counterpart in almost every job, those hectored from above finding compensation in hacking at those below. The situation is made all the worse because the regime's penchant for violence gets tied into the entire productive system. Violence used as punishment for those who do not perform or conform on the job constitutes, naturally enough, a chief source of job dissatisfaction.

Individuals can operate effectively under great pressures. But not indefinitely. Loyalty to nation can be heightened if the people achieve a sense of accomplishment against adversity. But duress and crisis cannot be permanent commodities. Weariness and disbelief, hopelessness and protest, grow. The antidotes of the totalitarian state—whether they be fully paid vacations for the workers or wars against foreign foes—seldom strike at the root cause of discontent and often carry their own immense penalties. A government presiding over a society of structural strain in the long run finds the loyalty of citizens similarly strained.

In the Soviet Union the large population group least tractable to control by the state is the peasantry. The history of Soviet farm policy is one of ever tightening controls over the peasant population, marked by brief periods of respite. The peasant's loyalty is tentative despite—and because of—this increasing state control. The process of replacing individual landholdings with collective farms has been brutal; millions have suffered and died. A deep residue of resentment remains.

More fundamentally, the peasant way of life demonstrates the relative intractability of some population groups to control from the top. The geographic dispersion of the farm population makes difficult their continuous enlistment in political acts. It is hard to supply them with trained political leadership. They are less available as subjects of propaganda. They have traditional strong family ties, strong religious bonds, and a heritage that values ownership of the land. Soviet leaders have had serious difficulties in making a loyal group of the peasantry. The alternate hardening and easing of repressions demonstrates that this difficulty is still by no means overcome.

Russian peasants illustrate the relative failure of dictatorships to extend total control over entire population groups. Dictatorships cannot crack loyalties to all groups not controlled by the state, and they cannot overcome all ideas not acceptable to the state. We have seen that this very failure masks dissidence; it allows some people to live happily in a dictatorship, even though opposed to the regime. But, in the long run, the existence of uncontrolled non-national loyalties is a source of national disloyalty in all totalitarian states.

The peasant in Russia is by no means the only example. Once state policies attempt to cut completely through affections for family, village, profession, and culture, then loyalty to the totalitarian state becomes prejudiced. The point finds corroboration in strange places. In the Soviet Union, some individuals attempt to escape suspicion and to ease their lot by joining with others in informal associations for mutual protection. They do not report one another, they gloss over minor (in some cases major) deficiencies, they help one another in maintaining good relations with those who watch them, they sometimes indulge in outright corruption. Soviet literature is filled with denunciations of such groups. They exist in the party, in the bureaucracy, in factories, and on the farm. They have an illuminating name: "family circles." Families—those related by blood as well as those united for self-preservation—cannot exist independently in totalitarian states. Yet no totalitarian system has managed to destroy them or completely to control them.

Other groups in the Soviet Union also express opposition. They do so most frequently under duress and sometimes only as the result of almost accidental factors. They have found themselves able to flee as the result of war or occupation duty; they have been captured by enemy forces; they have found a means of egress after being shocked by the death or disappearance of friends or after having found themselves facing a similar fate.

The Soviet leaders of the principal wartime opposition to the Soviet regime—the so-called "Vlasov movement"—apparently would not have become opponents of the regime, had they not been captured by the Germans. None of the key figures surrendered voluntarily to oppose their nation. Yet great disaffections did appear in the Soviet Union during the war, sometimes due to anti-Russianism as well as antitotalitarianism. Whole villages and regions welcomed German armies as their saviors. The evidence for this is not German testimony but rather the repressive measures taken by the Russian masters against their own people. During the war itself, four autonomous republics were dissolved. In the language of a later ratifying decree concerning two of these republics, the repression was necessary because "during the great patriotic war . . . many Chechens and Crimean Tartars, upon the instigation of German agents and in detachments organized by the Germans, voluntarily . . . waged an armed struggle against units of the Red Army." Armed forces of Soviet citizens also fought in the rear against their own countrymen. And the decree further asserts that the inhabitants of the states concerned "did not give opposition to these traitors in the native land."

No exact estimate is available of the number of people actually involved in open warfare, though several millions of people from the areas concerned were probably later dispatched to forced-labor camps or to the frontier regions of Asia. For two of the republics involved, the official decree makes it appear that their entire populations "were resettled in other districts of the Soviet Union."

A Pomeranian general officer might—many did—regard the horny-handed illiterate Crimean peasant as some species of lower animal. But some German generals acted exactly like some Russian peasants in one respect: they elevated another loyalty above their nation. Members of the German officer corps were, by and large, skeptical of Hitler during his early days of power. But they were confident that they could use the Nazi leader to promote their own professional group and their own view of the national welfare, just as they had used the Weimar governments. Early successes of the regime cut away the officers' independence and stifled their opposition to Hitlerian policies. The personal rewards, professionally and socially, were great:

> Marshal's batons and Knight's crosses, gifts, estates and building permits, silenced such pangs of conscience as may, from time to time, have assailed them. They were not disposed to overthrow their Führer while he still had these honours within his gift.

Yet from the very first, some members of the corps—Colonel-General Ludwig Beck, chief of the general staff, was an outstanding example—were opposed to the Bavarian corporal and his policies. They had elaborate plans for a coup d'état, including the arrest of Hitler, even before the Czechoslovakian crisis in 1938. These plans, like many others, miscarried, and for the period of Hitler's outstanding success—from the Polish campaign in 1939 to Stalingrad in 1943—the thousand-year Reich seemed a reality, and the resisters to Hitler among the officer group found few converts. After Stalingrad and especially after the Allied invasion of the Continent, German defeat seemed more and more certain, and the number of conspirators increased. They grew so numerous as to be embarrassing to the secrecy of the plotters.

As in other cases, choices for loyalty and disloyalty turned on highly personal reasons. The commander-in-chief of the army, Field Marshal von Brauchitsch, believed as a soldier that Hitler's policies were ruinous to the nation. He was considered anti-Nazi, but his wife was a "200 per cent rabid" Nazi. In the conflict of loyalties between profession and wife, he chose his wife and, in so doing, attached himself to the regime. At one point Field Marshal von Witzleben was prepared to take violent action against Hitler, but, before striking, the field marshal decided he had to be in the best physical condition. He suffered from Frederick the Great's ailment; and Hitler's regime was at this time spared a new assault because, at the propitious moment, Field Marshal von Witzleben was in the hospital having his hemorrhoids removed. And Field Marshal von Manstein was leading troops on the Eastern Front when approached by the conspirators. He indicated willingness to join the "Generals' Strike" against Hitler. But he would not do so immediately. He wanted first to capture Sebastopol. The strategic problem interested him; and, anyway, Von Manstein wanted another medal before joining the plotters.

The military plot, aided in various ways by civilian groups, reached its climax on July 20, 1944, with the unsuccessful attempt on Hitler's life. The plotters paid for their final failure with their lives, by suicide if they were fortunate (as in Beck's case), by torture and slow strangulation if they were not (as in Von Witzleben's case). They died bravely. They felt justified in their treason to the regime because they conceived their action necessary to preserve the army, in which they had an almost mystic faith; and this desire, in turn, was linked in their minds to the preservation of the fatherland. "The one motive which was common to all within the conspiracy was a deep desire to save their country from a catastrophe of cataclysmic proportions and in this, whatever else they may have been, they were patriots."

So the generals put loyalty to their class and to their fatherland, when they were threatened, above loyalty to government or leader. Other German groups found other prime loyalties. Members of the so-called "Kreisau Circle," under the leadership of Helmuth von Moltke, held firmly to conservative Christian principles and died almost joyously for them. In his last letter to his wife before being executed, Von Moltke wrote: "I stood before [Hitler's court] not as a Protestant, not as a great landowner, not as a noble, not as a Prussian, not as a German even. . . . No, I stood there as a Christian and nothing else." The views of the Circle were close to those of the Protestant and Catholic clergymen who saw Dachau because of their opposition to Hitler. Trade-union leaders, young professionals, remnants of the old German Center party, and university students were also represented among Hitler's opposition.

The totalitarian state faces disloyalty because its citizens put other things first. A democracy runs the same risk; but in most circumstances independent smaller groups put their energy to work for state purposes. The totalitarian state attempts to achieve the same parallelism of non-state and state loyalties and in large measure succeeds. But the power apparatus tends to turn the smaller groups to *ersatz*. Control from the center is, by definition, what makes a totalitarian state total. Every group that exists uncontrolled is, *ipso facto,* a source of national disloyalty. The long run again produces an unhappy paradox for totalitarian leaders: national loyalty can be secured only if the state becomes less total.

One obvious difference between democratic and totalitarian societies is that the democratic citizen can find little political relevance for most of life's dissatisfactions. He has other places to look, other institutions to blame, if life is sour. Even if the political factor is apparent, traditions of free association and redress tend to make him work within the system, to cement his loyalty in the very process of expressing his complaints.

But where the state attempts to control all of life, every discontent can be attributed to the state. For the totalitarian citizen, all disquiet has a plain political base, whether it be a shoddy shoelace or a turn of foreign policy, a poor sleeping-room or the operation of the railroads, unpalatable coffee or the inadequacy of power machinery in the steel foundry. More than this, there is little scope for protest. Whatever the promises of such devices as "self-criticism" and "democratic centralism," protest is treason if it does not fall within narrowly defined boundaries of acceptability.

This difference between the democratic and totalitarian situations, as important as it is, only reflects other less tangible but more fundamental contrasts. We have seen that individuals in a democracy face conflict as the result of multiple-group memberships and multiple loyalties. This source of individual difficulty is also a source of social strength. For the overlapping of membership imposes very great "restraints and conformities upon interest groups on pain of dissolution or of failure." If the members of a labor union are also strongly religious, the union's leadership, no matter how radical it may be, cannot attack the church and still remain leaders or still maintain a union. If the business members of a "taxpayers' " group (the pseudonym for tax-cutting groups) are also members of school boards and highway-improvement associations, the group's drive to reduce taxes must be mitigated by the knowledge that it will lose members if it strongly attacks school or highway appropriations.

The existence of overlapping memberships is in all cases a leavening force. It tends to decrease social conflict and make for reconciliation among population groups. The blunting effect is all the greater because of the potential of the unorganized and disorganized to come together in new organizations when the old ones are no longer sufficiently accommodating.

Multiple groups and loyalties have another related, but independently important, stabilizing effect. Non-national loyalties, as we have seen, are the prime ingredient of democratic national loyalty. Their very number and diversity provide a stable foundation for national loyalty. Like a prudent businessman, the democratic citizen has investments of loyalty in many places, and, in one way or another, most of these loyalties link him to his nation. Few blades cut so wide a swath as to sever all these ties. Barring the deepest depression or the most destructive war, he retains areas of fellowship, of deference, of power. When family ceases to be important, he buries himself in business; when business palls, he attends American Legion or Rotary meetings; when he quarrels with his professional group, he turns to the church.

The existence of many voluntary groups, the overlapping allegiances to these groups, and the freedom to form new groups all give resiliency and bounce to the democratic social structure. They constitute a great force for maintaining social stability and for preserving national allegiance in the face of hardship and catastrophe.

The totalitarian situation is markedly dissimilar. There exist many fewer memberships and therefore many fewer ties relating the citizen to the state. In theory at least—and reality does not mirror the theory—the bond is the single, direct one. When this direct tie with nation snaps, all life must be reorganized. No resources for patriotism remain. Indeed, what the theory does not provide for makes the process all the more complete: when the state control apparatus becomes weakened, the smaller group loyalties that secretly exist as a defense against the nation appear with a vengeance.

If the direct tie to nation explains the ease with which totalitarian loyalties can be mobilized, it also explains why totalitarian loyalties are easily smashed. For the pendulum is held by a single thread. Once cut, there are no restraining forces. The fullest wrath is unleashed by those who have been held to obedience by fear, by those who have assuaged guilty consciences through frantic activity, by those who have preserved small joys of life by accepting large evils, by those who have been loyal only because they could not be disloyal and live. Even those who are sincerely committed find that life has no focus, and their loyalties shift rapidly and completely. Large-scale social change—revolution—comes suddenly. New totalitarianisms have an open season.

The prospects for widespread totalitarian disloyalty are not encouraging to those who cherish democratic values. The totalitarian citizen is coerced and propagandized by the state. He is bribed by the satisfactions offered by the regime. He shelters himself from political demands, and this makes life more tolerable and disloyalty less likely. His compliance, even to himself, becomes indistinguishable from conviction. He solaces himself that his fatherland is being served. He has no alternative to obedience.

Yet the strengths of the regime conceal many weaknesses. The long-term cultural drift tends to impair totalitarian loyalties. Terror destroys allegiance. Anti-intellectualism is a slender reed on which to build for the long run. The regime completely controlled is one of great structural strain. Loyalty built upon a single tie to the state is a loyalty that disintegrates rapidly when the state is no longer strong.

The disloyalty potential is the impossibility over long periods of time of keeping large population groups in a state of controlled alienation, destroying the joys of life that spring from social relationships uncontrolled by the state and substituting state programs as the monopolist of time and energy. In practice, no totalitarian nation has completely succeeded in this endeavor. The more it tries, the greater the potentiality of unrest.

From one perspective this argues in favor of the natural decline of totalitarianism from within, the loosening of controls, the reduction of tensions, the conscious building of non-national groups and of an indirect strand of national loyalty. Such a view credits totalitarian leaders with a sensitivity to social process that they may not in fact possess. Even if they did, they might thereby lose their positions, if not their lives. Nevertheless, the gradual decline over the years of totalitarianism from within is not an unlikely possibility. American experts on the Soviet Union are almost unanimously agreed that the regime would have little to fear in the way of popular opposition if the standard of living were improved, the pace of life slackened, the fear of the secret police reduced, and the collective farmer assured of his private plot.

These changes are rendered more likely by the increasing

productivity of Soviet industry: those who have food and shelter need no longer be so fearful of those who do not. And widespread realization that atomic war means total or near-total destruction for all concerned may bring not only a diversion of goods from armaments to consumption items but also a slow shift away from totalitarianism in the direction of a less rigidly controlled society. This would mean, in turn, the development of a pattern of loyalties more similar to those in democratic states.

A second possible development is the emergence of a dictatorship so skilfully manipulative that people would not recognize it. This would see the surface disappearance of terror and maximum political participation on a basis that would appear voluntary to the participants. It would mean masking, rather than glorifying, the total dependence upon direct nation-person ties and therefore the apparent removal of large areas of life from political concern. The result would be a totalitarianism of subtle psychology, less brutal than the present system but no less firmly controlled from the top.

A third possibility is the collapse or weakening of the totalitarian apparatus of control. In modern times this has occurred only when the state has been chopped down as the result of war. But conquest from the outside is not the only possibility. Totalitarian collapse could also occur if the executive power is weakened, as when one leader must be chosen to succeed another; or if the distrust that is generated between internal power groups breaks out into open warfare, as in a conflict between the armed forces and industrial leaders. The more complete the totalitarianism has become, the more likelihood of revolt under these circumstances. A rift at the top or a piercing of the system from without is an invitation to social explosion.

PART IV

Where Are the Disloyal?

10 Disloyalty and the Social Structure

Are some social groups more likely than others to contain traitors or potential traitors? Can these groups be defined?

The relationships set forth in the analysis of groups are probability statements. They state only that within the group more (or fewer) individuals will exhibit certain attitudes and actions than individuals in some comparable group. The statistician's cold numbers, except for the rare situations where correlations are perfect, say little about any single warm individual. A chart demonstrating that fifteen out of a hundred persons will live to be more than eighty does not reveal which eighty-five die and which fifteen live. Similarly, neighborhoods of high delinquency rates have produced presidents and peers; and from the "best" neighborhoods, where crime rates are exceedingly low, there have emerged murderers, embezzlers, and rapists.

The existence of individual differences limits the usefulness and accuracy of group analysis. Our present knowledge of society does not produce the elegant nicety which we believe, often falsely, exists in the physical sciences. The difficulties are compounded when discussing disloyalty because acts of disloyalty are relatively rare and because information concerning the disloyal is relatively fragmentary. Nevertheless, it is useful, in a completely speculative vein, to attempt to relate disloyalty to group characteristics. This is done in *relative* and *situational* terms: relative in the sense that individuals in some groups are more likely to be disloyal to the nation than individuals in other groups; situational in the sense that disloyalty is the product of specific social facts which change with time and which, even without change, are subject to changing evaluations by the persons concerned. The assumption is that group characteristics are so influential that they produce relationships to national loyalty and disloyalty despite the influence of factors that may not be related to group membership.

The framework for the group analysis consists of three questions:

1. What are typical satisfactions and dissatisfactions for given groups?

2. To what extent can these happinesses and sorrows be related to the nation-state?

3. To what extent are alternatives to national loyalty available?

A person is dissatisfied with life if there is a discrepancy between life-expectations and life-achievements. The sponge fisherman who lives in poverty but desires no other life is not dissatisfied. The executive vice-president who savagely desires to be chairman of the board, but is blocked from that post, is dissatisfied. Dissatisfaction may cover only one area of life and may be compensated for by joys in other areas. So dissatisfaction is important only when it colors all of life, when it overbalances joys. And joy today may be sour tomorrow: once the vice-president achieves the chairmanship, the view from the top may reveal how puny his hill looks against the near-by mountains.

The linkage of dissatisfaction to nation exists most readily when the state can be identified as the source of dissatisfactions. The clear case is the businessman gone bankrupt as the direct result of government programs or the churchman whose religious practice is proscribed by government decree. Here the linkage is real. But it may be real in the minds of the deprived persons, even though it may, in fact, not exist at all. When bad weather leads to poor crops, farmers vote against the government in power.

No alternatives to national loyalty have meaning if people are broken, if they are used to misery and avoid all new experience out of fear that it will make them more miserable. This group aside, there are two possible alternatives to national loyalty. One is loyalty to another nation. The alternative to democracy, in today's world, is the Soviet Union, and it is most readily available where a party cell or Marxist study group exists. It is more available to college students than to farmers, to factory workers than to fishermen. The second alternative to national loyalty is provided by non-national groups and is best supplied by a group willing to direct the entire life of its members. Certain churches are most likely to meet this requirement.

Simple patterns of response to the three questions indicate the potential for loyalty and disloyalty among members of given groups. Two idealized extreme patterns are as follows:

	Dissatisfaction	Linkage to Nation	Alternative to National Loyalty
Group I.......	Yes	Yes	Yes
Group II ...	No	No	No

Members of Group I are more dissatisfied with life, can more easily link their dissatisfactions to the nation-state, and have an alternative to their current national loyalty more readily available. More individuals in Group I than in Group II are likely to be disloyal to their nation.

This, of course, is absurdly oversimple. But, before leaving the easy ground of the paradigm, it is worth noting that seven additional combinations of the three factors are possible. Each defines the circumstance of a group, and each encourages a different political posture by members of that group. Thus

	Dissatisfaction	Linkage to Nation	Alternative to National Loyalty
Group III.....	Yes	No	No

presents a picture of deprivation unlinked to the nation and unleavened by the possibility of an alternative to national loyalty. If social action follows as a consequence of dissatisfaction, it is not likely to be political in content. There are plenty of other means of expressing reaction to deprivation, including those in the private spheres of life. And one reaction, of course, is no action: withdrawal, with or without acceptance of the unhappy circumstances. The pattern

	Dissatisfaction	Linkage to Nation	Alternative to National Loyalty
Group IV.....	No	Yes	Yes

produces the radical dilettante. Here associations with those on the edges of lawful politics are available, the avenue to disloyalty is open, the nation is felt to be inadequate, but life-conditions do not impel political action. We have seen that this pattern can turn into disloyalty as promises held forth by the alternative loyalty produce discontent with the current situation.

On the other hand,

	Dissatisfaction	Linkage to Nation	Alternative to National Loyalty
Group V......	Yes	Yes	No

produces discontent with the current system but little chance for association with those pledged to overthrow it. With the spread of modern communications and widespread literacy, few groups remain in this position. It most probably leads to political activity within the legal system; where this does not suffice, it produces expressions of hatred against the nation.

A formal paradigm of this sort could be infinitely elaborated, by adding other relevant categories (personality types, for example) or by breaking each category into smaller ones. However enjoyable the exercise, it has only limited utility. Probably no group falls neatly into the categories the system provides, and the dimensions of such a logical pattern can never be sufficiently subtle to describe completely the situation of any actual group. Moreover, in the shifting hierarchy of each man's loyalty, there are many ways by which one loyalty can come to take precedence over another. The scheme of weighing dissatisfactions, of relating them to nation, and of assessing them in terms of available alternatives probably does not describe the thought-processes of any individual. It does not claim to represent any actual sequence of acts. Rather it is a descriptive tool, an aid for social analysis. It is meant to be helpful in the same way that the concept of the magnetic field is a helpful construct in the physical sciences. For the analysis of groups, the model is useful as a guide for observation and as a pattern against which observed facts can be compared.

A number of Chicago night-club and banquet waiters were studied during 1952 by Milton Millon, to see whether their group characteristics could be related to national loyalty and disloyalty. These waiters work in one of the lowliest professions. They are so rated by others, and they so rate themselves. As one waiter put it: "When you put on this black tie you put on the mark of a jackass, to be spit on and kicked." And another: "When I was a bus boy I was the dirtiest of the dirt; now that I am a waiter I am just dirt." Most of these waiters hate to see a familiar face at work. "Boy, if my mother or sisters knew what I was doing I'd die. Nobody knows my business. My folks—well, they think I work in a machine shop."

Feelings of inferiority at work carry over into other aspects of life. The waiter lives low because he feels low. Most of those in the group studied had neither stable families nor decent homes. They drifted from rooming-house to rooming-house, entering brief alliances with bar girls or prostitutes. They gambled away their earnings and spent freely during brief periods of riotous living. A few saved compulsively. Their friends were almost exclusively fellow-waiters, and their talk centered almost exclusively upon job discontents.

The waiters hated their jobs, their employers, and their customers. They commonly referred to the night-club or banquet guest as a "rich [or lousy] bastard." They exercised considerable ingenuity in devising ways and means to steal both from the guest (by charging him for what he did not receive) and the "house" (by collecting for food and drink outside the usual channels of cashiering and accountancy). The more elaborate the methods evolved for preventing such thievery, the more artful the waiters became in making it possible.

The folklore of the profession consisted largely of stories about successful thefts and of even greater depredations: of urinating into drums of ice cubes and spitting into soup; of glass unintentionally broken but intentionally not removed from foodstuffs. Many of the waiters claimed to be prepared at all times—with guns and knives, with "Mickey Finns" and laxatives—to retaliate against the guest as the occasion demanded. Much of this was bombast. Even if no action were suited to the words, the words themselves are revealing. In fact, however, there is ample evidence that the waiters expressed their hostility with far more than talk. Attacks upon guests and upon fellow-waiters were not uncommon. Millon himself, active as a participant observer, joined a group of waiters testing their skill at spitting from a distance into a bowl of salad dressing.

This description does not fit all waiters. It is not applicable to the middle-class women who take waitress jobs in order to augment the family income and who enjoy the social contacts that the job provides. It does not fit the waiter in the upper-class restaurant who looks upon his regular customers as if he were a family retainer. It does not fit the situation of some immigrant waiters who are happy in their jobs; Mexican immigrants in Chicago, for example, viewed waiting on table as a highly desirable task because it was superior in both income and prestige to the laboring jobs commonly available to members of their group.

The night-club and banquet waiters shared none of these attitudes. They had only a distaste for their occupational role, and this established their distaste for the larger world. Except for membership in the union, which was compulsory, the waiters belonged to virtually no other organization; and the union itself was often the object of suspicion and distaste. No happier area of life offset the occupational role.

Their resentment did not stem from low income. In 1952, weekly earnings of $100 a week were common, and $150 was not uncommon. These were good earnings even for an inflationary period. What rankled was that some proportion of this income had to be stolen and that an even larger portion came from tips. Income from tips was often considered more demeaning than theft. The tip makes waiters suffer fools with good humor. Income depends upon ingratiation, and this is perhaps the central clue to the waiters' depreciation of their lot. They must perform service of low status in constant contact with an observing and demanding public. They are forced into a servile and inferior role under circumstances that all can see.

If members of an occupational group feel that the "public" treats them "like dirt," it is not unlikely that society will be repudiated by that group. And their attitudes toward the nation will be especially affected if the nation itself is thought to be responsible for the low status of the occupation. The night-club and banquet waiters could not directly relate their occupational status to state action. But they made the connection indirectly and in no uncertain terms. They identified the high-and-haughty spenders whom they served and hated as representative of the nation. The customers were an obvious and rankling elite, possessing women, money, and leisure. They were responsible for the waiters' low status. Hatred against those served was frequently expressed as hatred of the "system," the nation, or the government.

Discontents were plain, and their linkage to nation was easy; but an alternative to national loyalty was not readily found. On the one hand, there were few night-club waiters with strong ties to family, church, or ethnic group; there were, in more general terms, no strong non-national groups available to which they could give primary loyalties. On the other hand, the waiters had few possible links with other nations. They did not have contacts with radical groups. Union activities were recreational and economic, not political, in nature.

The waiters consequently had little political interest or competence. They raged against fate, turned their hatred upon themselves, and gained whatever compensation they could by mocking the suckers who ate steaks garnished with cigarette ash and who paid for what they did not drink. Having virtually no loyalties at all, the waiters under proper circumstances might build very strong direct patriotic ties to their nation. But, by the same token, with proper cultivation by the proper outside nation, it can be predicted that such a group would supply a higher proportion of traitors than other groups.

This kind of analysis can also be applied to age groups. The so-called "radicalism" of young men and women is well known. Young people traditionally have been most prominent in international migrations. Public opinion polls in many countries indicate their relatively greater willingness to leave their native land. Young people join radical movements, both left and right, in disproportionate numbers. Outside the political sphere, youth rebels in many ways, fighting with parents at one extreme, becoming involved in criminal behavior at the other.

The age period for such activity in the United States usually comes as the young person leaves high school. Up to this point in his life, he has in most cases been provided with firm primary-group relationships: family, school peers, playground friends. He has reasonably well-established social orbits in which to operate. Some of his roles—football player—may produce high prestige, while others—glee-club member or simply classroom attender—may have no such glamour. But all tend to provide a secure and satisfactory network of personal relationships. The many problems that exist for the individual at least have familiar guidelines within which solutions may be sought.

High-school graduation frequently brings about a great change. The individual is faced with what Everett Hughes has called "status shock"—he has no audience to which his prowess and good (and poor) qualities are well known. He has no easy pattern of expected action or reaction. He is either in the lowly position of looking for a job (full employment and high wages ease the transition) or in the lowly occupation of a college Freshman. And it is precisely at this moment that relationships with his parents become strained. Now parents expect the child to act like an adult; but the child under the circumstances is able to make noises like an adult only at home, and there only by refusing, by his lights, to act like a child.

A sophisticated commentator on these problems, Erik H. Erikson, has named this interval between youth and adulthood a *psychosocial moratorium*. It is the time of life in which one must identify one's self with some section of society. And yet it is also precisely the time when the individual has not yet been able to translate childhood identifications into acceptable adult ones and when he is faced with maintaining "the most important defenses against the onslaught of sexual maturation." The individual has not yet developed a sense of where he is going, nor has he received recognition from those people he considers to be important.

The adolescent, in short, faces alienation. And he tries to solve his problems like any other alienated person: by making efforts to bring some sense out of the social and psychological chaos that confronts him. In most cases this has no relevance whatsoever to national disloyalty. Time, social class, economic circumstance, and other factors define more or less recognized *rites de passage* in which a satisfactory sowing of wild oats—or relative withdrawal from the world—is followed by a satisfactory set of relationships in an emerging adult life. Even in antisocial manifestations—the street-corner gang, for example—the revolt against family and the vote on behalf of bohemianism are likely to take the politically neutral form of petty and not-so-petty delinquency, gang fights, and competitive sexuality.

In contrast to this kind of social radicalism, the college student's "radicalism" is more likely to have a political flavor. The dissatisfactions of the college student are markedly similar to those of youths not in college; and the relationships of dissatisfactions to the nation are therefore similar. But the intellectual community of the campus is more likely to provide a recognition of alternative political schemes. And this, in turn, may lead individuals to define dissatisfactions as if they were related to the nation. As in other cases, political commitment may follow a search for companionship, and the political apathetic may become a revolutionary in the process of looking for romance.

The very exposure of college students to new idea systems, including Marxism, leads some to question established political loyalties and to seek new ones. Here, again, intellectual grounds for changing loyalties become apparent. As always, the intellectual and social factors go hand in hand, each influencing the other. There is less political expression of adolescent alienation where marriages are contracted early or where, as in rural areas, work programs are relatively fixed, demanding of time and energy, and productive of satisfactory relationships to enterprise, work companions, or family groups.

The youth's commitment, when it is made, is likely to be extreme and negative. The roles that he is expected to achieve may be so unattainable that he prefers to identify totally with precisely what he is not supposed to be. This sort of negative identity often brings relief. A young man said: "I would rather be quite insecure than a little secure"; and a young woman, "At least in the gutter I'm a genius." The late adolescent sometimes "would rather be nobody or somebody bad, or indeed, dead—and this totally, and by free choice—than be not-quite-somebody." When turned to politics, this extreme need for identity is expressed as a fanatical devotion to a cause or a leader. It can be mobilized either for or against the nation.

The youth movements in Germany before World War I illustrate this ambivalence. Groups of all sorts existed under many auspices and for diverse purposes. All in common represented a "revolt of discontented bourgeois youth against a liberal bourgeois society and all its works."

> . . . they thought that parental religion was largely sham, politics boastful and trivial, economics unscrupulous and deceitful, education stereotyped and lifeless, art trashy and sentimental, literature spurious and commercialized, drama tawdry and mechanical, . . . family life repressive and insincere, and the relations of the sexes, in marriage or without, shot through with hypocrisy.

Yet these rebellious youth almost unanimously supported the German cause during World War I. Thousands went to their death in support of the empire.

This case beautifully illustrates how, under the stimulus of an outside threat, rebelliousness can be mobilized in small groups for patriotic purposes. But it is not difficult to imagine other masters being followed. German youth after World War I flocked to join the Free Corps groups and ultimately joined the Nazi movement. Patriotic slogans were as important for Hitler's youth groups as they had been twenty years earlier. And other similarities in the two situations may easily be found. But the point here is one of contrast. In 1914 the youth of Germany marched in support of the duly constituted nation-state; in the 1930's German youth marched to smash the Weimar Republic.

Strong loyalties to non-national groups, rather than alienation, may also lead to national disloyalty. Under these circumstances, individuals express disloyalty to one nation without choice of another nation. They choose in favor of a non-national group. From the partial viewpoint of the nation, they are the dangerously socialized.

Most conflicts between national and non-national loyalties do not, as we have seen, produce disloyalty at all. Even when nation is put second to family, church, business, or friends, the issue is rarely defined as one of disloyalty. Furthermore, when such choices against the nation are most likely to become disloyalty—when the nation is threatened from outside—they are least likely to be made. The threat to the nation is interpreted as a threat to all within it, and every attempt is made to adjust loyalties to other groups so that they reinforce the demands of the nation.

Conflicts between nation and non-national groups are nevertheless capable of producing overt acts of national disloyalty. The greatest potentiality in this direction occurs when the non-national group attempts to control the whole life of its members and is willing to contest with the nation for primacy of control in conflict situations. Religiously based, closed agricultural communities—like those of the Doukhobors of Canada—illustrate such groups. Every attempt is made in these communities to maximize the members' identification with the community. Meaningful contacts with the "outside" are discouraged, and any unauthorized contact may be severely penalized. Under such circumstances, conflict between the nation and the community can cover issues ranging from marriage customs to service in the armed forces. And the tighter the community, the more likely that its demands—and not those of the nation—will be met.

The United States once contained the equivalent of many such cultural islands. In some cases, as with the Mormons, religion was the distinguishing feature, later reinforced by relative geographic isolation. In other cases, as with eastern European immigrants in New York, the cultural distance of language and religious differences was as important as geographic distance in establishing closed communities. In still other cases, as with Chinese and Japanese immigrants, skin color was added to religion, language, and other cultural differences. In all such cases, loyalties to the community were likely to be stronger than loyalty to the nation; and the community controlled large areas of life, including child training, education, and leisure activities.

American society—and, as we have seen, loyalty to the nation—has been successfully built upon such non-national loyalties. Furthermore, the passing of years has resulted in a continuous decrease of the conflict potential between ethnic and cultural groups, on the one hand, and the nation, on the other. The pull of the larger culture has destroyed in large measure the influence of the American ethnic islands. Loyalties to such groups still exist, as voting statistics demonstrate, but they are loyalties more and more easily accommodated to the direction of the nation.

Membership in certain religious groups is more likely to produce non-national loyalties that directly challenge national ones. Sir Thomas More, condemned for refusing to swear to the supremacy of a Protestant king, went to his death with the remark, "I die the King's good servant, but God's first." The challenge of religious loyalties no longer contains its old potency, armies are not recruited according to religious beliefs, and reconciliation today often consists in compromising religious standards in response to national demands. Nevertheless, strong attachment to church precepts may still create conflict with nation.

The danger of a nation-religion clash is not acute when the issue is limited to restricted areas of activity, as in saluting the flag. It becomes more grave when religious affiliation results in a refusal to serve in the armed forces. And even more fundamental and comprehensive clashes potentially exist. The Catholic church, for example, attempts by prescription to direct education and family life; it is fundamentally international in character; and its militancy is aided by effective central leadership and a corps of obedient and dedicated officials. Moreover, its universal principles are considered more worthy than worldly, national ideals; and this belief in the primacy of spiritual powers is, when attacked, capable of producing martyrs.

It is therefore not surprising that national demands will in some cases conflict with Catholic doctrine. The church responds by accommodating itself in different ways to different political situations. The sharpest conflicts occur, of course, where the state extends control over areas of life that the church considers its own, and does so in a fashion that the church disapproves. Thus the church has been in implacable opposition to the totalitarianism of the Soviet Union; it has found less to complain about in the totalitarianisms of Mussolini's Italy and Franco's Spain; and the church's conflict with the Peronist government of Argentina illustrates how friends become foes when politics reaches further outward than the church will allow.

In the democracies, including the United States, accommodation on both sides prevents, or greatly mitigates, the church-state conflict. On one side, for example, principles of freedom allow for the existence of parochial schools; on the other, the church lives peacefully with laws and practices it considers inimical—from doctrines of free conscience to laws permitting contraception. The practice of men softens doctrine, and Catholicism in America, from the days of the Revolution, has been consistent with Americanism.

Yet it is not difficult to imagine circumstances wherein conflict might occur, just as it is not difficult to imagine serious conflicts in loyalty for Americans whose Jewish faith attracts them to the cause of the new state of Israel. The latter case involves another nation, as the Catholic case does not. But in both, where religious affiliation is taken seriously and where religious demands overlap those of nation, difficulties follow, sometimes only in the minds of men, sometimes in social action. As always, it is difficult in such cases to draw judgments of right and wrong. Some Catholic groups in Nazi Germany were traitors to the duly constituted government; but they were heroes to most of the world, including most Americans.

The scheme of balancing joys and sorrows, assessing their linkage to current loyalties, and measuring the availability of alternatives, provides a way of looking at shifts in all sorts of loyalties. The problem of marital infidelity, for example, can be viewed as we have viewed national infidelity. A husband's potentiality for unfaithfulness can be measured in terms of his unhappiness as related to the institution of marriage and to available alternatives. As in the case of national disloyalty, a shift in any factor can have effects on the others: if "alternatives" are numerous, a little unhappiness can be used to justify a great amount of infidelity.

As with changes in national and marital loyalty, so with changes in religion. The histories of Christian denominationalism can be read in the terms used here. So can, indeed, the emergence of Christianity itself. But the point perhaps can be best illustrated by the simple and dramatic story (derived from a monograph by David Mandelbaum) of the Kota tribe in the Nilgiri Hills of southern India.

The Kota were severely struck in 1924 by an epidemic of relapsing fever, and, in one village, more than half the inhabitants were dead before the epidemic was over. In the immediately following years, a new set of religious practices became prevalent. The new gods were eagerly adopted by some of the villagers, accepted slowly by others, and completely rejected by still others.

The most influential person in the development of the new religion was Kusvain. When all the old priests had been killed by the epidemic, the villagers in their usual ceremony prayed for the appointment of successors. But no supernatural seizures took place. No man was possessed as a priest or diviner. Soon afterward, however, Kusvain was possessed; but the voice that spoke through him was the voice of a Hindu god, not the traditional Kota god. This god instructed the village to build new temples and to follow new rituals.

Kusvain was a person who felt keenly the dissatisfactions of life. He had once been a diviner, but, because of the death of his wife, the old tradition barred him from this position of esteem. Aside from this, he was a person without prestige. Status among the Kota could be achieved by craftsmanship or wealth or hunting ability or skilful argumentation in council.

> Kusvain often has to beg for his food, is not a craftsman at all, has never gained particular acclaim in the buffalo chase, does not open his mouth in council. Several informants characterized him as a shiftless ne'er-do-well.

Only as a diviner could Kusvain distinguish himself. The old religion barred him from this role. The new one gave him access to it.

Next to Kusvain, the most instrumental person in establishing the new religion was Sulli, the schoolmaster. He was the only Kota who had been educated among the Hindus and who had extensive contact with the English. He was the only Kota to hold a governmental post. He had advised the villagers during the epidemic to abandon their traditional funeral rituals, which were expensive in food and fuel, and to bury the dead simply and without ceremony. He was first to advocate acceptance of the new priests, whose supernatural seizures were expressed in the name of new gods. Sulli was "a rebel and a reformer . . . everlastingly advocating change."

On the surface, Sulli had less cause than Kusvain for dissatisfaction with the old religion. But, for Sulli, sensitivity for what the alternative promised was very great. Knowing what life was like in the outside world, he found the village oppressive. More than that, he found Kota ways an impediment to his acceptance elsewhere. He therefore favored diminishing the marks that distinguished Kota from others. He urged, for example, that the tribesmen should cut the long hair that each wore in a bun at the nape of his neck. Sulli saw this hair style as "lowly and mean, degrading and distasteful." He had often been refused admittance to teashops outside the village because his hairdress identified him as a Kota, a representative of a carrion-eating group who were looked upon with repugnance by caste Hindus. Other Kota felt no meanness in their tribal status. They had not experienced the extra-Kota world, as Sulli had, and they did not feel hurt at being barred from other places because they knew no pleasure in these places.

Sulli's advocacy of the new religion was clearly a part of his desire to break down the differences between Kota and Hindu. The new Kota religion borrowed heavily from Hindu ritual. This was a direction of change that he desired and from which he hoped to achieve new satisfactions.

The leading opponent of the new religion was Ka·Kn, an elder member of the community. He was neither a diviner nor a priest, but he was highly regarded in the community because of his mastery of ritual and his knowledge of ceremony. He regarded the new religion with its ceremony as "the blocking of his road to glory." He saw that his competence would no longer be needed if the new religion became established, and he therefore bent his efforts to maintain old ways and to discredit the new.

The new religion was a direct road to higher status for Kusvain. For Sulli it was a step in the direction of joys he already partially knew. For Ka·Kn it was a menace to his happiness and security.

These were people in a primitive culture, and their choice involved religion. Yet they followed the same social processes that characterize citizens of more complex cultures when the choice is the nation. When sorrows overbalance joys, when the cause of sorrow can be traced to an existing allegiance, and when an alternative is available, the stage is set for a shift in loyalty.

11 Accidents, Personality, and Ideas

Shortly before the Civil War, a young man of northern Tennessee found himself at odds with his friends and neighbors. He expressed loyalty to the Union cause, and he left no doubt that he would join the Union armies if war came. But his plans were frustrated when he was suddenly and unceremoniously impressed into southern service. He marched sullenly to his first battle, deeply sensitive to the guns of his own officers. Yet he served with the highest distinction through four years of campaigning, and he was ultimately promoted to a captaincy.

His home town welcomed him as a hero at war's end. His old friends were curious. Why had he so suddenly lost his convictions, why had he served so long and gloriously for the South? He responded with heat. The South's cause, he still believed, was absurd and hateful. Yet he could easily explain his war service. He attempted to desert during that first battle, he said. The Yankees shot at him just as if he were an ordinary rebel. What could he do but shoot back?

The authenticity of the story is good, but this is less important than its perception of causes of loyalty and disloyalty. Only some of these causes are related to group membership. Others are too elusive for such categorizing. They are products of individual action. They are idiosyncratic. We learn much from looking at groups, but to understand the acts of an individual, we must know him individually.

The important political choices of some people are made only after soul-searching deliberation and with full consciousness that great and significant acts are taking place. Whittaker Chambers has recorded that his two important political decisions—to join and to break with the Communist party—were of this sort. But another large number of political choices are certainly made without design, without intent, and without comprehension of consequences. They result from the political accidents of life.

Incidental and accidental factors serve equally to bring people into, and to keep them out of, left- or right-wing movements. Caprice was largely controlling when Mary McCarthy failed to join the Communist party, just as it was when she entered anti-Communist ranks.

For a number of years after college, Miss McCarthy played joyfully on the fringes of the party. She drank at Communist social events, and she marched in Communist parades. She didn't join the party largely because she and her husband were fully occupied with each other and with their careers. Significantly enough, "the summer my husband and I separated . . . I came closest to the gravitational pull of the Communist world." But again the party became subordinate to personal plans: a Reno visit and a projected new marriage. When the new marriage did not materialize, Miss McCarthy once more drifted close to the party. And this time she was saved from membership because she casually approved of political asylum for Leon Trotsky. She did this unwittingly and without any clear knowledge of the issues. But it made her an anti-Communist, a role that was strengthened when she was forced to defend it against her erstwhile friends. She did not at all mean to do what she had done, and she discovered what it was only when she heard it labeled "anti-Communist." She summarizes this political career: "The 'great' decisions—those that I can look back on pensively and say, 'That was a turning point,' have been made without my awareness. Too late to do anything about it, I discover that I have chosen."

One can just as nonchalantly go in the opposite direction. Personal friendships, unlinked to politics, can lead persons into dissident political groups and to disloyal acts. A chance acquaintanceship, the casual reading of a book, the impression of a single lecture, a sudden personal aversion—all these can be catalysts, guiding dissatisfactions into political channels. The process by which this may be turned to national disloyalty is often slow, subtle, and unrealized by the person concerned. It is accidental in origin and frequently accidental in its progress. It is also accidental in the eyes of the person concerned. Like a newly married man, a traitor may find himself at new thresholds of life without being able to retrace the steps by which he arrived.

More generalized events, accidental in that they are unplanned by those affected, also lead to disloyalty. Many Germans did not join the plot against Hitler because they were not asked; others joined because they were. The latter, to be sure, would not have died for their effort at assassination if they had not shared—or could not be brought to share—some sentiment against the regime. It remains true that they, rather than others, took overt action because of accidents of companionship, of location, and of social situation.

In a similar way, when a nation is invaded by an enemy army, some collaborate as a consequence of relatively capricious factors. Can the household be saved, or has it already been destroyed? Is the family threatened? Are there "decent" people among the invaders? Even among the heroic resisters of totalitarianism, there are many who acquire political dignity by accident: because they are forced to steal food, or because they become hunted—and perforce hunters—as the consequence of relatively trivial offenses against the occuping authorities. Many people will suffer utter indignity and still remain cowed; others will persevere in resistance despite (or because of) great hardship. But for large numbers, perhaps most, the misfortunes of war lead to desperate decisions in the face of immediate situations. If the Yankees had not shot at the Tennessee soldier, the Rebel army would have lost a good officer.

Human personality can be viewed as the inclusive, internal organization that creates persistence in an individual's attitudes and actions. This persistence is shown in many ways. A person, for example, demonstrates stability of outlook over a whole range of activities. His political and social attitudes are clearly related to such matters as attitudes toward sex, family, and disease. He reacts to varying situations in a more or less predictable fashion. The changing experiences and conditions of life affect and alter personality. But an "inner rhythm" persists, characterizing the person; the degree of change in this rhythm with the passage of time is itself an index of personality stability.

A good example of consistency of viewpoints is provided by the so-called "authoritarian" personality. Childhood experiences marked by "basically hierarchical, authoritarian, exploitive" relationships with parents are carried over into adulthood. Adult attitudes are well integrated. Such persons believe in the importance of power, they depend upon others, and they exploit this dependence. Their political philosophy and social outlook have "no room for anything but a desperate clinging to what appears to be strong and a disdainful rejection of whatever is relegated to the bottom." The authoritarian person is the conforming person. He has strong loves and hates. He is anti-Semitic, anti-Negro, anti-Catholic. He needs strong leadership, and he is capable of expressing this dependency with sudden, hostile acts against those he considers weak.

Some political positions and groups are relatively congenial to given personality types. For example, communism in the United States and Great Britain (where the party is not respectable) has a particular appeal for those whose personality traits include a high degree of hostility and feeling of isolation. So fascism is attractive to the authoritarian. Personality type is thus, like other group categories, a useful tool of political analysis. A given personality establishes a predisposition toward given types of action.

It would be a great error to conclude from this sort of evidence that personality alone is decisive in determining loyalty choices; that traitors are born, not made; or even that traitors are formed in the childhood years that are so crucial for personality development.

Personality itself is the product of social factors. We know virtually nothing about the biological determinants of personality as that personality is acted out in social and political roles. Personality emerges from sequences of social experiences in which individuals first test themselves and the reactions of others and, finding a given role congenial, establish their own characteristic mode of action, Personality, in other words, develops in the course of experience.

In addition, the achievements of all are limited by what the society defines as permissible or possible. Only the rare genius or madman transcends these ranges. The traitor needs a social opportunity. There could be no atom bomb without a century of preceding mathematics and physics, neither a George Washington nor a Benedict Arnold without a British colony in disaffection.

Most important, personalities do not themselves make political movements, and political behavior does not directly grow out of personality characteristics. There is no evidence that even a large number of so-called "authoritarian" personalities could produce an authoritarian political movement or manage an authoritarian state. The same personality can serve a variety of political masters. The near-paranoid who is rated highly susceptible to fascism also finds communism congenial; or he may function happily and successfully as a post-office clerk in a democratic nation. Personality needs can be served in a variety of ways, and neither national loyalty nor disloyalty is a necessary fulfilment of any known personality factors.

The authoritarian personality can be used to illustrate the last point. Such personalities, tests show, exhibit a "blind attachment to certain national cultural values, uncritical conformity with the prevailing group ways, and rejection of other nations as outgroups." Other nations and nationality groups are regarded as "backward, immoral, and threatening." In one view, therefore, the authoritarian personality is patriotic, naïvely and uncritically so. In another view, however, the authoritarian is ambivalent; his need for dependence leads him to cling to the nation if it is strong but equally leads him to turn away from the nation if it is weak. He can fulfil his personality needs by both loyal and disloyal attitudes and acts.

These factors argue heavily against the view that personality type is decisive in producing loyalty or disloyalty. Personality may limit political action, just as that action may be limited by class, sex, occupation, and other social factors. But boundaries of action, however established, also define areas of freedom. Within these areas, a person does make his own choices. He does not, for example, join all the groups that he might; he joins those he finds most congenial. The very limitations imposed by cultures and subcultures may serve to challenge and stimulate, rather than to deaden and confine. Despite all limiting factors, free choices remain. Dynamic and responsive individuals follow no determined political life-pattern. They are able in varying degrees to shape their own environments.

It is fashionable to talk about the importance of personality; this may simply be a new perspective for what traditionally has been considered the importance of ideas and ideals. As with personality, some regularities of idea systems can be related to social situation. As the personality protects itself by selecting from the environment those cues that are most congenial to it, so idea systems are built by a process of selective assimilation and rejection. As personality structures alter and mature with time and circumstance, so idea systems are seasoned, built, and rebuilt.

Political action is often a means of meeting personal problems. In some cases, political justifications for personal prejudices are transparent; the maxim that politics is the public expression of private motives is clearest (and probably fallaciously oversimple) when the bedroom sadist becomes the public executioner. Moreover, it is often possible to relate ideas to social groups. Rich Protestants in New England are more likely than poor Catholics to vote for the Republican party. White southerners argue in favor of school segregation on the grounds of national welfare, but the economic and sexual bases for their argument can be easily revealed; and these in turn can be related to regional, class, and other group categories.

If all political ideas could be so categorized, there would be no need to postulate ideas themselves as an important impetus to social action. But, in fact, it is frequently impossible to relate ideas and ideals to social and economic position. How explain, in such terms, Aristotle or Machiavelli, Spinoza or Tom Paine?

Many ideas and ideals possess a thrust and a career of their own. Some American revolutionaries sought economic gain when they demanded independence from Great Britain. But they were inspired by the liberal doctrines of Locke, Rousseau, and others; and very soon the idea of independence itself became paramount. Personal sacrifices—far greater than the economic deprivation originally suffered—were readily endured for this cause. For many, death became preferable to continued dependence. Other causes may be brought forward to explain their determination, ranging from social position, to loyalty to comrades, to fear of penalty by the British. But for many patriots these causes were not controlling. Whatever else they fought for, they fought first for freedom.

The intensity with which different persons hold political ideas is also only poorly related to measurable personal situations or social conditions. Personal or social characteristics frequently do not distinguish a militant Communist from a person completely apathetic to politics. Radicals have explicit political demands; they are willing to work in politics; they believe that political action can change the course of events; and they have strong identification with political groups and symbols. Non-radicals neither hold such ideas nor identify themselves so strongly with political groups. Radicals and non-radicals can be separated according to social position, ethnic background, personality needs, or any number of other categories. But the radical group is most sharply distinguished from others by the idea system itself, not only its content but also the intensity with which it is felt and expressed.

A related factor is that some individuals are far more firm than others in adhering to ideas and ideals. Some Frenchmen fought against American invaders in North Africa in 1943, despite the fact that they welcomed the Allied assault upon the Vichy government; they believed so thoroughly in the sanctity of their service oath that they died rather than violate it, even though they died defending a cause they detested. A number of anti-Hitler German generals displayed the same fidelity but greater casuistry. They would not consider violating their personal oath to Hitler as supreme commander of the German armed forces; but they were willing to disobey his direct operational orders and thus "merely refuse to recognize him as Commander-in-Chief of the Army."

Observation in more commonplace situations—in business, government, universities, leisure groups—reveals great variety in the extent to which ideas are maintained among persons from the same economic and social stratum. One person is consistently guided by a system of ideas, seeking social reinforcement when he can find it but sometimes content to stand in opposition to solid social pressure. Others may enunciate the same ideas, but they renounce them when strongly opposed, or, more likely, they discover compelling competing ideas which allow the original ones to be shunted aside, sometimes joyously, sometimes with pious platitudes of regret.

Future advances in scientific analysis may satisfactorily explain political accidents, individual differences in personality, and the varying extent to which ideas and ideals influence action. Perhaps what appears to be randomness is only a deficiency of exact understanding. Theories that relate accidents to the needs of personality may be perfected. The psychological wave of the future may throw up finer and finer relationships between attitude and personality. Personality type may be related certainly and with precision to political act. Ideas and ideals may be established as inevitable correlates to social and personality factors that are presently unidentified.

Whatever the future may hold, the present seems to preserve areas of free political choice for many individuals. They transcend social situation, preserve the mystery of personality before the most determined psychological assault, confound socioeconomic correlations, and pursue courses of action that are consistent with their own ideas and ideals. This is a source of perturbation to the social scientist, whose mission in life is to reduce such irregularities into some general system of explanation. The scientist's defeat in this case is the citizen's joy. Individuals, in fact as well as in democratic theory, exercise freedom.

12 The Traitriot

Mr. N. was a Japanese American whose loyalty to the United States, established during World War I, was a casualty of World War II.

From every evidence available, Mr. N. was an exemplary American before Pearl Harbor. He had been honorably discharged from the American army following service in the first World War. He was a member of the Veterans of Foreign Wars and the American Legion. He belonged to a Christian church, he was a college graduate and a financial success. He had never visited Japan. He spoke convincingly of the values of the American democracy, and he was identified with a newspaper of markedly patriotic endeavors. After the war began, he applied unsuccessfully for defense-related jobs in which his skills as a ship navigator and radio operator could be utilized.

Mr. N. moved voluntarily to the Manzanar Relocation Center. He did so, he later explained, because he wished to cooperate with his government and to take advantage of special privileges promised voluntary evacuees. But he reacted adversely to the living conditions at the center and soon became known as a bitter critic of the evacuation. He was prominent as an opponent of those "spineless Americans" who urged cooperation with center authorities.

Mr. N. refused to answer the government's loyalty question in February, 1943; subsequently renounced his United States citizenship; and sailed from the United States for Japan in November, 1945. Before leaving this country, Mr. N., literate and angry, explained his shift in national loyalty. He wrote of the "abominable existence" he found at the Relocation Center:

> Being a citizen and a veteran . . . and having made every effort I could to further this present war effort . . . I found that my being treated as an alien was more than I could bear. This treatment has caused me to swear severance of my allegiance to the United States forever.

In another document he explained:

> I . . . will not forgive this government of the United States as long as I live. I have . . . become 100 per cent pro-Japanese. . . . To live as a Jap is the greatest pride we can enjoy in life.
>
> Who made me so?
>
> . . . Did the [U.S.] treat us like citizens? No! . . . What does the government think? Does it think we are degenerates? Or does it think we are illiterate savages? Or does it think we are without pride?

Mr. N. believed that all Japanese Americans would have retained their loyalty to the United States if they had been treated with "honor, justice, and humanity instead of harshness, injustice, and oppression." He thought anybody "with the slightest spark of manhood" had to react as he did, with an open desire "to fight for Japan against the United States." This course of action was also demanded by other weighty considerations.

My enemies call me vociferous, pro-Axis, fanatic, trouble maker, and everything else. . . . I am . . . proud of it. . . . Where are the virtues of American democracy? . . . I am not a hypocrite. I do not hide behind the veil of hypocrisy and wave the American flag. Neither am I a coward. *I will voice my conviction like a man and will fight like an American.*

Thus loyalty swings full circle to disloyalty. Disloyalty to democratic America becomes an expression of democratic ideas and democratic standards of action, the result of no failure to learn American principles but of success in making such principles a serious guide for life. The most loyal person becomes the most disloyal. Complete commitment to cause turns to the strongest attack, once the cause has been compromised. And the attack is all the more vigorous and all the more bitter because it is waged in terms of the original commitment.

This is one meaning of *traitriot.* So former Communists become the most bitter anti-Communists. So strong hatred is akin to strong love.

Any person who believes completely in another person, a cause, or an institution may cast himself in Mr. N.'s image. Any attempt to order loyalties into a hierarchy of values may end in national disloyalty unless the nation is judged supreme. The complete Christian is a traitriot because he would be a traitor to everything but his God; the lover, a traitor to everything but his love. The honorable may betray virtue, king, country, home; but the honorable do not betray their conception of honor. Those who put first things first may head their list with mankind, world government, salvation. If these come into conflict with nation, nation is put second.

All this happens with no change in the individual's beliefs. He stands but the world moves. What was loyalty today may be disloyalty tomorrow. His consistency to values that he places above the nation makes him a traitor. This is a second meaning of traitriot.

A third meaning of traitriot exists at levels of allegiance unrelated to the nation. Here disloyalty can be seen as a way of life—acceptable, necessary, and very frequently admired. This is characteristic of the fluid society of the United States, with its ideal of social and economic "success." It is also true of the other kind of fluid society in the Soviet Union, where an important road to achievement is adherence to a succession of radically shifting programs and rapidly recruited program leaders.

The desirability and necessity of quickly changing loyalties within the Soviet Union needs no elaboration. In simplest terms, one must shift loyalties with shifting leaders or die. The same desirability and necessity, less violently enforced, exists among the Western democracies and especially in the United States.

The improvement of social position is the great American game. The American injunction is "Better thyself." The most important American dream is "from rags to riches." In all areas of life, open competition for improved status offers Americans an unending series of choice points for new companions, new group affiliations, new jobs, new neighbors. This flexibility of social life demands a flexibility of loyalties. "Go West, young man," is advice to drop old loyalties and to seek new ones.

Disloyalty as a socially desirable fact can be traced in virtually every aspect of American life. The courtship pattern of marriageable girls is a pattern of changing loyalties. Despite the virtues of "going steady," the girl who is engaged several times before marriage is smiled upon rather than censured; she has every right to make the best match possible. In a similar fashion, persons of talent are admired for seeking new life-ways, and the trail from log cabin to White House is a long journey of loyalties made and unmade.

Of greater significance is the ordinary drive of the vast majority of Americans to improve their wealth and position. The prototype is supplied by the son of immigrant parents. He finds distasteful the speech accents, the food habits, and the living conditions of his family. As a youth in school, he avoids bringing friends from non-immigrant families to his home. As a young adult, he leaves his parents, perhaps for the less comfortable quarters of a bachelor's rooming-house, and he marries outside his parents' church and without the Old World ceremony. As a striving middle-aged businessman, he establishes his family in another and more desirable area of the city. To a greater or lesser extent, he cuts himself off from—is disloyal to—not only his family but also old friends, those who have "never become Americanized." And as he shifts jobs or businesses, as he gains wealth and prestige, he is forced continuously to trade one set of work associates and leisure companions for another.

There are many exceptions to this pattern. One point of access to better things is through leadership of the underprivileged group rather than through leaving it. Those who leave it, once they are securely established, may display nostalgia and attempt to re-establish old ties: as when Mr. Andrews (changed from Andreuccitti) serves spaghetti cooked according to his mother's recipe to his old friends on the new patio. Furthermore, the schematic presentation does not do justice to the difficulty of achieving shifts in status. Established loyalties are not easily replaced. The pull from the past is strong, and new groups demand new living patterns which are hard to learn, as the caricature of the social climber illustrates.

Ideals of trustworthiness and fidelity sometimes conflict with the ideal of success and interfere with the shifting of loyalties that is demanded by social improvement. Persons who cannot be trusted or who cut old friends are universally held to be contemptible (though the most brutal are admired if their success is great), and many persons must make uneasy compromises, trying equally to preserve old associations and to cultivate new ones. Most frequently, the old friends and associates are not cut; they simply become no longer an important part of one's life. The boss may occasionally play poker with the boys. He may enjoy being with his old friends from the shop more than he does with new ones at the country club. But his position—the very social drive that made him boss—almost invariably demands that the old be dropped and the new elevated.

All qualifications aside and whatever the conflict of ideals within the minds of men, the America of fluid classes is a society in which the breaking of old loyalties and the forging of new ones is characteristic. This can be traced in the history of all immigrant and underprivileged groups, which is the history of most of America. It is the pride of the melting pot and the hallmark of our way of life.

America is a culture of shifting loyalties. The shifts must be made without flagrant disregard for standards of trustworthiness. If this is accomplished, disloyalty in situations not involving nation is looked upon with high favor.

These considerations lay bare the deepest meaning of traitriot: all patriots are potential traitors.

The paths to disloyalty are closed to no man. In a democracy the completely "normal" citizen—happily married, in a good job, the pillar of his church, committed to the nation's value system—faces the possibility that his loyalty to those very groups and ideals which give him happiness may produce disloyalty to nation. His risk is greatest when the best of all worlds begins to crumble; when the welfare of his family or the security of his income is threatened by national policies which appear to him contrary to the nation's ideals; when he can maintain what he loves only by action inimical to the nation.

If the best of all worlds should disappear, or if, indeed, it never existed, the second path of disloyalty beckons. Here is the man devoid of loyalties to smaller groups, alienated in society, without status or values. His disloyalty to nation results not from the priority of one allegiance over another. Rather, he searches for stability and sense and achievement in life by grasping a cause, by saluting a leader, or by drifting into close relations with others who are pledged to the destruction of the going system.

The universal potential for disloyalty among citizens of a dictatorship rests in part upon these same factors. The more total the state tries to be, the more likely it is to inspire attitudes and actions against itself and in favor of family, church, and friends. The policy of using state-dictated programs to fill forcibly alienated lives results in a single strong bond to nation, which, if it snaps, leaves no base for allegiance whatsoever. This is true even for those who completely accept the system. The Soviet idealist can turn only against the state if he believes the state has perverted the precepts of Marxism. The Soviet careerist can turn only against the state if he is not protected in his job and cannot realize his career aspirations. The Soviet conformist can turn only against the state if he feels that the society no longer offers him security and safety.

The totalitarian potential for universal disloyalty is clear-cut for some reasons that are unknown to democracy. Those loyal because they have been duped by lies about their own and other worlds are fierce in anger when the truth is unfolded.

Those who blindly follow one master bow easily before another. Those loyal out of fear must be loyal to those most feared.

The totalitarian terror masks dissidence. A very wide gulf can thus separate attitude and action concerning the totalitarian state. Great displays of patriotic action may mask great hatreds for the regime. Patriots can become traitors, terribly, suddenly, and en masse.

Democracies, to the extent that they are sensitive to public opinion, do not face these dangers. Yet democracies must tolerate a thin line between patriotism and treason. Loyalties to democracy are built largely from loyalties to smaller groups. The latter cannot be destroyed without destroying democracy itself. And so the alienated masses of democracy, those without any loyalties, those that most observers consider the greatest internal threat to democracy, are joined by the socialized masses, those whose loyalty to nation is prejudiced because their other loyalties may be more powerful.

The social processes that bring individuals to commit treason are the same processes that produce patriotism. Traitor and patriot alike relate sorrows and joys—through identification and rejection, obedience and revolt—to the nation. The traitor frequently justifies himself in patriotic terms and believes that he serves his nation. The rare exception is the person who has been bribed, who knows it, and who suffers guilt pangs.

So all of us are potential traitors. The situation of people marginal to the larger culture—racial minorities are a good example—is different only in degree from the situation of those who are solidly within the dominant group. The white Protestant businessman—like the Japanese American Buddhist-laborer—may at some point be forced to choose between the demands of his nation and the demands of his religion or business or lodge or family. Or, as the consequence of factors completely beyond his control, he may find his social moorings wrecked, his once stable position only an angry point of contrast with new poverty or other severe deprivation. All people may at one time or another, for one cause or another, find themselves in a marginal position in relationship to the nation, lacking the ability to respond without hesitation to the nation's call.

Disloyalty comes for the alienated when he joins the crowd behind a new leader or embraces the religion of a new cause. Disloyalty comes to the socialized when he can no longer successfully juggle his numerous loyalties, when he places family or job or friend or church above the nation.

No person is a complete patriot or a complete traitor. All are traitriots. Just as all men have a little neurosis in them, so it is that all have a trace of the traitor.

PART V
Some Policy Conclusions

13 The Reverse Consequences of National Loyalty Investigations

Scientific analysis, no one need be told in the age of the uranium atom, has more than an intellectual kick. Social science cannot compete with recent accomplishments of physical science in influencing social policy. But the insights of social science can nevertheless be used to foster, for good or evil, a variety of practical programs. With sufficient refinement, the explanation of what produces disloyalty could be turned by an unfriendly government to spot areas of potential disaffection in the United States. No data given here would enable a foreign agency to name, at a distance, specific individuals ready to perform treasonable acts. But population groups, defined by job or age or place in the social system, might conceivably be singled out as those most likely to produce traitors. On the other hand, if appropriate additional information were at hand, the analysis might be used equally well by Americans to identify and nourish traitors in some other nation.

Scientific insight can be turned to building loyalties rather than destroying them. It can be a tool for assessing the effectiveness of specific governmental investigations of loyalty. It can provide a base for more general programs by which a democratic nation can encourage and maintain the loyalty of its citizens.

All nations are concerned with safeguarding themselves against their own disloyal citizens. How effective are the current loyalty-security programs of the United States? Do they promote national loyalty, discourage disloyalty, uncover actual and potential traitors? Consider the situation of American scientists, those most frequently and most intensively subject to loyalty investigations.

Some factors in the situation of scientists in the United States, after World War II, undoubtedly lead toward a very strong national allegiance. For one thing, the state of the world is regarded by scientists, along with others, as something abnormal and (hopefully) impermanent. It represents crisis and demands sacrifice. As we have seen, there is almost no limit to what men will suffer and remain loyal to their nation. Sacrifice and grief raise patriotism to its highest level, and scientists may achieve a great sense of recompense for their efforts, even if these involve hardship, in the urgent cause of the nation.

The compensation is not merely psychic. Scientists have a new high social status as a consequence of their wartime successes. And their position has been further raised as the government has supplied new funds, new laboratories, and new positions of trust. For many, these developments have produced substantial work satisfactions. They have become directly involved in the affairs of the nation, and their scientific careers have become dependent upon continued contributions to nationally defined goals. All this has strengthened the scientists' positive identification with nation.

New professional importance is matched by new political importance. Opinions of physicists and chemists on national and world affairs are twice weighed, and scientists find here new areas of self-esteem. Even when unsuccessful in influencing policy, their political activity is a catharsis for discontent. And their contribution to great programs of government is both a source and a symbol of loyalty.

Finally, scientists are not a separate breed of men. Like other men in Western culture, they cherish a set of Western values, some of which—such as the value of freedom—they find indispensable to their work and work satisfaction. These values do not lead to extravagantly proclaimed national loyalties, but they certainly militate against an easy identification with nations where work freedom is heavily restricted. Democratic beliefs are thus a source of energy as scientists work politically to encourage national policies which will most aid their professional effectiveness. These values sustain loyalty during the crisis period.

On the other hand, powerful forces push toward weakening the loyalty of scientists to the United States. Scientists are not bound to nation by direct ties of great strength that might be demonstrated, for example, in love for a political leader. They do not achieve gratification through what we have called the "religious" quality of patriotism. To a greater extent than for almost any other occupational group, the life-satisfactions of scientists issue from work. Their identification with the nation is filtered through their careers. And it is precisely at job and career that loyalty-security programs and secrecy restrictions hit hardest. Professional life can be destroyed by an adverse security ruling or by the publicity which accompanies congressional investigation. "To have once been dropped for security reasons is for the average person . . . a professional catastrophe."

The loyalty-security investigations have adverse effects whether they are conducted secretly or in public, whether one is cleared or not. Those cleared without personal interrogation feel the foreboding hand of investigation. They worry about the political views of their neighbors and distant relatives, find it difficult to make new friends or retain old ones, and speculate openly about whether the work they are doing is worth the personal stress imposed upon them. Clearance after intensive investigation and interrogation may be won at the price of losing a large part of what is conducive to national allegiance.

> The shattering financial, psychological, and practical consequences of even a wholly successful defense against [disloyalty] charges are commonly recognized, for the stigma is not erased by a clearance and nothing can replace the harrowing months of uncertainty and the loss of friendships that are usual concomitants of loyalty proceedings.

These consequences are probably less likely when the investigation is conducted according to careful administrative procedures rather than by congressional committees; but their effect is aggravated as the administrative criteria for "loyalty" or "security" change and as individuals are consequently subject to investigation and reinvestigation many times.

Great scientific programs, involving the national defense, inevitably become the object of political concern and the subject for political controversy. A scientist who takes a stand for or against a given development or the utilization of a given weapon finds that he has made political enemies. He discovers that politics exists within the scientific fraternity. He also finds that government administrators and military officers, as well as congressmen and senators, are concerned with the control of scientific development. Issues of disloyalty and security become confused with issues of policy. What is easier than to charge an opponent with being a security risk, especially if the accuser is a non-scientist, suspicious of intellectualism, and uneasy because recondite information available to the scientist is only a puzzle to him? Great stakes—in money and in the nation's welfare—are involved. So loyalty and security become political weapons. Norbert Wiener, commenting on the Oppenheimer case, remarked that a scientist, "participating in what has become a moving crap game, must expect to get slugged occasionally."

Getting slugged is most likely for those scientists who have emerged from the laboratory to become research entrepreneurs and, perforce, political figures. It is a risk taken for the joys and privileges of participation in directing great programs of government. But all scientists suffer in another way from loyalty and security programs. These programs impose restrictions on the free interchange of scientific information, restrictions which run radically counter to the scientists' creed.

Their fraternity is world-wide. The professional guild from which a scientist acquires prestige and cues for action is confined to no national boundaries. Scientific progress depends upon free, world-wide communication. Science proceeds slowly, in cumulative steps, and every scientist depends upon the work of predecessors and colleagues, wherever they may be. Scientists therefore tend to be internationalists. The search for truth, they believe, should be unconfined. Few, if any, deny that some measures of secrecy are needed in today's troubled world. But scientists tend to localize secrecy to small areas of weapon technology. They believe more extensive restrictions impair the nation's total scientific effort and do not prevent armament development by other nations. Legislators and administrators, who are not scientists, are tempted to take the opposite course of maximum secrecy. Clashes occur, to the frustration of both sides, scientists in their own view suffering because of the ignorance of non-scientific policy-makers.

The eminent physicist and British traitor, Dr. Allan Nunn May, declared that he gave official secrets about the atom bomb to Russian agents because he believed that both science and mankind were endangered if the results of Anglo-American nuclear research were not made available to all scientists throughout the world. These are not merely the extreme views of the traitor. They are commonplace among the scientific fraternity, and they have found their most explicit statement in novels by authors who are intimate with scientists. The theme of secrecy (and national welfare) versus science (and international welfare) is central to Nigel Balchin's *A Sort of Traitors*. Here the scene is Great Britain, and the field is biology. Michael Amrine's *Treason* concerns nuclear physicists in the United States, and its protagonist declares:

> Where does a man's loyalty lie? Is loyalty to the race larger than loyalty to a nation? . . . I am a scientist, dedicated to truth. If I cannot speak the truth, I have no reason for existence. If I lie, I am false not only to you, but to myself, to my science, to my civilization, and, as I believe, false to the best interests of my country. . . . Science can never submit to censorship. That is not science. . . . It is madness.

One cannot doubt that many scientists in the United States believe that loyalty-security investigations unfairly threaten them with the loss of their jobs and reputations, the alienation of their friends, and the foreclosure of new opportunity. These views have been enormously strengthened by the case of Professor J. Robert Oppenheimer. Furthermore, the secrecy imposed upon research and publication is widely regarded as detrimental to the progress of science.

These programs of the government have apparently produced few traitors. This assumption must be made because evidence is lacking to the contrary, even though the very nature of the problem does not admit conclusive proof. Successful traitors do not, after all, give evidence of their existence. Investigative logic might find this lack of evidence a sign of guilt: at least one government employee has been condemned because he published anti-Communist articles. But we abide by the evidence available, and we can find good reasons for the inefficiency of the loyalty-security and secrecy programs in turning scientists against the United States.

For one thing, as already noted, the successful scientist can find many aspects of life that are gratifying and that bind him to nation. These overbalance his frustration and distaste. Even the person subject to trial before a congressional committee or caught up in lengthy administrative hearings knows that the investigation represents only one segment of a diverse society. He does not find the entire world against him. A few staunch friends will encourage and aid him. Though the community may be laden with fear, colleagues will collect money for his legal defense and living expenses. A lawyer or an organization concerned with civil liberties will offer assistance. A newspaper reporter will carefully present both sides of the case. A clergyman will venture words of praise before the congregation. A few neighbors will throw a sympathetic beer party. This kind of support provides the congenial face-to-face contact that is so important for personal satisfaction and equally important as a basis for a positive view of the society as a whole. It indicates that the whole nation has not set its hand to indiscriminate life-smashing.

If the person investigated receives this support exclusively from a group pledged to disloyal acts, his loss to the nation becomes most probable. The group effort will be to convince him that his troubles do not result from an aberration, or a temporary stage, of the political system but rather are a central manifestation of that system; that the future is forever clouded unless radical political changes take place. But there are few groups available to capitalize in this fashion on the discontent of those investigated.

A final reason for the continued national loyalty of scientists, despite investigatory pressures, is that the principal alternative national loyalty—to the Soviet Union—is unpalatable. The Marxist dialectic, with its finely wrought "scientific" overtones, has appealed in the past to many scientific men, as the large numbers of open Communists among physicists and chemists in prewar Britain testify. The scientist, whose business is to understand and change the physical world, can easily be attracted to Marxism, whose business is to understand and change the social world. But in recent years the enchantment has worn thin as the intellectual brutality of the Soviet Union has become less disguised inside Russia and more widely understood outside. Scientists who chafe in America under pressures for conformity, threats of investigation, and regulations demanding secrecy must believe under most circumstances that their lot would be infinitely worse in the Soviet Union.

So the government's loyalty-security and secrecy programs have probably not led many scientists to embrace communism. Yet these programs seem greatly to increase the possibility that a scientist might be driven to perform a traitorous act as a momentary expression of protest, dissatisfaction, and disgust, despite the pressures operating to discourage such an act. To assume that disloyalty cannot come in this fashion and that it must be the result of more rational and deliberate processes is to ignore a large portion of the evidence we have concerning the ways in which men become traitors. Disloyal acts are probably less frequently the consequence of mature deliberation than of immediate reaction to unhappy circumstance.

The pernicious consequences of loyalty-security and secrecy programs are not principally measured by the hypothetical occasional traitor which those programs might produce. The consequences are more subtle, as scientists face unhappy choices when the nation aligns itself in seeming opposition to professional ethics, job security, and family welfare. Some individuals have great tolerance for such ambivalences. They submerge themselves in work, tell themselves with conviction that the disabilities of American security regulations are temporary and inconsequential, or that they are a necessary evil, or that they do not exist at all; and these scientists labor effectively for both science and nation. Others have no such tolerance. With the basis of old national loyalties cut away as the result of loyalty-security and secrecy programs and with a new national loyalty forestalled by the image of Russian despotism, these scientists react by retreating into a state of powerless frustration or diffuse hostility.

The reaction pattern takes a number of forms. Some scientists emptily follow the rituals expected by government, accepting research contracts as they come, sticking close to their laboratories, and refusing to involve themselves in any discussion of politics, including the politics of science. A smaller number fly to the opposite pole: they refuse to work in any program of classified government research because they define the conditions of such work as intolerable. This critical view has led some scientists to intense political participation. A third group has been alienated from both nation and science; they develop a national neutralism, search out other focal points for political loyalty—a world peace organization, for example—and expend their energy on behalf of that organization's cause.

One competent observer has remarked that "the scientist as a class always seemed to be quarreling with military officers as a class, even while they were developing one of the most effective partnerships in history." The short-run effectiveness of the military-scientific alliance cannot be doubted, in so far as such things are measurable: the superbombs have been built. The very freedom of scientists to criticize the military has not only revealed difficulties but has also decreased hostile pressures. Nevertheless, in the long run the loyalty-security and secrecy programs of the federal government, including the army, may produce very great harm to both science and the nation.

These programs result in a withdrawal of affection and competence from the nation. The withdrawal of affection is summarized in the statement of a prominent scientist that he did not believe it would be very much different to live and work under a Soviet master. The withdrawal of competence is in part unknown. How can one assess scientific opportunities lost because of secrecy regulations? Only the direct impairment of competence can be weighed, as when scientists refuse to work on government programs under conditions they define as unbearable; when rigidities of the program prevent competent persons from being employed; when the interchange of ideas and information is strictly curtailed; when suspicion, distrust, and fearfulness impede the effectiveness of research and the creativity of researchers. The withdrawal of affection may lead to disloyalty. The withdrawal of competence leads to research inefficiency and, in the long run, to a decline in scientific progress. Damage to the nation may be as great from one as from the other.

What is true of scientists is also true of other groups subject to continuous loyalty investigation. Civil servants are one such group. Screened and rescreened under the various loyalty and security programs of two presidents and fair game for congressional committees, very many employees of the national government have become demoralized, suspicious, and unhappy. Teachers are perhaps even more resentful of investigation, partly because traditions of academic freedom are so strong and partly because the scrutiny of teachers cannot be justified in terms of any immediate danger to the nation. Teachers, furthermore, have in recent years been widely investigated by state legislative committees. These committees, to an even greater extent than national groups, have attacked individuals without adequate evidence, have equated non-conformity with danger, and have carried to extremes the doctrine of collective guilt.

Many teachers and civil servants have been convicted of guilt "for offenses not always defined in law" and punished through the destruction of their reputations and the loss of their livelihood. A much larger group has suffered as the result of worry, fear, and suspicion arising from the act of investigation and, in some cases, the vehemence of the investigators.

The withdrawal of affection from nation by civil servants and teachers has been expressed bitterly: "I must leave my government job; I'm not afraid of any investigation of my past, but I am afraid of what investigation might make me do in the future." In other cases, it is expressed jocularly: "This God-damned committee makes me feel as if I should go out and give away some secrets to Russia." These reactions and others like them do not indicate treason, but they certainly are danger signs pointing to an increased potentiality for disloyalty. Those who see the investigations as an affront to human dignity and as characteristic of democracy do not make the best defenders of their nation.

The withdrawal of competence by civil servants is marked by growing caution and conformity, a decline in initiative, and a discouragement of critical ideas. The loyalty-security programs have destroyed many effective working groups. Men of ability have left, and others have been discouraged from entering, the government service. Marked inefficiencies have resulted, in agencies from the post office to the foreign service. In the Department of State, five distinguished former diplomats have testified that loyalty-security programs threaten to cripple the entire foreign service:

> The conclusion has become inescapable . . . that a Foreign Service officer who reports on persons and events to the very best of his ability and who makes recommendations which at the time he conscientiously believes to be in the interest of the United States may subsequently find his loyalty and integrity challenged and may even be forced out of the service and discredited forever as a private citizen after many years of distinguished service. A premium therefore has been put upon reporting and upon recommendations which are ambiguously stated or so cautiously set forth as to be deceiving. When any such tendency begins its insidious work it is not long before accuracy and initiative have been sacrificed to acceptability and conformity. The ultimate result is a threat to national security.

An impartial professional authority, Professor Hans Morgenthau, has come to an even more damning conclusion: as a result of loyalty-security investigations, the Department of State "is hardly competent to serve any government, totalitarian or otherwise."

In education the programs have also resulted in timidity, discouragement, and withdrawal. The edge of inquiry and teaching has been dulled, from those lower grades in some communities where discussion of the United Nations has been forbidden, to those universities in some states where scholarly research on political matters and comment on public affairs are discouraged, whether by fears of open reprisal from self-styled patriotic organizations or by timidities resulting from the more subtle pressures of community sentiment seeping through the adjectives and resolve of trustees and administrative officers. Teachers in some areas must sign special loyalty oaths. Others are forbidden to assign books concerning the Soviet Union. To subscribe to technical journals or to read books devoted to analyses of communism may be culpable. The consequences often extend into all areas of life. Neighborhood discussion as well as classroom teaching must be cautious and circumspect. To live safely, for many teachers, means to give up their life of free investigation.

On the one hand, the loyalty-security programs have prejudiced the effectiveness of American foreign policy when that policy must be effective if the world is to survive. On the other hand, these programs, extended to the schools, have reduced intellectual freedom and weakened the institutions best able to provide the democratic virtues of examination, evaluation, and dissent.

Governments must guard themselves against harm and destruction, and there can therefore be no criticism of the objectives of loyalty investigations for government employees and scientists who work on government projects. The ill consequences of the investigations might be risks fairly taken if the investigations effectively turned up individuals whose threat to the nation was great and if there were no better methods of discovering these individuals. Neither of these conditions is fulfilled.

What administrative and congressional investigation of government employees and scientists has accomplished in the way of protecting the nation is not easy to judge. If effectiveness could be measured by newspaper headlines, the investigations could be acclaimed an unqualified success. But that test is not a fair one. Reports of government offices—listing separations for security and other reasons and including persons whose files contain "derogatory" information—are similarly unrevealing. On the other hand, it is also unfair to evaluate the investigations by the harshest test available: by asking how many persons, as the result of the investigations, have been convicted of treason, sabotage, or espionage. From all the presently available data, the answer to this question is: None. Some persons have been sent to jail as the result of action taken by congressional committees, but in every instance these have been cases of contempt or perjury, offenses against the committees themselves. There is no evidence that the congressional or administrative loyalty-security programs have in any single instance been followed by a conviction for substantial acts against the nation. Persons tried and convicted for crimes of disloyalty such as espionage or sabotage—the Rosenbergs, for example—have been uncovered by regular law-enforcement agencies, principally the Federal Bureau of Investigation.

The failure to uncover acts of disloyalty punishable by law does not mean that the investigations have been a complete failure. A number of persons have been dismissed as a consequence of loyalty proceedings, and a far larger number have resigned—or failed to apply for government employment—as a consequence of their disinclination to be subject to investigation. Some of the persons in these categories may have prejudiced the security of the United States in the jobs they held or might have held. Furthermore, some of the information turned up by congressional and administrative investigation has undoubtedly proved useful to the regular law-enforcement agencies, even though the latter are most often the source, and not the recipient, of such information.

These are positive results of the loyalty-security programs. Yet even when the investigators claim to be most successful, the nation is adversely affected. Success is achieved when a past, or current, member of the Communist party is "uncovered," when a person is demonstrated to have a "sensitive affiliation" (through being related by blood, marriage, or friendship) with party members or fellow-travelers, or when he is shown to have been a member of an organization defined as Communist or dominated by Communists. The usual result is that the person "exposed" loses his job. The attendant publicity prejudices his friendships, his community status, and his future career. The success of loyalty investigations is in part a success in manufacturing conditions conducive to disloyalty.

Security-loyalty investigations carried out under executive orders of Presidents Truman and Eisenhower have been, in comparison with congressional committees, far more sensitive to the rights of those being investigated, more careful in procedure, and less prone to declare persons guilty by publicity. The congressional committees, in turn, have been less open to criticism on these grounds than most of the state investigatory groups. But these are differences only in degree. The end results are often the same. And the individuals concerned do not often make nice distinctions between the executive and the legislature, between state and national agencies. In every case it is the government or nation that is the source—what is felt to be the unjust, arbitrary source—of their difficulty; at the least, the nation countenances what is done. Many people are able to relate discontents to the nation despite the fact that the true source of their difficulty may be completely unrelated. In loyalty investigations the relationship between nation and deprivation is immediate and direct. The nation causes the person's trouble, and the nation may be cursed. All the investigation programs suffer from common frailties and lead to similar undesirable results. More appropriate and more efficient means for combating subversion in government are available.

To achieve a more desirable program requires new administrative arrangements as well as deeper understandings of the ingredients of loyalty and disloyalty. Don K. Price has admirably set forth some of the necessary administrative steps: a need to have the highest responsible officers concerned with security, on the grounds that "anyone who disapproves of lynchings has to be ready to serve on a jury"; a stronger central administrative system and a career service capable, among other things, of withstanding the temptation to consider workers as publicity rather than as security risks; and restraint of congressional committees, a control that is difficult to achieve because it can come only from Congress itself. Such suggestions will themselves go far in building a more effective and more responsible program. But, as the Oppenheimer case has illustrated, even the highest officials, acting under the most careful procedures and in a most restrained fashion, do not necessarily achieve wisdom. What is also needed is an accurate understanding of what loyalty and disloyalty are.

Those responsible for security should recognize that loyalties change with time and circumstance. They should recognize that affiliations of the past are less important than actions of the present. They should recognize that investigation can erode loyalty as well as disclose disloyalty. They should recognize that men properly have multiple loyalties in a democratic state, that superpatriotism is not always a desirable attribute, and that judgments concerning security are more limited and easier to make than those concerning loyalty. They should recognize that all men have a disloyalty (and loyalty) potential, that some risk is therefore inevitable in all government enterprise, and that "absolute security is likely to result in nothing save absolute sterility." They should recognize that patriotism may be discouraged by measures that indicate national weakness and jitters, just as it is fostered by measures that show the nation's strength.

A loyalty program based upon these principles would take into account that diversity of opinion is essential to democratic life. It would adhere to "a basic concept of our laws and Constitution that persons should be penalized for their conduct, not for their beliefs, and not for the acts of those with whom they associate." It would not have the negative emphasis of rooting out clerks with ancient leftist affiliations but would seek affirmatively for attributes of intelligence, resourcefulness, and integrity in public servants. It would realize that investigation is a technique of the most limited usefulness in encouraging the desirable attributes of public service. It would penalize, through regular administrative and legal procedures, criminal, inefficient, and untrustworthy officials. It would recognize that post-office clerks, elevator operators, county agricultural agents, and the vast majority of government workers have little to do with the nation's immediate security, and it would therefore confine close scrutiny to those relatively few officials in positions of great sensitivity. It would not expose scientists and others to repeated inquiry covering the same facts. It would provide for traditional safeguards, wherever possible, in the handling of evidence. It would rigidly separate dissent from disloyalty. It would make known the administration's trust, not suspicion, of the great mass of workers, encouraging loyalty by assuming loyalty.

It would not hold up to public odium those investigated but would observe the maxim that the best investigation is the quietest one. The proper loyalty investigation would not cast out into unemployment those removed from their jobs. Rather it would, as an essential part of its task, establish a re-employment center to find posts of less strategic importance for those removed from positions of greater importance, thus avoiding the situation of men wandering in the alleys—angry, embittered, and perhaps waiting to strike back.

There is, in sum, no way of justifying the current executive and congressional investigations of disloyalty on the grounds of their efficiency. More desirable methods of administration and more exact knowledge of the ingredients of loyalty and disloyalty would better protect the nation and simultaneously avoid the many undesirable by-products of the present system. A loyalty-security program worthy of its name would, above all else, attempt to build and not destroy democratic loyalties in the process of maintaining the nation's security.

National loyalty comes easily to an individual if his job and career are secure, if he participates amiably in work and leisure with colleagues and friends, if he feels accepted and secure, if his relationship to the larger community is not strained. Destroy his career, disrupt his work and play groups, isolate him, persecute him, show your disdain for him, and you plant the seeds for his disaffection. His allegiance will withstand maltreatment. But the multiplication of abuses will weaken his loyalty; and, as abuse continues, loyalty erodes away. It erodes all the more completely and all the more rapidly if he believes that the government is directly responsible for his difficulties.

A frequent criticism of the loyalty-security programs is that they utilize undemocratic procedures for democratic goals. The danger is that the means swallow the ends and that the loyalty-security programs consequently undermine the very traditions of American democracy that they seek to strengthen. The analysis presented here adds another conclusion, by its very nature beyond complete proof, but nevertheless strongly suggested by all the materials available and by the understanding of the nature of national loyalty gained through analysis of those materials. The loyalty-security programs produce reverse consequences. They weaken national loyalties rather than strengthen them; they undermine, not increase, competence; they create more traitors than they uncover.

14 Democratic Values and Democratic Loyalty

For more than a hundred years observers of industrial civilization have looked back upon older times for a point of envious comparison. They have described pre-industrial society as characterized by an acceptance of common beliefs and by the social stability that results from happy, sustained human relationships within residential, work, and family groups. This state of affairs has been contrasted with modern society, where, it is held, industrial urban conditions have destroyed enjoyment, and even understanding, of life. Ferdinand Tönnies, in terminology that has been widely accepted, identified the earlier, pre-industrial way of life as "community" (*Gemeinschaft*), and industrial civilization as "society" (*Gesellschaft*). The "gemeinschaft grouse" is the criticism of modern Western society by those who believe it a generally unhappy place; it is especially the criticism which emphasizes the deficiencies of industrial civilization by comparison with an earlier way of living; but it also includes the critique that looks forward, rather than back, to a society that is regulated, uncomplicated, and serene.

The grouse extends far more widely than is commonly understood. It is by no means confined to the Marxists, whose original criticism of capitalist industrialism was savage and whose portrait of the coming socialist society was extremely ambiguous. The grouse represents the mainstream of social commentary during the last century.

Max Weber's view of the modern world illustrates the critical view. Weber believed that unceasing work, characteristic of industrial society, was originally abetted by the Calvinist injunction to seek a calling. In the early days of industrialization the worker could solace himself with the belief that his unremitting labor was an evidence of eternal salvation. But, with industrialization full blown, the religious ethos lost its power. One worked only for work's sake. The business of business was confused with the business of life. Life consequently became meaningless, and the future of industrial civilization was black.

Like Weber, Émile Durkheim saw many virtues in industrialization: high productivity, for example, and the development of talent and personality that results from the division of work and specialization. But Durkheim believed that industrial society produced bitter conflicts of class interests and destroyed religious beliefs held in common. These were fatal cultural faults. They could be remedied only by the device of enforced and directed co-operation, a corporate system which Durkheim sketched in 1902 and which was fairly duplicated, though without any need for the Durkheim model, by the Italian Fascist state in 1922.

Thorstein Veblen raged against the domination and exploitation of industrial civilization by business groups. These groups perverted productive capacities to non-social ends. For the majority of people, life was reduced to a rat race of meaningless work and conspicuous competitive consumption. Neither work nor the products of work produced happiness.

Though Sigmund Freud was less self-consciously concerned with assessing industrial culture, he finds a place in the front ranks of the grousers. Freud clearly cast his vote in favor of civilization, and it is a misreading of his work to place him as an advocate of life in any primitive past. But he was certain that the development of culture made men suffer, and he was equally certain that the culture he saw made men suffer too much. The culture's restrictions upon sexual activity loaded men with frustration, and the culture's restrictions upon aggressiveness filled them with anxiety and guilt. The price of civilization was unhappiness.

These are only samples—brief and therefore simplified, but not inaccurate—of the gemeinschaft grouse. Marx, Weber, Freud, Durkheim, and Veblen span a century and two continents and range in discipline from medicine through sociology to economics. Their differences are many, but they are at one in criticism of industrial society and in their belief that this society of conflict and confusion inadequately serves the needs of mankind. All find valuable things in the society, but all believe that these are overwhelmed by the pernicious. And all look to more stable and more secure societies. It would be difficult to find five other persons of equal influence on scholarship and, through scholarship, on popular culture.

The grouse is still a dominant note in contemporary social analysis. For example, C. Wright Mills, the Thomas Wolfe of American sociology, describes the great middle class of white-collar workers as having "no firm roots, no sure loyalties to sustain . . . life and give it a center." The white-collar worker is the "new Little Man." He is in a "frantic hurry" because "he does not know where he is going," and he is "paralyzed with fear" because "he does not know what frightens him." These many Americans, we are told, suffer from the "root fact" that "in our politics and economy, in family life and religion—in practically every sphere of our existence—the certainties of the eighteenth and nineteenth centuries have disintegrated or been destroyed and, at the same time, no new sanctions or justifications . . . have taken hold." For members of the middle class, "there is no plan of life." They are "morally defenseless as individuals and politically impotent as a group."

Such views are widely shared. A political scientist (S. de Grazia) sees political cohesion resting only upon a common system of orders and a ruler that all men love. Western civilization is in a sad state because it possesses neither of these requisites, and consequently men are "directionless, rudderless, ruleless." A sociologist (P. Selznick) believes that Western democracy is weak because the mass of men spread incompetence into all areas of life; having no common system of values, these men can easily be mobilized and manipulated for non-democratic ends. A political theorist (W. Kendall) argues the need of a political system that will put meaning into empty lives by making demands upon the energies of all and that will build a "community whose members willingly accept a single belief-system." A philosopher (B. Brownell) mourns "the disintegration of the community and its slow extinction in the Western world." Trends of urbanization and centralization "may well be a tendency toward death." "Survival in any form that matters is the survival of the small community in its implicit freedom, friendliness, and fullness of human association."

Western culture embraces much that these criticisms imply, but it is accurately described by none of them. Alienation, described in an earlier chapter as one path to disloyalty in democratic states, is an ill that the grousers have correctly identified.

And we have seen how trend lines in the direction of mass alienation can be consciously steepened as both a cause and a product of the strong nation-person tie that characterizes totalitarian states. But neither the relatively few alienated democratic citizens nor the totalitarian masses are characteristic of industrial culture. Much that is observable does not correspond to what the critics describe as Western culture, and evidences of social consensus exist despite the critics' assurance that the society lacks any basis for unity. We look at the United States and ask: What have the grousers missed?

America's complexity is America's strength. The crazy quilt of ethnic, economic, recreation, and religious groups; the clash of ideas and ideals; the struggle for prestige and power—these are the very marks of democratic social order. They take their toll as individuals strive to reconcile sometimes irreconcilable claims upon their energies and allegiances. But they also add immeasurably to the mature pleasures of life. We may be appalled by the picture of Americans who seem to vacillate between doing everything and doing nothing; but it would be far more appalling to be caught in a society where we could do only what we were told. We may be harried by choices so innumerable that they appear meaningless, and thus we may sympathize with those who are weary of freedom. But we would feel immeasurably more impoverished if we had no freedom to fly from, no free choices to make.

The bewildering variety of the American social system is neither neat nor easy to understand. The social reformer is tempted to simplify and to organize; he tries to bring order out of apparent chaos by urging all men to accept certain ideas and by mobilizing individuals into larger and larger "action" groups. Even so passionate a democrat and so wise a reformer as Karl Mannheim traveled in this direction.

True wisdom dictates another course. For both ideas and organizations, the prescription should be more, not fewer. The real ill is not that we become confused because of the complexity of social organization or the competition of idea systems. Rather, the difficulty is that organizations and ideas are not sufficiently numerous or diverse. The range of choice should be wide enough that all Americans—with all their differences of character, culture, interest, and intelligence—can associate themselves successfully with others in pursuit of their own goals. These goals may appear selfish, petty, and unrelated to the national interest. Yet we have seen, in fact, that members of such groups relate themselves positively to the nation in varied and complex ways. There is always some risk that these groups will pursue antisocial or antidemocratic programs. This is a risk democracy must take, protecting itself largely through informal social procedures and through law when that is essential. With rare exceptions, the voluntary groups build democratic loyalties and strengthen the democratic state.

The unregimented character of this society leaves room for loneliness; and the free organization of groups allows for snobbishness in membership policy and despotism in internal organization. These again are strains that the system generates by its virtues and bears because of its strength. And they are ills which can be self-cured. Loneliness, when it is not enjoyed, is overcome by multiplying opportunities for meeting others. Exclusion from one group can be an invitation to join, or form, another; and the same courses of action are available when leaders of voluntary organizations operate dictatorially. The danger of such groups is less than the danger of the totalitarian state because the former have less power to direct a person's whole life and less power to discourage competitors. They are consequently more amenable to control by their members. Individuals can rarely separate themselves from their state, but they can almost always join another voluntary group or find new friends. The tendency of American Legion posts and departments toward control from the top by cliques would be more alarming if there did not also exist the American Veterans Committee, the Veterans of Foreign Wars, the Disabled American Veterans, Jewish and Catholic veterans groups, and various associations based upon prior membership in military units, as well as government facilities which overlap the services of all these groups.

Many urbanites do not attend the formal weekly meetings of social or political organizations. To conclude from this evidence, as some observers do, that urban life provides no opportunity for satisfying group activity is to miss much of the richness and freedom of our culture. The most important and most enjoyable aspects of life are largely unorganized: friends or acquaintances who come together to play bridge, to trade stamps, to bowl, to fly model airplanes, to look at museum pictures, to sing in barber-shop quartets, or to drink beer while complaining about television commercials. The list is unending because the opportunities for such activity in the industrial culture are beyond count.

The diversity of the industrial system lends it strength. It provides opportunities for life-satisfactions to all individuals and all groups. It supplies, within the system, channels for protest and disaffection that under less fluid conditions would show themselves in repression or revolt. It gives resiliency to society as it ties, in innumerable crosshatching lines of strength and subtlety, individuals and groups of individuals to the nation-state.

In the United States today, most elections attract only a minority of the voters. Even in national elections, well over one-third of those eligible usually do not participate. Most of those who do go to the polls cast their votes not on the basis of principle or interest but as a consequence of family, class, and ethnic pressures. Voters cannot distinguish important issues, and they are in large part influenced by the personalities of the candidates. Reason, rationality, and calculation are less important in determining votes than sentiment and tradition. These facts encourage breast-beating on national holidays. They serve other democratic purposes throughout the rest of the year. Political apathy in a democracy is a good thing.

The uninterested and the apathetic soften the bitterness of political warfare. Those least interested in politics are those who change their minds most frequently. This makes it easier to resolve conflicts and allows for flexibility in political policy. The uninterested also make the two-party system more universally acceptable, since they can more readily compromise their differences within a large party.

On the other hand, those who hold extreme political beliefs become extreme partisans. Partisanship is also emphasized when the politically uninterested are brought to politics. Political newcomers are the political naïve. They seek easy and quick solutions and move to political extremes. The largest electoral gains of the Nazi party during the crucial 1928–30 period came from votes of more than four million people who had previously been non-voters. "It was the radicalization of people who had not [previously] participated actively in party politics and who had been too young to vote which gave a major impetus to the rise of fascism."

The Nazi experience indicates that the apathetic can be exploited by demagogues. But demagoguery alone cannot produce the mass political participation of former non-participants. The basic additional ingredient is widespread social and economic distress. Under democratic conditions, such distress almost invariably leads to political participation. Political apathy, to be sure, may also be a reaction to defeat and despair. But only in the short run if politics are free. For large numbers over longer time spans, apathy in politics often indicates satisfaction and preoccupation with affairs outside politics. This sort of apathetic response also indicates approval of existing political institutions.

Non-participation not only positively serves the democratic system as a leavener of controversy. It may also be evidence of that system's political stability and of social strength and activity outside politics.

One must conclude that citizen participation in politics is not the hallmark of democracy. On the contrary, no populations have been more completely mobilized in programs of direct political action than the populations of Nazi Germany and Soviet Russia. Participation is always present in dictatorships. Apathy and non-participation are never evidence of totalitarianism, but only of democracy.

The baldness of such a conclusion must be immediately qualified. Apathy is far preferable to participation that is manipulated; but informed, interested, and rational participation is even more to be desired. This ideal is never completely realized, but it has been approximated in some American communities, in the Scandinavian countries, in Switzerland and the United Kingdom, and in other places.

Under any circumstances, all democratic societies need political interest and political wisdom. Apathy can serve democracy negatively by making change easier; but change needs to be initiated, and it needs to be directed at strengthening the democratic order. Apathy in some people must in all cases be balanced by political interest in others. Democracy cannot exist if some of its citizens do not believe that politics is important. They must support that belief by devoting time and energy to political problems. The apathetic constitute followers. The system must also produce leaders of political opinion and political action.

Of equal importance, the apathy we have described may be more apparent than real. It is characterized by a disinclination to do anything directly about political problems. But this may hide very deep beliefs concerning the proper role of government. It may also hide a kind of political participation which is very genuine, even though not always recognized as such.

Beneath the surface of individual apathy there lies the tremendous activity of interest groups. These groups play decisive political roles. Organized on the basis of profession or work, ethnic or religious affiliation, regional or other special interest, they represent their constituents in politics at all levels of government and throughout the entire institutional structure of American life. The persons who lead such groups are often also active in the political arena. But many individuals, apathetic on the scene usually labeled "political," play decisive political roles within these groups. They do so by formulating and supporting policies that are continuously represented to legislative members and administrative officers as the group's policies. This kind of political activity leads to an effectiveness that is far beyond the capacity of an individual working alone in politics.

A decisive power of rejection is held by the organizations of these "apathetic" people. It is not far from the truth that "the only leaders of national scope left in the United States today are those who can placate the veto groups." Yet the veto power of those already organized is not so significant as the affirmative power of the potentially organized. Their freedom includes the basic freedom to capture existing groups as well as to form new ones, to initiate programs as well as defeat them. The latent power of populations to enter politics and to exercise decisive power lies behind surface apathy. Political power is real and important even when it is not activated.

The affirming and vetoing function of interest groups, expressing the political choices of their memberships, represents one proper democratic relationship between leaders and followers. Leaders must have independence to carve out great programs of government. The public is competent on many issues to give only the broadest guidance, in the form of "Aye" and "Nay" votes. This guidance can be recorded directly at the polls. More typically, it is expressed through the continuous pressures of groups on all links of the governmental decision-making chain.

The necessary factor is that the leaders must always look back over their shoulders to be certain that the followers still follow. And it is the distinction of democratic populations that, through existing groups and groups to be formed, they may choose not to follow and still remain alive and outside barbed-wire fences. This is a far more significant mark of political participation than masses marching in lock step to political rallies, more significant even than large numbers flocking to the polls.

All this does not minimize the great tasks still to be solved by democratic populations: tasks ranging from conquest of neighborhood slums to liberation from threats of atomic annihilation. One cannot look even casually at the American scene without discovering at every hand deficiencies in the sensitivity of population groups, wide areas of political ignorance, shadows of political corruption, and institutional arrangements that seem designed to thwart the popular will, even if it were expressible and expressed. No gloss need be applied to these conditions, and to stress the values of political non-participation constitutes no argument in favor of do-nothing government. Democracy needs strong and active government for survival. The collapse of democracy follows the collapse of democratic leadership, when civic crisis is allowed to fester and popular needs are unfulfilled.

Civic reform is accomplished in part by direct citizen action, in part by leaders leading and citizen groups wielding their decisive power of approval or disapproval. Large numbers of citizens can play their political roles most effectively by being active in voluntary groups which themselves are active in politics. An important objective is to create conditions under which groups can be formed and re-formed easily. An equally important and more delicate job is to achieve democracy within such groups, making them more effective as exchange points of information and opinion and as proving grounds for the politics of freedom. Just as the national loyalty of democratic citizens is in largest part established indirectly through voluntary groups, so the political participation of these citizens, even as voters, may be secured.

The alternative, often suggested, is to stimulate widespread political participation by the organization of action groups, by the enlistment of citizens in programs of reform, by propaganda or education leading to the mass acceptance of goals and beliefs. Such programs, carried to enthusiastic points of great effectiveness, are characteristic of totalitarian states. To whip up, certainly to enforce, participation is to endanger democracy. Those who enforce participation must in the end dictate to the participants.

Apathy—the neglect of political institutions—is an acceptable political posture of a democratic citizen. In contrast to the apathetic, there are citizens preoccupied with politics, but in a spirit of critical inquiry. They compare what exists with what might be; and they labor to improve the state according to their image of the ideal. Their perspective and activity contribute to the welfare of the nation.

Critical appraisal, including criticism that contemplates an alternative national loyalty, is often turned to socially creative ends, to new programs of government, new accommodations of society, new definitions of the good and the possible. It is easy to trace how this process has worked in the past: to take an extreme example, the call to the terrible new loyalty of 1848—the *Communist Manifesto*—has affected the Western world in many ways, not least of all because a large part of its program has long been legislated and accepted as commonplace. Criticism challenges the authoritarianism of majorities. It brings strengthening change to society. It prepares the way for accommodation to new situations. Without it, nations would become complacent and stagnant. They would be weak before forces of the changing years.

Advantages of critical appraisal also accrue to the individual. One type of desirable democratic citizen has experienced other ways of life or the challenge of other political systems. He works effectively on behalf of the public welfare because he knows the promise and the delivery rate of other loyalties. The knowledge need not come from actual personal commitment. (It is a fool's argument that only the victims of tuberculosis understand it and can fight it.) Yet the constructive effect of a temporary commitment to an alternative national allegiance, if it is too easily overrated, can also be too easily dismissed. The trip into and out of the Communist party, for example, can produce highly desirable attributes of character and democratic allegiance: of character because joining and breaking may provide choice points which test and establish courage and independence; of allegiance because an intimate view of communism is often a great impetus to labor on behalf of democracy. The larger point is not the special virtue or extraordinary value of ex-Communists to democracy. It is that wisdom, including political wisdom, comes from inquiry. The point has been stated best by Socrates, who himself was accused of criticizing the customs and gods: "The unexamined life is not worth living."

All this has immediate practical relevance. For one thing, it argues in favor of the inalienable right of all Americans to youthful radicalism. We have seen that social processes encourage this radicalism. We can now add that it is proper and desirable for the democratic community. For, plainly, allegiance to nation, once subjected to the heat of critical appraisal, is stronger, more meaningful, and more socially useful than allegiance accepted on the basis of tradition, or ignorance, or faith, or fear. This has been completely unheeded in the loyalty-security investigations that have followed World War II. Those charged with youthful radicalism have apologized for it and excused their actions as follies of immaturity. On the evidence, it would be far more proper to praise such radicalism. It is likely to make desirable democratic citizens.

The point extends further than considerations of youth and immaturity. In baldest terms the democratic system of limited government presupposes that national loyalty will be a limited loyalty.

One meaning of this limitation has been explored in preceding chapters: a democratic citizen has many other loyalties on which the strength of national loyalty depends. It follows that the democratic state must be cautious in creating demands that conflict with those of other groups to which loyalty is given. The state should promote social diversity and preserve the ambiguities in the meaning of national loyalty; it should make harmony among loyalties easy and conflict difficult.

Congressional committees investigating the "leftist associations" of university professors and patriotic groups reading history textbooks with a wary eye for the word "revolution" narrow the definition of what may be regarded as loyalty to the nation. So do loyalty boards which find it culpable that a scientist aims to keep faith simultaneously with friends, profession, and nation. Wise leadership would move in the opposite direction: toward encouraging the reconciliation of multiple loyalties.

These are not radical views. Indeed, the great conservative spokesman of the eighteenth century, Edmund Burke, gave them classic expression when inveighing against the extremes of the French Revolution:

> To be attached to the subdivision, *to love the little platoon* we belong to in society, is the first principle . . . of public affections. It is the first link in the series by which we proceed towards a love to our country, and to mankind. . . . [and later] We begin our public affections in our families. . . . We pass on to our neighbourhoods, and our habitual provincial connexions. . . . Such divisions of our country [are] so many little images of the great country in which the heart found something which it could fill. The love to the whole is not extinguished by this subordinate partiality.

A final step must be taken. Burke's statement assumes an easy convergence of loyalties that, in bleak fact, often does not exist. In most cases the individual can reconcile the strains and cross-pressures of his many loyalties. But this is not always possible. And there may come a time when fundamental human values tip a person away from the nation and toward another cause.

A doctrine of limited loyalty to nation must recognize that other loyalties may be given precedence. Criticism may be followed by action—the withdrawal of support from the nation or the support of groups antagonistic to it. Prudence dictates that long-established governments should not be changed for light and transient causes. But a long train of abuses and repeated injuries and usurpations may become destructive to the good society and intolerable to individuals. The people may find that neither life nor liberty nor the pursuit of happiness is possible. Under such extreme circumstances, individuals and groups find it a right and a duty to disobey—or to discard—their government and to provide new guards for their future security.

A theory of limited loyalty to limited government must recognize the sometime value of national disloyalty.

As a brief aside, it is worth noting that the limited loyalty of democratic nations is the only model for building a world state that need not be a slave state.

One way to achieve a world state is by the destruction of all lesser allegiances. This follows the model of the totalitarian nation. The fear that a world government would impose this pattern has led men of the greatest good will to doubt whether it would be worth the candle, even if such a government could achieve world peace. Their argument is the proud argument of free men: it is better to die on your feet than to live on your knees.

But these may not be the only alternatives. Burke's vision saw the compatibility of loyalties extending from the "little platoon" to all of mankind. We have seen that national loyalty in a democracy reaches its high point when the welfare and strength of the non-national groups to which men pay allegiance are related to the nation. Just as non-national loyalties have the potentiality for strengthening the democratic national state, so democratic national loyalties may strengthen the international state. The cases are plainly analogous.

The strategy of building loyalty to an international state is also suggested by the contrast between national loyalties in democratic and totalitarian nations. To avoid the totalitarian pattern, indirect links between individual and world government should be forged. World government needs no man on horseback; it needs rather to relate life-satisfactions in a whole vast range of human activities to the idea and institution of world government.

Industry and science have created a single world during the precise period in which national loyalties have been established and have flourished. The latest developments have been the most spectacular. The choices increasingly seem to be one world or no world. "Nationalism and the split atom cannot co-exist in the planet." The immense difficulties in building some sort of international state are not even discussed here. The point simply is that the model of democratic loyalties to the nation-state is the desirable model for loyalties to a world state. The alternative model—the totalitarian way of smashing other allegiances—is a pattern for world empire and mass enslavement.

The diversity of American life, the real and imagined political apathy of Americans, and the limited loyalty paid to the limited American government combine to give the impression of disunity and mass alienation. They make it appear that Americans have no beliefs in common, that loyalty to nation is non-existent or so unstable that a militant antidemocratic movement could readily capture the support of large masses of Americans.

Americans speak easily of their discontents and find it difficult to talk about abstract beliefs. This does not mean that they hold no beliefs in common. Their ease in voicing dissatisfaction may indicate that their most widely shared ideals are negatives: that the state should *not* intrude into the sphere of intimate human relations; that speech, education, and religion are *not* to be regimented; that associations are *not* to be controlled from outside. Justice Brandeis precisely defined these beliefs when he said that the most valued and comprehensive right of civilized men was "the right to be left alone."

The obverse of these negatives is a belief in liberty. Americans shy away from loosely using the word, yet "no one who reads our national literature, who listens to our daily speech, who mingles in the common course of our living, can fail to hear that note rising above all others in which we express ourselves." However the tenets of liberty may from time to time be violated, the ideal is a strong and continuous one, the most important commitment of the largest number of Americans. And from their belief in liberty, Americans derive other values held in common: the dignity of each individual's personality, the importance of family life, the necessity for equal opportunity, the need for impartial courts of justice.

These values, identified with the nation and widely held by the citizens, are a direct linkage between individuals and the nation, an element in the religious quality of patriotism. Yet the importance to Americans of such values does not spring from their mystical, cement-like qualities that are said to bind a nation together. Democratic values play a dual role—as ideas held in common and as definitions for life that can be realized. They ultimately establish the individual—not the leader, not the blood principle, not the state—as the highest value.

So there exists a crucial relationship between what we have called the direct and the indirect strands of loyalty. Americans do hold beliefs in common, and these beliefs are an important ingredient of American national loyalty. But the larger significance of commonly held values lies in the expectations they establish for the ordinary routines of life, where the indirect tie between person and nation is nurtured. Freedom of religion is important as a belief, but it is more important as an activity in a community church. Equality of opportunity is inspiring as an ideal shared by all citizens, but it is most meaningful in the experience of a person and his friends scaling economic, social, and professional ladders.

Today's stylish patriot sings songs of xenophobia and conformity. It is unfashionable to praise democracy for its diversity of social and moral systems, to find virtue in the political uninterest of democratic citizens, or to suggest that the democratic state must share the loyalty of its people with many other groups and institutions. Fads, styles, and fashions are no more reliable in defining patriotism than they are in establishing standards of beauty. Today's fashion in patriotism leads in the direction of the totalitarian model of loyalties. For all its chaotic appearance and apparent frailties, the democratic model is the patriotism to be preferred.

It reflects a more stable social structure. If it encourages more skeptical loyalties, it also makes them more durable. Such loyalties, not the totalitarian pattern, have a better chance of maintaining the national order through time. This is to say that democratic loyalties are more efficient. But the preservation of worthless institutions has no value, and efficiency is not the only criterion for evaluating loyalties. A more important test is that democratic loyalties more appropriately fulfil human needs. And they are more difficult, in their diversity and decentralization, to misuse for the perversion of human life, for subverting human loyalty to inhuman ends.

Human potentials of personality, inclination, and talent are endlessly varied. These potentials can be realized fully and freely under conditions of democracy, and to the greatest extent within urban, industrialized democracy. The human personality needs the free society for its full development. The free society includes the distastes that freedom spawns; it provides no neatness of social structure and suffers gaps which may be filled by the joys of self-pity and self-destruction and the terrors of surfeit and loneliness. But it also provides infinite and infinitely varied life-ways that fulfil the self or serve the community and frequently do both.

This is a culture of social maturity. It needs and develops mature individuals. The unified village community is the bored community. The community always attended by the father-substitute is the community of children or patients. The community mobilized for the achievement of grandiose state purposes is the totalitarian community, and its citizens are ciphers. All are unpalatable alternatives to democratic industrial society.

Democracy is both product and producers. It is at once achievement, achievers, and a method of achievement. If democracy promises freedom, it need not immediately deliver freedom, but it must then demonstrate to its citizens that freedom is being sought. If democracy promises equal opportunity for education and for advances in real income and status, it need not make those opportunities immediately real, but its citizens must believe that realization will eventually come. If democracy promises that men's homes are inviolate and their lives safe from official harassment, it may smash doors and capriciously slander, but only as a temporary aberration and only if the citizens believe that the promises will in the end be fulfilled. The achievement may be postponed, but the achievers must always be able to proceed with the method of achievement. This is the method of protest, of taking organized action to redress wrongs, of reanimating institutions toward desired ends. The method allows the governed to change the governors, the critics of programs to become program masters.

Totalitarian systems promise great things and in many ways fulfil popular desires. They remain totalitarian because the individual remains subordinate to the state and because there are no methods for popular protest or for securing the peaceful change of political leaders. The system produces fanatic loyalties, but loyalties that wilt when the stiffening of terror is no longer available.

Yet the allure of totalitarian systems is great. Universal literacy has produced universal sensitivity to alternate social systems. Populations become easily impatient and disenchanted with democracy when it falters and does not provide what it promises.

To sustain the loyalty of its citizens, democracy must work for the achievement of the promises held forth by democratic beliefs and made practical by the diversity and productivity of the industrial economy. The producers of democracy—varied in color, creed, interest, and profession—must know the products of democracy. The danger is not that individual persons will become disenchanted and turn to treason. The danger is not that industrial democracy will fail because it is inherently unable to supply the satisfactions that, indirectly but certainly, lead to strong national loyalty. The danger is not that democracy will fail on its merits. The danger is that democracy will fail because it fails to be democratic.

Postscript and Acknowledgments
Notes
Index

Postscript and Acknowledgments

I have conceived this book to be a contribution of the social sciences to an understanding of national loyalty and disloyalty. It is another voice in the great national conversation.

The social sciences do not, of course, speak with a single tongue, and some of my fellow-scientists can claim that I have not used our idiom with the precision that it ought to have. I cheerfully admit the charge. Perhaps some day national loyalty as attitude can be measured as precisely as specialists now measure attitudes toward race or toothpaste, and perhaps some day national loyalty as act can be counted with the same elegant exactness that the act of voting for a presidential candidate is now counted. Perhaps even the reasons for national loyalty and disloyalty can be explained some day with the certainty that we now explain the growth of the great urban centers. But these are far-distant days at best. I have considered national loyalty and disloyalty of sufficient interest and importance to examine them now, with imperfect instruments, with imperfect data.

The resulting product can claim to be no more than a general statement, supported by examples. What it lacks in precision, I hope it gains in pertinence.

This immediate grappling with immediate social problems is a valid task for the social scientist, as scientist. I assert this, without attempting to prove it here. The bulk of the book (chaps. 1–12) represents one scientist's attempt to order facts about loyalty and disloyalty into generalizations that, with further information and refined techniques, may be tested—and proved or refuted. I have also suggested (especially in chap. 10) agenda for further work. In this game all research is prologue and all conclusions are thin tracings to be tested against the next man's data.

At the same time, I have not scrupled against expressing judgments (in chaps. 13–14) about social policy. I conceive these judgments to be based upon the preceding analysis and yet derived from, rather than intrinsically a part of, that analysis. Again I make no apologies. Scientists need to be philosophers, willing or not, and I choose to express my philosophy in this way—as a citizen presenting policy arguments that are linked to scientific understandings. Other policies may possibly flow from the scientific analysis. Those I present seem to me appropriate, indeed necessary, to our democratic order of things.

I am deeply indebted to many people for assistance in preparing this book. Perhaps my first debt is to those who are responsible for the administration of the University of Chicago and through them to the institution itself. Certainly this book would never have been conceived by me if it were not for the learning process made possible by teaching in the exciting Chicago program of general education after World War II. My teachers were my students and my colleagues, the latter a distinguished and disputatious group whose members, now widely scattered, gave me my first genuine insights into the limits and promises of the social sciences. We were never unanimous about anything but the lovely vigor of intellectual activity. The university has also made it possible for me to pursue problems of loyalty and disloyalty in seminars with graduate students, the brash and abrasive graduate students who stalk weakness and hoot at glibness. And this experience, in turn, has led to happy and profitable relationships with scholars in the many disciplines that are grouped in Chicago's Social Science Division. Finally, the university has liberally supported my work through a series of grants from its Social Science Research Committee. One of these grants, which also gave financial aid to several of my students whose theses have been cited in the text, had its ultimate source in a gift from the Ford Foundation behavioral science program.

As for the manuscript itself, perhaps no book of such slight proportions has ever had the benefit of criticism from so large a number of heavyweight minds. These include Dr. Nathaniel Apter, Elisabeth Mann Borgese, Ralph S. Brown, Jr., Reuel Denney, Ruth Denney, Philip Glick, Charles Hardin, Robert Horn, Herbert Kaufman, Avery Leiserson, C. Herman Pritchett, Milton Singer, Herbert Simon, Edward Shils, Leo Strauss, Howard B. White, and Leonard D. White. All these persons read all or part of the manuscript and gave me valuable advice. In addition, four friends read the entire manuscript with special care and supplied me with the kind of detailed commentary that makes its mark on virtually every page: Harold Guetzkow, Louis Kriesberg, Milton Mayer, and David Riesman. I am especially grateful to them for their sustained critiques, the unselfish service that adds to the pleasure of book-writing. I must add that those who have criticized the manuscript have also increased the difficulty of the job. They are responsible for my sensitivity to the inadequacies that remain in the book: I am presently unable to answer some of the questions they asked.

The editors of the *American Journal of Sociology*, the *Public Administration Review*, and the *Bulletin of the Atomic Scientists* have allowed me to use the pages of their respective journals to try out some of the ideas now presented in this book. Eleanore Ray Carruth and Lila Butler performed efficient research and secretarial services during early stages of work.

Doreen Herlihy, from first draft to proofreading, has been an invaluable secretary, research aid, critic, colleague, and friend. She has taken particular responsibility for the difficult task of checking all references and for compiling, in the first instance, the note section. She has been an inexhaustible source of encouragement and help. My indebtedness and gratitude to her are beyond calculation.

Ruth Grodzins, as always, has been the best of critics on matters of both substance and style. She remains the master pin-wielder for all verbal balloons. She has been an essential part of the enterprise at every stage and in every way. The book is her product, as well as mine.

One of the satisfactions in writing a book of this sort is that I have been able to say in the last two chapters what I believe to be true about some of the pressing problems of our nation and world. These chapters, like others, were read by a number of scholars before publication. I prize most a comment written by a friend, once a student in my seminar, now himself a teacher. What he scrawled in a margin of the manuscript is what I would choose, both for the policy statements in this book and for my larger political views, as epitaph: "God, a true believer in democracy."

M. G.

Notes

PAGE

ii. Medieval oath quoted in Lewis Mumford, *The Culture of Cities* (New York: Harcourt, Brace & Co., 1938), p. 78.

George Washington, *The Writings of George Washington* (George Washington Bicentennial Commission ed. [Washington: Government Printing Office, 1934]), XI, 286; see John Jay's similar views in the *Federalist Papers*, No. II.

CHAPTER 1

3. The story of the thief is taken from George Dixon, of King Features, "It's All in Your Point of View," reprinted in *Reader's Digest*, LX, No. 359 (March, 1952), 84. For similar stories of similar incidents see *Washington Post*, January 19, 1953, p. 1; and Donald Powell Wilson, *My Six Convicts* (New York: Rinehart & Co., Inc., 1951), pp. 216–17: "Convicts . . . are hotly patriotic"; William R. Morrow in T. W. Adorno *et al.*, *The Authoritarian Personality* (New York: Harper & Bros., 1950), pp. 817–90.

4. *In re:* prisoners in Korea see *New York Times*, January 22, 27, and 28, 1954; Harold Lavine, "Twenty-one G.I.'s Who Chose Tyranny," *Commentary*, XVIII (July, 1954), 41–46.

PAGE

4. The rational basis of patriotism was stated as early as the beginning of the nineteenth century by William Hazlitt: "Patriotism, in modern times, and in great states, is and must be the creature of reason and reflection. . . ." See "On Patriotism.—A Fragment," in *The Collected Works of William Hazlitt,* ed. A. R. Waller and Arnold Glover (London: J. M. Dent & Co., 1902), I, 67. For modern statement of agreement see Hans Kohn, *The Idea of Nationalism* (New York: Macmillan Co., 1946), chap. i.

5. For irrationality of patriotism see Sergei Chakhotin, *The Rape of the Masses,* trans. from 5th ed. by E. W. Dickes (London: G. Routledge & Sons, Ltd., 1940); Adolf Hitler, *Mein Kampf,* ed. and trans. John Chamberlain *et al.* (New York: Reynal & Hitchcock, 1940), *passim.*

   Last paragraph. Academic writing is largely the making of definitions, and academicians reading this book may look for a brief definition of national loyalty. They will look in vain. The whole book is in one sense that definition. It may be said, in this aside, that the difficulty of dealing practically with matters of loyalty and disloyalty is the difficulty of definition. Individuals and groups smaller than the nation define loyalty (as both attitude and act) in various ways. And a man, by his own lights, may be loyal to his nation even when he is being hanged as a traitor. Here individual and official national definitions differ. Whatever the ultimate right or wrong of the matter, a man is a traitor or disloyal when so declared by legal authorities of the nation acting legally. In democracies, such an officially defined norm usually exists only for a severely limited number of acts, notably for treason, espionage, sabotage, and related crimes. The effective definitions of loyalty and disloyalty are therefore, under most circumstances, unofficial social norms; and groups compete to establish these definitions as they compete in other spheres of life.

6. Loyalties as habit patterns. See John Dewey, *Human Nature and Conduct* (New York: Modern Library, 1930), Part I.

7. The aid of group ties. R. R. Grinker and J. P. Spiegel speak of the threats and dangers to an individual arising from interpersonal relations, from the hammering of his conscience, and from actual or imagined external physical causes. They write: "The ego must deal with all these forces and maintain its cool objective discrimination in order to preserve its existence. Alone it would fail; as part of a group, its span is often large enough" (*Men*

PAGE

under Stress [Philadelphia: Blakiston Co., 1945], p. 441); see also M. Sherif and H. Cantril, *The Psychology of Ego-Involvements* (New York: John Wiley & Sons, Inc., 1947), pp. 114–15.

7. "In so far as. . . ." Charles Horton Cooley, *Social Organization* (New York: Charles Scribner's Sons, 1927), p. 38.

8. "The supreme loyalty. . . ." Hans Kohn, *The Idea of Nationalism,* p. 16.

9. For Plato's view see *The Republic,* trans. A. D. Lindsay ("Everyman's Library" [London: J. M. Dent & Sons, Ltd., 1935]), Book V. For quotations from Cicero and others see William Edward Lecky, *History of European Morals* (New York: D. Appleton & Co., 1880), I, 201.

The long quotation ("They . . . had no affection . . .") is from Edward Westermarck, *The Origin and Development of the Moral Ideas* (London: Macmillan & Co., Ltd., 1908), II, 179. St. Augustine's views praising great deeds for the love of *patria aeterna* rather than for an earthly city are well known (see Augustine, *The City of God,* trans. Marcus Dods, in *A Select Library of the Nicene and Post Nicene Fathers of the Christian Church,* ed. Philip Schaff [New York: Charles Scribner's Sons, 1887], Vol. II, especially Book V, chap. 18).

9–10. The quotations about Machiavelli and about the Jesuit general are from Edward Westermarck, *The Origin and Development of the Moral Ideas,* II, 181, 179.

10. For the views of Machiavelli see *The Prince* and especially *The Discourses* (New York: Modern Library, 1940).

The loyalties of men of the Middle Ages are discussed in Francis W. Coker, "Patriotism," *Encyclopaedia of the Social Sciences,* XII (1934), 27; Carlton J. H. Hayes, *Essays on Nationalism* (New York: Macmillan Co., 1926), p. 28; Edward Westermarck, *The Origin and Development of the Moral Ideas,* II, 180.

11. For an example of research indicating early dating of nationalism see Ernst H. Kantorowicz, "*Pro patria mori* in Medieval Political Thought," *American Historical Review,* LVI (April, 1951), 472–92.

Rousseau's discussion of a "civil religion" is contained in *The Social Contract,* ed. Charles Frankel (New York: Hafner Library of Classics, 1949), Book IV, chap. viii.

PAGE

11. "Children belong . . ." is a statement of Barère in French National *Evolution of Modern Nationalism* (New York: Macmillan Co., 1950), pp. 62–63. Cobban's analysis is similar to mine, but he makes a distinction between the "classical idea of patriotism," i.e., "loyalty to the state and its ruler," and national patriotism, i.e., loyalty to the nation itself (see Alfred Cobban, *Dictatorship* [London: Jonathan Cape, 1939], pp. 163–65).

13. For the status of Western man before industrialization see Sir Henry James Sumner Maine, *Ancient Law,* introd. Sir Frederick Pollock (4th Amer. ed. from 10th London ed.; New York: Henry Holt & Co., 1906); Henri Pirenne, *Economic and Social History of Medieval Europe* (London: Kegan Paul, Trench, Trubner & Co., Ltd., 1936). For an illuminating discussion of the concept of status see Robert Redfield, *The Folk Culture of Yucatan* (Chicago: University of Chicago Press, 1941).

15. David Riesman's discussion of social personality is contained in Riesman, *The Lonely Crowd* (New Haven: Yale University Press, 1950), and Riesman, *Faces in the Crowd* (New Haven: Yale University Press, 1952). These personality traits may also be displayed by those in non-industrialized culture; indeed, Francis L. K. Hsu has argued that the Chinese are the true "situation-centered" people and that Americans are more "individual-centered" than Riesman has described them (see Francis L. K. Hsu, *American and Chinese: Two Ways of Life* [New York: Henry Schuman, 1953]).

16. "All serious political writing. . . ." Howard B. White, "The Problem of Loyalty in American Political Thought," paper presented at meeting of American Political Science Association, Washington, D.C., September, 1953.

    E. B. White, *The Wild Flag* (Boston: Houghton Mifflin Co., 1946), p. x.

16–17. "Our whole history . . ." is a statement of Theodore Parker (see Henry Steele Commager, *Theodore Parker* [Boston: Little, Brown & Co., 1936], p. 193).

17. For Joyce's statement see Rebecca West, *The Meaning of Treason* (New York: Viking Press, 1947), p. 181; see also J. W. Hall (ed.), *Trial of William Joyce* ("Notable British Trials Series" [London: William Hodge & Co., Ltd., 1946]).

PAGE

18. For the Marxian critique of patriotism see *The Communist Manifesto;* Emma Goldman, *Patriotism: A Menace to Liberty* (New York: Mother Earth Publishing Association). For non-Marxian criticism of nationalism on economic grounds see a report by a study group of members of the Royal Institute of International Affairs, *Nationalism* (London: Oxford University Press, 1939), p. 296.

    Thorstein Veblen, *The Nature of Peace* (New York: Viking Press, 1945), p. 33; see also Thorstein Veblen, *Imperial Germany and the Industrial Revolution* (new ed.; New York: Viking Press, 1942); *Essays in Our Changing Order*, ed. Leon Ardzrooni (New York: Viking Press, 1934).

    Samuel Langhorne Clemens, *Mark Twain's Notebook*, ed. Albert Bigelow Paine (New York: Harper & Bros., 1935), p. 332.

19. Aristotle's *Politics,* trans. Benjamin Jowett (New York: Modern Library, 1943), iii. 1276b.

    "The love of. . . ." J. G. Zimmerman, *On National Pride*, trans. from the German (London, 1771), quoted in Clarence Reidenbach, *A Critical Analysis of Patriotism as an Ethical Concept* (Ph.D. dissertation, Yale University, 1918), p. 99.

    Ralph Waldo Emerson, "Essay on Politics," *Essays, Second Series* (Cambridge: Riverside Press, 1883), p. 199.

CHAPTER 2

21. First full paragraph. I have profited here from reading an unpublished paper by Harold Guetzkow, "A Framework for a Study of Loyalty."

    Identification of "we" with nation. See the discussion of "The Charismatic Character of Mission" in Robert Michels, *Der Patriotismus* (Munich and Leipzig: Duncker & Humblot, 1929), chap. i.

22. See Rudyard Kipling's poem "The Stranger."

    For elaborate documentation of ethnocentrism see Edward Westermarck, *The Origin and Development of the Moral Ideas,* II, 171 ff.; and William Graham Sumner, *Folkways* (Boston: Ginn & Co., 1906). Sumner believed patriotism was simply a manifestation of ethnocentrism.

PAGE

22–23. Anatole France, *Penguin Island,* trans. A. W. Evans (Cornwall, N.Y.: Cornwall Press, Inc., 1930), pp. xi, xii.

23. For discussion of how personal hostilities are handled by society see Talcott Parsons, "Certain Primary Sources and Patterns of Aggression in the Social Structure of the Western World," *Psychiatry,* X, No. 2 (May, 1947), 167–81.

26. "An element of worship. . . ." Bertrand Russell, *Why Men Fight* (New York: Century Co., 1917), p. 55.

26–27. "To the modern national state. . . ." Carlton J. H. Hayes, *Essays on Nationalism,* pp. 105–6.

27. "What attachment can. . . ." Hector St. John de Crèvecœur in *Letters from an American Farmer* ("Everyman" ed. [London: J. M. Dent & Sons, 1862]), p. 43. Carl van Doren in *Mutiny in January* (New York: Viking Press, 1943), p. 33, quotes a letter from General Anthony Wayne to Joseph Reed which eloquently makes the same point.

28. For discussion of life-satisfactions see William I. Thomas, *The Unadjusted Girl* (Boston: Little, Brown & Co., 1928); Harold D. Lasswell, *Politics: Who Gets What, When, How* (New York: McGraw-Hill Book Co., Inc., 1936); and "Democratic Character" in *The Political Writings of Harold D. Lasswell* (Glencoe, Ill.: Free Press, 1951), pp. 474 ff. There is, Crane Brinton tells us, more widespread economic suffering after revolutions than before them (see *The Anatomy of Revolution* [New York: W. W. Norton & Co., 1938], p. 253).

29. "Neither a central. . . ." Adolph Löwe, *The Price of Liberty* (London: Hogarth Press, 1937), pp. 13–25, quoted in Royal Institute of International Affairs, *Nationalism,* p. 193; see also Harold D. Lasswell, *Politics: Who Gets What, When, How,* pp. 29–30.

30. Josiah Royce, *The Philosophy of Loyalty* (New York: Macmillan Co., 1924), pp. 16–17.

Loyalty as not disloyalty. This formulation includes the case of a person who once was loyal but in whom the feelings which gave rise to loyalty have disappeared. This is loyalty as residue; Georg Simmel believed this to be a principal source of loyalty. His example is an erotic relationship which arises because of physical beauty but which "may very well continue when the beauty has

PAGE

faded" (see *Soziologie* [Leipzig: Duncker & Humblot, 1908], pp. 438–43).

30. James Bryce, *Studies in History and Jurisprudence* (New York: Oxford University Press, 1901), pp. 463–502. On weight of inertia see also Alexander H. Leighton, *The Governing of Men* (Princeton N.J.: Princeton University Press, 1945), pp. 334–35. Simmel (in *Soziologie*) pointed out that relatively rigid and unchanging social forms preserved by loyalty, make it possible for emotions to change rapidly. Loyalty, in this view, stabilizes society.

31. On meeting dissatisfaction with resignation see Erich Fromm, *Escape from Freedom* (New York: Rinehart & Co., Inc., 1941), p. 209.

32. On patriotism as a career for mediocrity see Norman Hapgood (ed.), *Professional Patriots* (New York: A. & C. Boni, 1927).

34. Hostages insuring loyalty. I am indebted to Louis Kriesberg for suggestions incorporated in this and the preceding paragraphs. See "Lectures on the Principles of Political Obligation," *Works of Thomas Hill Green*, ed. R. L. Nettleship (London: Longmans, Green & Co., 1893).

CHAPTER 3

39. Ralph Linton, *The Cultural Background of Personality* (New York: D. Appleton–Century Co., 1945), p. 125; see also Charles Horton Cooley, *Human Nature and the Social Order* (New York: Charles Scribner's Sons, 1902), p. 36: "The more thoroughly American a man is the less he can perceive Americanism. He will embody it. . . ."

    William Graham Sumner, *Folkways*, p. vii.

40. Loyalties are common to all cultures. The differences among cultures are very great; but they are not without limit, and some broad similarities exist among virtually all people. "Capricious violence against a person of one's intimate group is everywhere regarded as an evil; very generally loyalty, hospitality, and courage . . . receive positive evaluation" (see Robert Redfield, *The Educational Experience* [Pasadena, Calif.: Fund for Adult Education, 1955], p. 19).

41. Primary group. In the rest of this section, I have borrowed heavily from my article, "Public Administration and the Science of

Human Relations," *Public Administration Review,* XI, No. 2 (spring, 1951), 88–102. The study of groups is a rapidly developing one. I have profited in reading an unpublished paper by Anselm Strauss on "Identification." Strauss believes the current study of groups is handicapped by concepts (primary, membership, reference groups) that are not subtle enough to catch reality. He believes that the key concept of membership should be *communication* and that an individual belongs to a group when he shares a terminology with others; Strauss believes that membership must be conceived entirely as a symbolic, not a physical, fact. For series of articles on experiments with small groups see the special issue of the *American Sociological Review,* Vol. XIX, No. 6 (December, 1954).

41. Primary groups in industry. See Elton Mayo, *The Human Problems of an Industrial Civilization* (2d ed.; Boston: Graduate School of Business Administration, Harvard University, 1946); E. Mayo and G. F. F. Lombard, *Teamwork and Labor Turnover in the Aircraft Industry of Southern California* (Boston: Graduate School of Business Administration, Harvard University, 1944); F. Roethlisberger and W. J. Dickson, *Management and the Worker* (Boston: Graduate School of Business Administration, Harvard University, 1934); O. Collins, M. Dalton, and D. Roy, "Restriction of Output and Social Cleavage in Industry," *Applied Anthropology,* V, No. 3 (1946), 1–14; J. R. P. French and L. Coch, "Overcoming Resistance to Change," *Human Relations* (London: Tavistock Publications), I, No. 4 (1948), 512–32; Donald F. Roy, "Work Satisfaction and Social Reward in Quota Achievement," *American Sociological Review,* XVIII, No. 5 (October, 1953), 507–14; "Efficiency and 'The Fix': Informal Intergroup Relations in a Piecework Machine Shop," *American Journal of Sociology,* LX, No. 3 (November, 1954), 255–66.

Jean Piaget, *The Moral Judgment of the Child* (London: Kegan Paul, Trench, Trubner & Co., Ltd., 1932), pp. 341 ff. Children can exhibit strong loyalties to diverse groups at the same time, reconciling contradictions among loyalties more easily than adults. Mitchell Grodzins, when she was twelve, demonstrated that these loyalties can be given fiercely, yet simultaneously, to a horseback-riding group, acrobatic colleagues, school companions, and others, the membership of each group being different and the standards of conduct varying markedly in each case.

PAGE

41. Warm friends transformed into enemies. J. H. Rohrer and M. Sherif (eds.), *Social Psychology at the Crossroads* (New York: Harper & Bros., 1951), pp. 388–424.

41–42. "If conformity to. . . ." M. Sherif and H. Cantril, *The Psychology of Ego-Involvements*, p. 276.

42. "I . . . have been, am still. . . ." Mark Benney, *Low Company* (New York: Avon Publishing Co., 1952), pp. 3–4.

On criminals working in groups see Clifford R. Shaw, *The Natural History of a Delinquent Career* (Chicago: University of Chicago Press, 1931), and *Brothers in Crime* (Chicago: University of Chicago Press, 1938).

To be called a "thief" is . . . honorific. Edwin Hardin Sutherland, *The Professional Thief* (Chicago: University of Chicago Press, 1937), p. 200.

42–43. The thief's "distress. . . ." Edwin Hardin Sutherland, *The Professional Thief*, p. 206; see also J. Landesco, "Organized Crime in Chicago," *The Illinois Crime Survey* (Illinois Association for Criminal Justice) (Chicago: Blakely, 1929), Part III, pp. 815–1090, 1043.

43. Face-to-face groups in business. See Louis Kriesberg, "Steel Distributors, the Federal Government, and the National Emergency" (unpublished Ph.D. dissertation, Department of Sociology, University of Chicago, 1953).

On morale of German troops see E. A. Shils and M. Janowitz, "Cohesion and Disintegration in the Wehrmacht in World War II," *Public Opinion Quarterly*, XII, No. 2 (1948), 314–15.

43–44. On American infantrymen in World War II see Samuel Stouffer *et al., The American Soldier: Adjustment during Army Life* (Princeton, N.J.: Princeton University Press, 1949), I, 414–20; Samuel Stouffer *et al., The American Soldier: Combat and Its Aftermath* (Princeton, N.J.: Princeton University Press, 1949), II, 324–61 [cited hereafter as *The American Soldier*].

44. "The . . . force necessary. . . ." R. R. Grinker and J. P. Spiegel, *Men under Stress*, p. 45. For additional data see the same authors, *War Neuroses in North Africa* (New York: Josiah Macy, Jr., Foundation, 1943).

PAGE

44. ". . . as a rule ran first. . . ." S. H. Prince, *Catastrophe and Social Change* (New York: Faculty of Political Science, Columbia University, 1920), p. 61.

44–45. The quotations about the Texas City explosion and the Oklahoma tornado towns are from Lewis M. Killian, "The Significance of Multiple-Group Membership in Disaster," *American Journal of Sociology*, LVII, No. 4 (January, 1952), 309–14 (italics added). There is an extensive additional literature on the role and importance of primary groups. For overview of literature see M. Sherif and H. Cantril, *The Psychology of Ego-Involvements*. For theory statement see George C. Homans, *The Human Group* (New York: Harcourt, Brace & Co., 1950). Of special practical importance are the several works of the late Kurt Lewin and his associates; see especially Kurt Lewin's *Resolving Social Conflicts*, ed. Gertrud Weiss Lewin (New York: Harper & Bros., 1948), Parts II and III. The importance of the face-to-face group has been recognized in the development of various group therapies. J. L. Moreno's work has been both stimulating and puzzling in this regard. For analysis of group therapies see G. W. Thomas, "Group Psychotherapy—a Review of the Recent Literature," *Psychosomatic Medicine*, V (1943), 166–80. The recent empirical research on the small group has many antecedents in the work of earlier scientists and social theorists, especially Jean Piaget, Émile Durkheim, and C. H. Cooley.

Political behavior is also influenced heavily by primary groups. The primary group's importance has been traced most carefully in voting behavior (see especially B. Berelson, P. F. Lazarsfeld, and W. N. McPhee, *Voting* [Chicago: University of Chicago Press, 1954]; also A. Campbell, G. Gurin, and W. E. Miller, *The Voter Decides* [White Plains, N.Y.: Row, Peterson & Co., 1954]); P. F. Lazarsfeld, B. Berelson, and H. Gaudet, *The People's Choice* (New York: Columbia University Press, 1948), pp. 137–49.

A valuable summary paper on primary groups is Edward Shils, "The Study of the Primary Group," in D. Lerner and H. D. Lasswell (eds.), *The Policy Sciences* ("Hoover Institute Studies" [Stanford, Calif.: Stanford University Press, 1951], pp. 44–69).

45-46. For discussion of reference group theory, see Theodore Mead Newcomb, *Social Psychology* (New York: Dryden Press, 1950), Part V; R. K. Merton and A. S. Kitt, "Contributions to the Theory of Reference Group Behavior," *Continuities in Social*

PAGE

Research, ed. R. K. Merton and P. F. Lazarsfeld (Glencoe, Ill.: Free Press, 1950), pp. 63 ff.; T. C. Schneirla, "The 'Levels' Concept in the Study of Social Organization in Animals," in J. H. Rohrer and M. Sherif (eds.), *Social Psychology at the Crossroads*, pp. 83–120; Eugene Hartley, "Psychological Problems of Multiple Group Membership," in J. H. Rohrer and M. Sherif (eds.), *Social Psychology at the Crossroads*, pp. 371–87.

47. William James, *The Principles of Psychology* (New York: Henry Holt & Co., 1910), I, 315.

"... the sort of sympathy ... aims of his will. ..." Charles Horton Cooley, *Social Organization*, p. 23.

Conscience, guilt, and shame. A distinction made frequently, and elaborated at length by Margaret Mead, is between guilt as internal and shame as public. This distinction is criticized and largely destroyed by Milton B. Singer, "Shame Cultures and Guilt Cultures," in G. Piers and M. Singer, *Shame and Guilt* (Springfield, Ill.: Charles C Thomas, 1953), pp. 45–79.

49. Charles Horton Cooley, *Human Nature and the Social Order*, p. 148.

William James, *The Principles of Psychology*, I, 294.

50. Universal brotherhood and otherhood. The phrase is borrowed, slightly altered, from Benjamin Nelson, *The Idea of Usury* (Princeton, N.J.: Princeton University Press, 1949).

CHAPTER 4

52. For evidence that conscientious objectors feel that their stand is a "genuine expression of citizenship" see John Graham, *Conscription and Conscience* (London, 1922), p. 337, quoted in John M. Gaus, *Great Britain: A Study in Civic Loyalty* (Chicago: University of Chicago Press, 1929), p. 34.

53. The language is quoted from the Smith Act (54 Stat. 671, 18 U.S.C. 11), held valid in 1951 by the Supreme Court, *Dennis* v. *United States*, 341 U.S. 494 (1951).

54. Some persons and organizations argue. See Theodore Mead Newcomb, *Social Psychology*, pp. 567–70.

For numerous examples of diverse groups claiming to promote the national welfare, see Merle Curti, *The Roots of American*

PAGE

Loyalty (New York: Columbia University Press, 1946); Charles A. Beard, *The Idea of National Interest* (New York: Macmillan Co., 1934); see also Harold D. Lasswell, *World Politics and Personal Insecurity* (New York: McGraw-Hill Book Co., Inc., 1935), p. 45. National patriotism plays a similar role in legitimating personal careers. Once proved a patriot, a person finds other careers relatively open. Army generals, not counting those elected to head the nation, become college presidents, business executives, and directors of large-scale welfare organizations. The winner of military medals can run a still with greater impunity than can others. Poor actresses who have entertained the boys overseas return to find better roles and more charitable reviews.

54. "No tolerably normal person. . . ." David B. Truman, *The Governmental Process* (New York: Alfred A. Knopf, Inc., 1951), pp. 508–9. The first extended and still pertinent description of role-segmentation was made by W. I. Thomas and F. Znaniecki, *The Polish Peasant in Europe and America* (Boston: Richard G. Badger, Gorham Press, 1919), III, 54–81.

56. On government as monopolist of legal force see Royal Institute of International Affairs, *Nationalism*, pp. 329–30.

59. On nineteenth-century arithmetic books and patriotism see Merle Curti, *The Roots of American Loyalty*, pp. 124–25.

Charles E. Merriam, *The Making of Citizens* (Chicago: University of Chicago Press, 1931), p. 289. The quotations concerning the four hundred textbooks are from Bessie L. Pierce, *Civic Attitudes in American School Textbooks* (Chicago: University of Chicago Press, 1930), p. 254.

60. It is good in itself and makes possible the good things in life. An extraordinary statement of the strength of the direct strand of patriotism to a democratic citizen is Marc Bloch, *Strange Defeat* (London: Oxford University Press, 1949), especially pp. 177–78. Compare with Simone Weil, *The Need for Roots* (London: Routledge & Kegan Paul Ltd., 1952).

61–62. ". . . to draw all people together. . . ." This quotation and those in the succeeding two paragraphs are from W. Lloyd Warner, *American Life: Dream and Reality* (Chicago: University of Chicago Press, 1953), pp. 2, 10–12.

62. A possible audience of seventy-five million. This estimate was

PAGE

made in the *New York Times*, January 21, 1953, p. 1. The 1957 estimate will undoubtedly be far larger.

62. "the least among. . . ." Carlton J. H. Hayes, *Essays on Nationalism*, pp. 161–62.

63. Churches and national policies. See Salo Wittmayer Baron, *Modern Nationalism and Religion* (New York: Harper & Bros., 1947).

Lenin's statement was made in 1919 at the Eighth Party Congress. For growth of Soviet nationalism see Royal Institute of International Affairs, *Nationalism*, pp. 57–80; S. N. Harper and R. Thompson, *The Government of the Soviet Union* (2d ed.; New York: D. Van Nostrand Co., Inc., 1949); Michael T. Florinsky, *Toward an Understanding of the U.S.S.R.* (New York: Macmillan Co., 1939).

65. Louis Kriesberg, "Steel Distributors, the Federal Government, and the National Emergency."

66. "The Pole in this country. . . ." W. I. Thomas and F. Znaniecki, *The Polish Peasant in Europe and America* (Boston: Richard G. Badger, Gorham Press, 1920), V, xiv–xv, Introduction.

66–67. A college student from West Virginia. These data concern a student interviewed by me in 1940. I subsequently followed his career through personal correspondence.

68. Hans Speier, " 'The American Soldier' and the Sociology of Military Organization," *Continuities in Social Research*, ed. R. K. Merton and P. F. Lazarsfeld, p. 115. The views of Edmund Burke on the strength of reinforcing loyalties are quoted in chap. 14. The early American political scientist, Francis Lieber, was also impressed by the way in which attachment to family and to local community contributed to national loyalty (see Francis Lieber, *Manual of Political Ethics* [2d ed.; Philadelphia: J. B. Lippincott Co., 1890], Vol. I, Book II, chaps. iv, v, vi).

CHAPTER 5

70. ". . . monistic, total, authoritarian. . . ." Franz Neumann, *Behemoth* (2d ed.; New York: Oxford University Press, 1944), p. 400; see also Mussolini on "The Theory of Fascist Loyalty" in *Enciclopedia italiana.*

". . . a man without group ties. . . ." Karl Mannheim, *Diagnosis of Our Time* (London: Routledge & Kegan Paul, Ltd., 1943), p. 95.

PAGE

71. Aldous Huxley, *Brave New World* (New York: Harper & Bros., 1946); George Orwell, *Nineteen Eighty-four* (New York: Harcourt, Brace & Co., 1949). The quotations are from the latter work, pp. 65–66.

72. The Nazis "suspected and attacked. . . ." Max Horkheimer, "Authoritarianism and the Family Today," in *The Family: Its Function and Destiny*, ed. Ruth Nanda Anshen (New York: Harper & Bros., 1949), p. 374.

"... its feasts, its farm years. . . ." Erika Mann, *School for Barbarians* (New York: Modern Age Books, Inc., 1938), p. 139. For legal approval see Franz Neumann, *Behemoth*, pp. 400–402.

72–73. The "ideal German family" joke is from Alfred Meusel, "National Socialism and the Family," *British Sociological Review*, XXVIII (1936), 166–86, 389–411, quoted in Lewis A. Coser, "Some Aspects of Soviet Family Policy," *American Journal of Sociology*, LVI, No. 5 (March, 1951), 432.

73. Labor unions in the U.S.S.R. Data from this section are largely from G. Bienstock, S. M. Schwarz, and A. Yugow, *Management in Russian Industry and Agriculture*, ed. A. Feiler and J. Marschak (New York: Oxford University Press, 1944); see also Sir John Maynard, *Russia in Flux* (New York: Macmillan Co., 1948), chap. xxi; Isaac Deutscher, *Soviet Trade Unions* (London and New York: Royal Institute of International Affairs, 1950); Solomon M. Schwarz, *Labor in the Soviet Union* (New York: Frederick A. Praeger, 1952).

74. For data on forced labor see J. Dallin and B. I. Nicolaevsky, *Forced Labor in Soviet Russia* (New Haven: Yale University Press, 1947); also Naum Jasny, "Labor and Output in Soviet Concentration Camps," *Journal of Political Economy*, LIX, No. 5 (October, 1951), 405–19.

75. Soviet youth are told. The quotations are from *Young Communists in the U.S.S.R.*, trans. Virginia Rhine (Washington, 1950), pp. 77, 79; quoted in Merle Fainsod, "The Komsomols—a Study of Youth under Dictatorship," *American Political Science Review*, XLV, No. 1 (March, 1951), 35, 37.

76–77. George M. Orwell, *Nineteen Eighty-four*, p. 287.

77–78. "The task of the totalitarian police. . . ." Hannah Arendt, *The Origins of Totalitarianism* (New York: Harcourt, Brace & Co.,

PAGE

1951), p. 403. The concepts of the "potential enemy" and the "possible crime" are also Miss Arendt's (p. 404).

79–81. The story of Marie is from Joseph Wechsberg, "A Reporter at Large: The Children of Lidice," *New Yorker*, XXIV (May 1, 1948), 34–36 ff. The long quotation is used with the permission of the *New Yorker*.

CHAPTER 6

83. Joys in follow-the-leader. Freud believed that a successful group, such as an army or a church, could be formed only as the result of the members' common affection for a leader. The love-tie that united the followers to the leader also bound the followers to one another. "The Commander-in-Chief is a father who loves all his soldiers equally, and for that reason they are comrades among themselves" (see Sigmund Freud, *Group Psychology and the Analysis of the Ego*, trans, James Strachey [New York: Boni & Liveright, n.d.], p. 43). Latter-day theorists have based a complete theory of national loyalty upon a parallel need by adults for the ministrations of a ruler (see Sebastian de Grazia, *The Political Community* [Chicago: University of Chicago Press, 1948]). Compare with view of Ranyard West, *Conscience and Society* (New York: Emerson Books, Inc., 1945), pp. 228 ff.

83–84. For the strength of the bond between Hitler and his followers as it affected army resistance see E. A. Shils and M. Janowitz, "Cohesion and Disintegration in the Wehrmacht in World War II," p. 304. For postwar attitudes see Milton Mayer, *They Thought They Were Free* (Chicago: University of Chicago Press, 1955).

84. A Communist biology, a Communist statistics. See George S. Counts and Nucia Lodge, *The Country of the Blind* (Boston: Houghton Mifflin Co., 1949).

"It postulates a preordained. . . ." J. L. Talmon, *The Rise of Totalitarian Democracy* (Boston: Beacon Press, 1952), p. 2.

84–85. On how true believers look upon their opponents see Crane Brinton, *The Anatomy of Revolution*, p. 234.

85. "Man in Fascism. . . ." Mussolini in *Enciclopedia italiana*, quoted in E. B. Ashton, *The Fascist* (London: G. P. Putnam's Sons, 1937), pp. 32–33.

86. Sir John Maynard, *Russia in Flux*, p. 429. José Ortega y Gasset said the same thing, remarkably early. Communism, he pointed

PAGE

out, presented "a gigantic human enterprise" in which men have "resolutely embraced a purpose of reform, and live tensely under the discipline that such a faith instils into them." He thought all Europeans might be "carried away not by the substance of the faith, but by the fervour of conduct which it inspires" (*The Revolt of the Masses* [New York: W. W. Norton & Co., 1932], pp. 198–200); see also A. Rossi, *A Communist Party in Action* (New Haven: Yale University Press, 1949), for the similar attractions of communism in France. Eric Hoffer, *The True Believer* (New York: Harper & Bros., 1951), is a spirited general analysis of the phenomenon.

86–87. The better life of the "little man" under Hitler is described by Milton Mayer in *They Thought They Were Free.* The quotations are from pp. 48–49, 222–24, 51–52.

88. New dignitaries must be created. Elite formation, says Neumann, is a cardinal principle of Nazi social organization (Franz Neumann, *Behemoth,* p. 402).

Dirty work. I am indebted to Everett Hughes for introducing me to this concept.

The more completely involved . . . the more congruence. Raymond A. Bauer, in his unpublished paper, "The Problem of Political Loyalty," has made this point. I am indebted to Mr. Bauer for allowing me to examine several of his draft manuscripts on the issue of national loyalty in the Soviet Union. He has used extensive data on Russian expatriates from interviews and questionnaires administered by the Russian Research Center of Harvard University. See also Raymond A. Bauer, *The New Man in Soviet Psychology* (Cambridge: Harvard University Press, 1952).

89. This kind of freezing. See Alex Inkeles, "Social Stratification and Mobility in the Soviet Union, 1940–50," *American Sociological Review,* XV, No. 4 (August, 1950), 465–79.

". . . to pay the price. . . ." Hannah Arendt, *The Origins of Totalitarianism,* p. 413.

90. Josiah Royce, *The Philosophy of Loyalty,* p. 41.

90–91. "In order to be a perfect actor. . . ." Bruno Bettelheim, "Remarks on the Psychological Appeal of Totalitarianism," *American Journal of Economics and Sociology,* XII, No. 1, 89–96. I have borrowed heavily from this article in the last two paragraphs on p. 90 and the first paragraph on p. 91.

PAGE

91–92. "The citizens have shared. . . ." Royal Institute of International Affairs, *Nationalism*, pp. 195–96 (italics added).

92. ". . . the Communist movement fought. . . ." Lewis A. Coser, "Some Aspects of Soviet Family Policy," *American Journal of Sociology*, LVI, No. 5 (March, 1951), 432.

". . . a chain for the working man and woman. . . ." "Excerpts from the Works of A. M. Kollontay," from "Communism and the Family," quoted in Rudolf Schlesinger, *The Family in the U.S.S.R.* (London: Routledge & Kegan Paul, 1949), pp. 66–67. The Schlesinger volume is a valuable collection. See also Rose Maurer, "Recent Trends in the Soviet Family," *American Sociological Review*, IX, No. 3 (June, 1944), pp. 242–49. Some of the data in this section were originally collected by Leonard S. Stein.

93. "Under Soviet conditions. . . ." *Pravda*, June 9, 1936, quoted in Schlesinger, *The Family in the U.S.S.R.*, p. 268.

The idea of a mass being like a primary group is somewhat anomalous. For discussion which tends to deny this possibility see Georg Simmel, *The Sociology of Georg Simmel*, ed. and trans. Kurt H. Wolff (Glencoe, Ill.: Free Press, 1950), p. 96.

96–97. ". . . even . . . terror is not omnipotent. . . ." David Riesman, "Some Observations on the Limits of Totalitarian Power," *Antioch Review*, XII, No. 2 (June, 1952), 155–68. The next quotation (". . . against the Soviet system's . . .") is from the same article.

97. With respect to antistate activity in the Soviet Union, I have profited from Raymond A. Bauer's unpublished paper, "The Problem of Political Loyalty [in the Soviet Union]."

". . . an ever increasing number of parasites. . . ." Franz Neumann, *Behemoth*, p. 634.

Bruno Bettelheim, "Individual and Mass Behavior in Extreme Situations," *Journal of Abnormal and Social Psychology*, XXXVIII (1943), 417–52.

98–100. The story of the Fermi family is taken from Laura Fermi, *Atoms in the Family: My Life with Enrico Fermi* (Chicago: University of Chicago Press, 1954); quotations are from pp. 73, 116, 120.

100. "The idea of the immortality. . . ." Paul Schmidt, quoted in Paul Seabury, "Ribbentrop and the German Foreign Office," *Political Science Quarterly*, LXVI, No. 4 (December, 1951), 555. Alle-

giance to the nation as the culture complex (in contrast to the state or government) is characteristic of many people in areas where a stable constitutional development or a strong, long-lived government has not existed. Despite the dictators' best efforts, this focus of loyalty is probably more important for their populations than for citizens of democracies, where the stability of the system through time tends to merge nation and state. So it is that very strong national loyalties can be exhibited where the state, as such, may be weak or non-existent (see Florian Znaniecki, *Modern Nationalities* [Urbana: University of Illinois Press, 1952]).

101. The story of Pastor Niemöller is adapted from Milton Mayer, *They Thought They Were Free*, p. 169.

102. "Exulting is he. . . ." The quotation is from an Egyptian text cited by John A. Wilson in *The Intellectual Adventure of Ancient Man* (Chicago: University of Chicago Press, 1946), p. 71.

CHAPTER 7

105–6. The story of the Manzanar speech was reported by a number of informants in the fall and winter of 1942. The speaker was identified as Mr. N., whose experiences are described more fully in chapter 12. It has been verified that the August protest meeting occurred and that Mr. N. was the principal speaker. But details of his speech are not completely verified, and some of them are probably apocryphal. That the speech as reported here was widely discussed and that Mr. N.'s stand was widely approved by evacuees are more important than the literal truth of the report.

106. Many Japanese Americans who declared themselves disloyal subsequently renounced their citizenship and then, after the war, wished to renounce their renunciations. Their legal situation is still clouded. In some cases the renunciations of citizenship have been declared invalid on the grounds that they were not the result of free choice but rather of fear, intimidation, and coercion. In other cases, however, no such clear conclusion has been reached, and the renunciants have become anomalous citizens without citizenship privileges or, in the words of one observer, "native American aliens." See *Abo* v. *Clark*, 77 F. Supp. 806 (1948); *McGrath* v. *Abo* and *McGrath* v. *Furuya*, 186 F. 2d 766, (1951); cert. denied, 342 U.S. 832 (1951); *Ex parte Abo* and *Ex parte Furuya*, 76 F. Supp. 664 (1947); *Barber* v. *Abo*, 186 F.

PAGE

2d 775 (1951); *Acheson* v. *Murakami,* 176 F. 2d 953 (1949); *Clark* v. *Inouye,* 175 F. 2d 740 (1949).

106. It was widely (and falsely) stated. The American Japanese, in fact, were among the defenders of Hawaii, served on the same basis as others in the American armed services, and fully participated in other ways in the American war effort. But these facts were largely ignored in the wartime public discussion of the "Japanese problem."

106–9. For the situation of Japanese Americans up to January, 1943, see Morton Grodzins, *Americans Betrayed: Politics and the Japanese Evacuation* (Chicago: University of Chicago Press, 1949); D. S. Thomas and R. S. Nishimoto, *The Spoilage* (Berkeley and Los Angeles: University of California Press, 1946); Alexander H. Leighton, *The Governing of Men;* U.S. Department of the Interior, War Relocation Authority, *WRA: A Story of Human Conservation* (Washington, D.C.: Government Printing Office, 1946).

107. With respect to economic losses of evacuees see L. Bloom and R. Riemer, *Removal and Return* (Berkeley and Los Angeles: University of California Press, 1949); United States Department of the Interior, War Relocation Authority, *WRA: A Story of Human Conservation,* pp. 155–62.

110. For details of registration program see "Army and Leave Clearance Registration at War Relocation Centers" (War Relocation Authority, Community Analysis Section, June, 1943 [mimeographed]). A wide range of materials about the registration was examined in the National Archives. In addition to the personal and official documents cited at later points, other important reports include: "Registration at Central Utah: 14–17, February, 1943" ("Project Analysis Series," No. 1; War Relocation Authority, Community Analysis Section, February, 1943 [mimeographed]); "Army Registration at One Relocation Center" ("Project Analysis Series," No. 2, War Relocation Authority, Community Analysis Section, undated [mimeographed]); "Registration at Manzanar" ("Project Analysis Series," No. 3, War Relocation Authority, Community Analysis Section, April 3, 1943 [mimeographed]); Evelyn Rose (Kitagawa), "Army Registration at Tule Lake Relocation Center" (April, 1943 [typewritten]).

111–12. "We are not dual. . . ." Morris E. Opler, "Studies of Segregants at Manzanar. II. United States Citizens Only with No For-

PAGE

eign Travel" (Manzanar Relocation Center, Community Analysis Section, October 26, 1943 [typewritten]) (hereafter cited as the Opler Report). This report was made on the basis of firsthand reporting by Professor Opler, then WRA community analyst at the Manzanar Center. I am indebted to him for permission to quote extensively from the report. The first quotation on p. 111 is from p. 4 of the Opler Report; the next two quotations are from pp. 14 and 58.

113. "I am loyal. . . ." From an eyewitness report of a Tule Lake observer, Robert Billigmeier.

Youthfulness of the citizen group. Japanese females immigrated to America considerably later than the males, thus producing an unusual age gap between alien parents and citizen children. For discussion of social effects of this bimodal age distribution see Shotaro Frank Miyamoto, *Solidarity among the Japanese in Seattle* ("University of Washington Publications in the Social Sciences," Vol. II, No. 2 [Seattle, 1939]).

". . . glowing accounts . . . of the future. . . ." Shotaro Frank Miyamoto, "The Career of Intergroup Tensions: A Study of the Collective Adjustments of Evacuees to Crises at the Tule Lake Relocation Center" (unpublished Ph.D. dissertation, Department of Sociology, University of Chicago, 1950), p. 335.

114. Quotations concerning the twenty-two-year-old unmarried man at Manzanar are from the Opler Report, pp. 23–34; this case was also discussed in "From a Nisei Who Said 'No' " (War Relocation Authority, Community Analysis Section, January 15, 1944 [mimeographed]).

116. "Father is dead. . . ." Opler Report, p. 65. The next quotation is also from the Opler Report, pp. 68–69.

118–20. It was also an administrative error to have army teams administer the registration. The army was the most hated and feared of the U.S. government agencies. Many evacuees were highly distrustful of army personnel and showed this in their complete refusal to co-operate. I am indebted for information on this point to my colleague, the Reverend Joseph Kitagawa, who interviewed many evacuees at the Minidoka Center during the registration. I also owe Mr. Kitagawa thanks for his critical reading of an early draft of this chapter.

PAGE

120. The following table recapitulates the registration results and shows the great differences among centers:

REGISTRATION RESULTS, LOYALTY QUESTION, CITIZENS OF JAPANESE ANCESTRY, SEVENTEEN YEARS OF AGE AND OVER, 1943*

Japanese American Citizens	Eligible To Register	"Yes" Answers	Non-affirmative: Did Not Register	Non-affirmative: Did Not Answer	Non-affirmative: Qualified Answers	Non-affirmative: "No" Answers	Per Cent "Yes" of Eligible	Per Cent Non-Affirm. of Eligible	Per Cent "No" of Eligible
All centers:									
Males	20,948	15,037	654	128	715	4,414	71.8	28.2	21.1
Females	19,212	15,749	732	226	586	1,919	82.0	18.0	10.0
Total	40,160	30,786	1,386	354	1,301	6,333	76.7	23.3	15.8
Central Utah:									
Males	1,707	1,167	....	....	108	432	68.4	31.6	25.3
Females	1,604	1,199	....	....	242	163	74.8	25.2	10.2
Total	3,311	2,366	....	....	350	595	71.5	28.5	18.0
Colorado River:									
Males	3,474	2,858	....	....	115	501	82.3	17.7	14.4
Females	3,274	3,119	....	16	22	117	95.3	4.7	3.6
Total	6,748	5,977	....	16	137	618	88.6	11.4	9.2
Gila River:									
Males	2,588	1,637	....	....	†	951	63.3	36.7	36.7
Females	2,394	2,142	....	....	†	252	89.5	10.5	10.5
Total	4,982	3,779	....	....	†	1,203	75.9	24.1	24.1
Granada:									
Males	1,580	1,474	....	....	24	82	93.3	6.7	5.2
Females	1,311	1,311	....	....	....	....	100.0	0.0	0.0
Total	2,891	2,785	....	....	24	82	96.3	3.7	2.8
Heart Mountain:									
Males	2,145	1,760	....	93	82	210	82.1	17.9	9.8
Females	1,684	1,561	....	33	22	68	92.7	7.3	4.0
Total	3,829	3,321	....	126	104	278	86.7	13.3	7.3
Jerome:									
Males	1,615	1,078	....	16	213	308	66.7	33.3	19.1
Females	1,588	1,163	....	27	121	277	73.2	26.8	17.4
Total	3,203	2,241	....	43	334	585	70.0	30.0	18.3
Manzanar:									
Males	1,907	918	....	11	1	977	48.1	51.9	51.2
Females	1,703	960	....	128	46	569	56.4	43.6	33.4
Total	3,610	1,878	....	139	47	1,546	52.0	48.0	42.8
Minidoka:‡									
Males	1,406	1,294	26	....	25	61	92.0	8.0	4.3
Females	1,459	1,416	....	....	33	10	97.1	2.9	0.7
Total	2,865	2,710	26	....	58	71	94.6	5.4	2.5
Rohwer:									
Males	1,578	1,324	....	6	147	101	83.9	16.1	6.4
Females	1,412	1,274	....	6	100	32	90.2	9.8	2.3
Total	2,990	2,598	....	12	247	133	86.9	13.1	4.4
Tule Lake:‡									
Males	2,948	1,527	628	2	†	791	51.8	48.2	26.8
Females	2,783	1,604	732	16	†	431	57.6	42.4	15.5
Total	5,731	3,131	1,360	18	†	1,222	54.6	45.4	21.3

* *Source:* United States Department of the Interior, War Relocation Authority, *The Evacuated People: A Quantitative Description* (Washington, D.C.: Government Printing Office, 1946), Table 73, p. 164.

† Not available; included with "Yes" and "No" answers.

‡ 13 male citizen responses at Minidoka and 21 male citizen responses at Tule Lake were unknown; they have not been included with those eligible to register.

PAGE

120–21. The contrast between the centers in the Western Defense Command and other centers was suggested to me by the late John Embree, who served during the war as chief of the Community Analysis Section of the WRA (see his letter of March 15, 1943, to Manzanar officials). All three centers having the highest proportion of disloyal answers for male citizens were located in the Western Defense Command (in each case the non-affirmative answers were at least 37 per cent of the total). The single center in the Western Defense Command not having a very high percentage of non-affirmative answers was the Colorado River settlement at Poston, Arizona (where 18 per cent of male citizens refused to answer "Yes"). This center had been directed from its earliest days by personnel drawn from the Office of Indian Affairs, who were experienced and skilful in establishing administrative programs for minority peoples. A near-riot situation, several months earlier, had been handled without violence.

122. D. S. Thomas and R. S. Nishimoto, *The Spoilage*, p. 105. Mr. Kitagawa noted the importance of block leaders at Minidoka.

122–23. The socioeconomic differences have been demonstrated by Dorothy Swaine Thomas, with the assistance of Charles Kikuchi and James Sakoda, *The Salvage* (Berkeley: University of California Press, 1952), pp. 95–105. Mrs. Thomas' data concern residents from three centers only, and she includes among the "disloyal" all those later segregated at Tule Lake, as contrasted with the citizens who replied non-affirmatively to the loyalty question, the group considered in the present volume. It is certain that the differentials she demonstrated are also true for the non-affirmative respondents considered here. By far the largest number of citizen segregants over seventeen years of age (for definition of segregants see *The Salvage*, p. 94) were those who gave non-affirmative responses during the registration. Mrs. Thomas' data are presented so that the aliens and citizens can be separated, and I have cited her data as they relate to citizens only.

Unrefined data of the War Relocation Authority, lumping all citizens of all centers together, show a significantly higher rate of "No" answers for (1) those with a family member in Japan; (2) those with three years' residence and two years' school in Japan since 1934; and (3) those who had previously registered with the Japanese consul to establish their Japanese citizenship (see WRA, "Army and Leave Clearance Registration at War Relocation Centers," p. 78, Table 3).

PAGE

123. The data for non-Buddhist, non-agricultural males are from Dorothy Swaine Thomas, *The Salvage*, p. 102.

124. Submissiveness and loyalty response. Mr. Kitagawa is the source of information on this point.

125. Loyalty responses as counterpart of actions of other marginal men. See Georg Simmel, *The Sociology of Georg Simmel*, pp. 383–84. I am indebted to Donald Campbell for calling my attention to some of these relationships.

"We fight two battles. . . ." Japanese Americans, in general, maintained loyalty during the registration for the following reasons: (1) the alternative of Japanese national loyalty was not attractive; (2) many evacuees looked forward to better things in America; (3) personal cordial contacts with Caucasians were influential; (4) the bulk of Japanese Americans were completely acculturated to American ways; (5) the Japanese political system was repugnant to them; (6) in some cases parents encouraged "Yes" answers because, though uncertain about their own futures in America, they knew their sons and daughters had no other.

127. Caution must be exercised. Many observers have gone beyond caution and have dismissed the case as having no meaning for the understanding of national loyalty. Japanese Americans have held to this view (see Opler Report, *passim*). Thomas and Nishimoto (*The Spoilage*, pp. 88–89, 103, 108) concluded that the disloyalty declarations of Japanese Americans were given for "reasons highly irrelevant to the matter of political allegiance." According to this view, the category of "irrelevant disloyals" included those who said "No" to the loyalty question (1) because they sought to retain the securities of relocation center life; (2) because of their "estimate of the rewards that would ultimately be reaped by the technically 'disloyal' if Japan won the war"; and (3) because of protests over abrogation of civic rights and losses of property. People in these groups, it is argued, contrast with persons who were "politically conscious adherents of Japan." The latter were the "convinced" and the "ideological" disloyal, to be sharply distinguished from those disloyal for "irrelevant" or "practical" reasons. A similar view is given by Robert W. O'Brien, *The College Nisei* (Palo Alto: Pacific Books, 1949), pp. 104–5.

PAGE

127. Statistics on volunteers. For Hawaii see Andrew William Lind, *Hawaii's Japanese: An Experiment in Democracy* (Princeton, N.J.: Princeton University Press, 1946), p. 151; for the mainland, United States Department of the Interior, War Relocation Authority, *The Evacuated People: A Quantitative Description* (Washington, D.C.: Government Printing Office, 1946), pp. 125–26. Other Japanese Americans, from both Hawaii and the mainland, were, of course, already in the armed services.

128. Josiah Royce, *The Philosophy of Loyalty*, p. 284.

CHAPTER 8

132. Content and discontent. "The basic postulate of behavior," Harold Lasswell has written, is ". . . maximization of indulgences over deprivations" (see *The Political Writings of Harold D. Lasswell*, p. 513).

132–33. The Gide quotations are from Richard Crossman (ed.), *The God That Failed* (New York: Harper & Bros., 1949), pp. 168, 166.

133. On the focus of loyalties see Ranyard West, *Conscience and Society*, pp. 225–27, 234–35.

133–35. The literature on alienation and kindred ills is voluminous. I have drawn largely upon the following works: José Ortega y Gasset, *The Revolt of the Masses;* Sebastian de Grazia, *The Political Community;* Philip Selznick, *The Organizational Weapon* (New York: McGraw-Hill Book Co., Inc., 1952) ; Robert K. Merton, "Social Structure and Anomie," in his *Social Theory and Social Structure* (Glencoe, Ill.: Free Press, 1949), pp. 125–50; Talcott Parsons, "Some Sociological Aspects of the Fascist Movements," *Social Forces*, XXI, No. 2 (December, 1942), 138–47; and Erich Fromm, *Escape from Freedom.* Many of the ideas in these books are founded on the earlier works of Marx, Durkheim, Freud, Weber, and others. The specific description of alienation on p. 134 is based almost completely on Marxian ideas, though for Marx the idea of alienation expressed a formal relationship rather than defining a personal malaise.

134. Segmentation of beliefs. See Herbert Agar, *A Time for Greatness* (Boston: Little, Brown & Co., 1943), pp. 46–47. Agar writes of those who are cynical, hopeless, angry, or frightened: "A great increase in their numbers means that civilization has become vulnerable to the disease of fascism."

PAGE

134. German middle classes and alienation. See Frederick L. Schuman, *The Nazi Dictatorship* (New York: Alfred A. Knopf, 1935); Hans Gerth, "The Nazi Party: Its Leadership and Composition," *American Journal of Sociology*, XLV, No. 4 (January, 1940), 527.

134–35. Unemployed and alienation. Philip Selznick, *The Organizational Weapon*, pp. 282–86; E. Wight Bakke, *Citizens without Work* (New Haven: Yale University Press, 1940); B. Zawadzki and P. Lazarsfeld, "The Psychological Consequences of Unemployment," *Journal of Social Psychology*, VI, No. 2 (May, 1935), 224–51 (a valuable review of the literature); R. C. Angell, *The Family Encounters the Depression* (New York: Charles Scribner's Sons, 1936); M. Komarovsky, *The Unemployed Man and His Family* (New York: Dryden Press, Inc., for the Institute of Social Research, 1940).

135. Crane Brinton, *The Anatomy of Revolution*, p. 141.

136–37. Conscientious objector, draft dodger, saboteur. Robert Horn first pointed out to me that the disloyal act is regarded and punished in a variety of ways.

138–39. On wartime price-fixing and butchers see Marshall B. Clinard, *The Black Market* (New York: Rinehart & Co., 1952), pp. 126–31. Data from this volume were supplemented by my own interviews with retail butchers in Berkeley, California, and Chicago, Illinois. The "rationale" given is patterned closely after that of a Chicago shop-owner, J. T., a friend and a ready and intelligent informant. The position of American butchers during World War II is writ large in every inflationary situation. Inflation is potentially as destructive as war to national welfare. But the weapons which nations possess to dramatize the necessity of obeying national dictates in wartime do not usually exist in periods of inflation. Penalties for non-compliance are less drastic; rewards for compliance less certain. The history of every modern inflation is a history of government pleas and government controls being sabotaged through actions dictated by non-national loyalties. In a society in which wealth—and the social status that goes with it—are so highly prized, national loyalty suffers when it conflicts with wealth-getting.

139–40. Richard Wright, in Richard Crossman (ed.), *The God That Failed*, pp. 118, 130, 120, 117.

PAGE

140–42. H.R.H. the Duke of Windsor, *A King's Story* (New York: G. P. Putnam's Sons, 1951). Quotations are from pp. 412, 256, 205, 260–61, 262, 411, 413. Edward was a far cry from the model of the non-political monarch which the British constitution requires. This is illustrated at many points in his own memoirs, not least of all by his hope in the middle of the marriage crisis that the Cabinet would consent to his making a broadcast so that he could present his side of the case. Edward comments, in a fashion foreign to all that the British monarchy represents, "With its rejection, disappeared my only possible means of rallying the whole nation" (*A King's Story*, p. 376). Edward's concept of his kingly duties undoubtedly accounts for a large part of the Cabinet's intransigence and their seizure of the marriage issue to make their supremacy clear, once and for all. The main point in the text is not altered—indeed, it is strengthened—by consideration of these issues of constitutional politics.

142–43. Douglas Southall Freeman, *R. E. Lee* (New York: Charles Scribner's Sons, 1934). The quotations in the text are from p. 422 (letter from Lee to Markie Williams, January 22, 1861); p. 428 (Lee speaking with Anderson); p. 421 (Lee writing to Custis); p. 429 (Lee speaking with Anderson); p. 443 (Lee writing to his sister, April 20, 1861). I have added the italics in the last quotation.

143–45. The case of William Joyce is extensively and brilliantly exmined by Rebecca West in *The Meaning of Treason.* The quotations, in order, are from Miss West's study, pp. 18–19, 19, 72, 116, 19, 83–84, 20, 21, 104; see also J. W. Hall (ed.), *Trial of William Joyce.*

145. The alienated person need not be disloyal. For important discussion of deviant behavior see Talcott Parsons, *The Social System* (Glencoe, Ill.: Free Press, 1951), pp. 249–97.

145–46. "When a person is ready. . . ." This quotation and the next one are from William Kornhauser, "Liberal and Radical Political Careers: A Study of Group Loyalty" (unpublished Ph.D. dissertation, Department of Sociology, University of Chicago, 1953), p. 101.

146. No political discontent need exist. See M. L. Ernst and D. Loth, *Report on the American Communist* (New York: Henry Holt & Co., 1952), pp. 66, 196 ff.; Gabriel A. Almond, *The Appeals of Communism* (Princeton, N.J.: Princeton University Press, 1954),

PAGE

pp. 230–97. Conclusions in the text are corroborated by Kurt Lewin and Paul Grabbe, who have stated that acceptance of new systems of belief and new values are "linked with the acceptance of a specific group, a particular role, a definite source of authority as new points of reference." New beliefs are not usually acquired item by item but rather "in a jump" or "as a whole" ("Conduct, Knowledge, and Acceptance of New Values," *Journal of Social Issues*, I, No. 3 [1945], 53–64). For learning theory see Clark L. Hull, *Principles of Behavior* (New York: D. Appleton-Century Co., 1943).

146. The cases cited in the text do not include the case in which a person is a radical because his parents are radicals. This is the circumstance of a person being socialized into radicalism from childhood. It is radicalism as a consequence of non-national loyalties rather than as a consequence of alienation. It is relatively rare in the United States, common in France and Italy (see Gabriel Almond, *The Appeals of Communism*, p. 226).

On spy ring in Canada, see *Canada: Royal Commission To Investigate Disclosures of Secret and Confidential Information to Unauthorized Persons* (Ottawa: E. Cloutier, printer to the King, 1946).

146–47. Klaus Fuchs. The first quotation is from the court testimony of the security officer at Harwell. The following quotations are from the transcript of Fuchs's confession (see *New York Times*, February 11, 1950, p. 2).

147–48. ". . . insulated and absorbed. . . ." The phrase is adapted from Philip Selznick, *The Organizational Weapon*, pp. 25–26. The rest of the paragraph is indebted to Talcott Parsons, *The Social System*, pp. 286 ff. The quotation at the top of p. 148 is also from Parsons, p. 294. During World War II, Joost A. M. Meerloo studied different types of traitors and collaborators. "Not one . . . would admit his disloyalty to be an act of treason . . . he surrounds his treachery with a complicated web of sophisms and rationalizations" ("The Psychology of Treason and Loyalty," *American Journal of Psychotherapy*, VIII, No. 4 [October, 1954], 648–66).

148. The revolutionary group in Chicago. These data are from my interviews with a member of the group in 1937 and 1938.

To prosper in membership. See William Kornhauser, "Liberal and Radical Political Careers," chaps. vii and viii.

PAGE

149. "Work is a potent drug. . . ." Arthur Koestler in Richard Crossman (ed.), *The God That Failed*, p. 65.

"... to living like a foreigner. . . ." This quotation and the next, longer, one are from Ignazio Silone in Richard Crossman (ed.), *The God That Failed*, p. 99. Erich F. Berendt, a Nazi Freikorps member during the days of the Weimar Republic, has written: "The Freikorps followed the inner voice of duty, which forced them to forget everything including their paternal home, family, profession, and life" (*Soldaten der Freiheit* [Berlin: E. C. Etthofen, 1935], p. 44).

150. Wright in Richard Crossman (ed.), *The God That Failed*, p. 162.

"An individual existence. . . ." Eric Hoffer, *The True Believer*, p. 85.

"Since many of my friends. . . ." Quoted in William Kornhauser, "Liberal and Radical Political Careers," p. 164.

151. *Coriolanus*, Act IV, scene 5. Shakespeare, who took the story from Plutarch, has his tragic hero illustrate still another important point on the social basis of loyalties. Coriolanus is prepared to sack Rome and desists only because his mother, wife, and son intercede before the city walls. His mother's plea sets the issue between city and son:

> "We must find
> An evident calamity, though we had
> Our wish, which side should win; for either thou
> Must, as a foreign recreant, be led
> With manacles through our streets, or else
> Triumphantly tread on thy country's ruin,
> And bear the palm for having bravely shed
> Thy wife and children's blood."

151–52. For Italian Americans see Harold D. Lasswell, *World Politics and Personal Insecurity*, p. 169; for Japanese Americans see chap. 7 above; for an example from a novel see William L. Shirer, *The Traitor* (New York: Farrar, Straus & Co., 1950).

152. For the story of Alcibiades see Plutarch's *Lives*, trans. John Dryden ("Modern Library" [New York: Random House, Inc.]). The quotation is from p. 248.

CHAPTER 9

PAGE

155. Soviet refugees. George Fischer, *Soviet Opposition to Stalin* (Cambridge: Harvard University Press, 1952), pp. 142, 151 ff. Merle Fainsod, *How Russia Is Ruled* (Cambridge: Harvard University Press, 1953), pp. 496–97. Most of what is known about cohesiveness and dissension in the Soviet Union comes from refugees, whose testimony is difficult to evaluate. Though their stories may be honest and accurate, their representativeness of the home population is always open to question.

156. Chepurnykh. See *New York Times*, February 14, 1954.

"Coupled with their helplessness. . . ." Alex Inkeles and Raymond A. Bauer, writing in the *New York Times Magazine*, quoted in George Fischer, *Soviet Opposition to Stalin*, p. 125.

157. Integration of even the disadvantaged. The long centuries of Russian autocracy and paternalism also make Soviet citizens far less resistant to totalitarian controls than those whose history is one of rationalism and liberalism. This point is emphasized by many commentators upon Russian totalitarianism. See George Fischer, *Soviet Opposition to Stalin*, pp. 127–28; Sir John Maynard, *Russia in Flux.*

158. A society characterized by surveillance and suspicion. Merle Fainsod, *How Russia Is Ruled*, p. 485.

Not covered in manuals and directives. Don Levine noted this during his visit to the Eastern Zone of Germany (see his unpublished Master's thesis, "Conformity and Deviation in the East German Youth" [Department of Sociology, University of Chicago, 1954]).

159. ". . . personal aspirations into cosmic. . . ." Harold D. Lasswell, *World Politics and Personal Insecurity*, p. 135.

Cynicism and totalitarianism. See Herbert Krugman, "The Appeal of Communism to American Middle Class Intellectuals and Trade Unionists," *Public Opinion Quarterly*, XVI, No. 3 (fall, 1952), 331–55.

159–60. Ignazio Silone, *The School for Dictators*, trans. G. David and E. Mosbacher (2d ed.; New York: Harper & Bros., 1938), pp. 157–58.

PAGE

160. Russian youth and propaganda. Merle Fainsod, "Controls and Tensions in the Soviet System," *American Political Science Review*, XLIV, No. 2 (June, 1950), 266–82.

161. On the Nazi state as competing power structures see Franz Neumann, *Behemoth*, pp. 365–98.

Struggle for power among Hitler's lieutenants. See Hugh R. Trevor-Roper, *The Last Days of Hitler* (New York: Macmillan Co., 1947).

162. Arrest leads to rejection. Some statistical data bearing on this point are presented by Raymond Bauer in his unpublished paper, "Trends in Sources of Alienation from the Soviet Union" (April 15, 1955). This paper is based upon a preliminary analysis of questionnaire responses by several thousand Russian refugees.

". . . the reliance on fear. . . ." Merle Fainsod, *How Russia Is Ruled*, p. 482.

163–64. Data and quotations concerning Soviet physicians are from Mark G. Field, "Structured Strain in the Role of the Soviet Physician," *American Journal of Sociology*, LVIII, No. 5 (March, 1953), 493–502. Like the works by Fainsod, Fischer, Inkeles, Bauer, Moore, and Berliner, cited elsewhere, this study is a product of the Russian Research Center of Harvard University, whose research is doing much to illuminate important areas of Soviet politics and society.

165. Virtually every memoir. See, among others, Vladimir Tchernavin, *I Speak for the Silent Prisoners of the Soviet* (Boston: Ralph T. Hale & Co., 1935); Victor Kravchenko, *I Chose Freedom* (New York: Charles Scribner's Sons, 1946); Bertha Fischer, *My Lives in Russia* (New York: Harper & Bros., 1944); *Thirteen Who Fled*, ed. L. Fischer and B. A. Yakovlev, trans. G. Fischer and V. Fischer (New York: Harper & Bros., 1949); Vladimir Brunovsky, *The Methods of the OGPU* (London: Harper & Bros., 1931). Data from memoirs have been collected and discussed by John Hepler in his "Soviet Disloyalty" (unpublished M.A. thesis, Department of Political Science, University of Chicago, 1951).

Victor Kravchenko, *I Chose Freedom*, p. 328.

166. Peasants as least controllable. See Merle Fainsod, *How Russia Is Ruled*, chap. xvi; W. W. Rostow, *The Dynamics of Soviet Society* (New York: W. W. Norton & Co., 1952), pp. 208–15; Bar-

PAGE

rington Moore, Jr., *Soviet Politics: The Dilemma of Power* (Cambridge: Harvard University Press, 1950).

167. On "family circles" see Merle Fainsod, *How Russia Is Ruled*, pp. 201–2, 329–30, 430, 476. For how managerial work cliques operate, sometimes in conflict with the demands of the Soviet Union, see Joseph S. Berliner, "The Informal Organization of the Soviet Firm," *Quarterly Journal of Economics*, LXVI, No. 3 (August, 1952), 342–65; see also Margaret Mead, *Soviet Attitudes toward Authority* (New York: McGraw-Hill Book Co., Inc., 1951).

None of the key figures surrendered voluntarily. George Fischer, *Soviet Opposition to Stalin*, p. 138; see also Merle Fainsod, *How Russia Is Ruled*, p. 498. An important unanswered question is how hard these opposition leaders fought before they were captured. No evidence indicates that they made their capture easy.

167–68. Five autonomous republics dissolved. See *New York Times*, June 27, 1946, p. 4. The autonomous republics concerned were the Volga-German, Kalmyk, Chechen-Ingush, and Crimean. In addition, the autonomous republic of the Kabards and Bolkars was destroyed.

168–71. "Marshal's batons and Knight's crosses. . . ." John W. Wheeler-Bennett, *The Nemesis of Power* (London: Macmillan & Co., Ltd., 1953), p. 536. Data on the German resistance to the Nazis, on which the following paragraphs are based, are taken principally from this book and from Hans Rothfels, *The German Opposition to Hitler* (Hinsdale, Ill.: Henry Regnery Co., 1948). See also Heinrich Fraenkel, *The German People versus Hitler* (London: George Allen & Unwin, Ltd., 1940); Ruth Andreas-Friedrich, *Berlin Underground* (New York: Henry Holt & Co., 1947). These books together contain a large bibliography on the German resistance.

169–70. Choices for loyalty and disloyalty. The data are from John W. Wheeler-Bennett, *The Nemesis of Power*, pp. 428, 527–28, 530.

170. "The one motive. . . ." John W. Wheeler-Bennett, *The Nemesis of Power*, p. 689.

"I stood before. . . ." *A German of the Resistance: The Last Letters of Count Helmuth James von Moltke* (London, 1947), quoted in Hans Rothfels, *The German Opposition to Hitler*, p. 49.

172. ". . . restraints and conformities. . . ." David B. Truman, *The Governmental Process*, p. 168.

PAGE

174–75. American experts agree. See Raymond A. Bauer's unpublished paper, "The Implications of the Succession Crisis in the Soviet Union for East-Western Relations," p. 10. The probable future of the Soviet Union, as it bears upon national loyalty, is also discussed in Isaac Deutscher, *Russia: What Next?* (New York: Oxford University Press, 1953), and Barrington Moore, Jr., *Terror and Progress USSR* (Cambridge: Harvard University Press, 1954). Moore believes that the Soviet Union may also evolve into a sort of rationalist technocracy or a limited and traditionalist despotism. Deutscher argues that a democratic regeneration of the regime is a distinct possibility.

CHAPTER 10

179–80. The existence of individual differences. For a statement that denies the utility of psychological data for group analysis see Reinhard Bendix, "Compliant Behavior and Individual Personality," *American Journal of Sociology*, LVIII, No. 3 (November, 1952, 292–303.

181. Weather, crops, and voting. See Seymour Martin Lipset, *Agrarian Socialism* (Berkeley: University of California Press, 1950), pp. 1–19, and the bibliography there provided.

183–87. Chicago night-club and banquet waiters were studied in 1952 by Milton Millon, then a student in my University of Chicago seminar and now a university teacher, who served as a night-club waiter in order to collect his data (see his "National Loyalty among Chicago Waiters" [unpublished M.A. thesis, Department of Political Science, University of Chicago, 1952]). Material in this section is largely derived from this work and from conversations with Millon.

184. One of the lowliest professions. See Robert E. Clark, "The Relationship of Occupation and Various Psychoses" (unpublished Ph.D. dissertation, Department of Sociology, University of Chicago, 1947); G. S. Counts, "The Social Status of Occupation," *School Review*, XXXIII (1925), 21; J. A. Nietz, "The Depression and the Social Status of Occupations," *Elementary School Journal*, XXXV (1935), 454–61; Mapheus Smith, "An Empirical Scale of Prestige Status of Occupations," *American Sociological Review*, VIII (April, 1943), 185–92.

PAGE

185. Middle-class waitresses. See William Foote Whyte, *Human Relations in the Restaurant Industry* (New York: McGraw-Hill Book Co., Inc., 1948). But, as Whyte makes clear, even waitresses in middle-class restaurants have status difficulties, and the "crying waitress" is a common phenomenon.

    Resentment did not stem from low income. The waiters were a group to whom high status did not come with high income. A good discussion of economic classes and national loyalty, showing how the changing situation of classes changed their relationship to the state, is Paul Kosok, *Modern Germany* (Chicago: University of Chicago Press, 1933); see also Frederick L. Schuman, *War and Diplomacy in the French Republic* (New York: McGraw-Hill Book Co., 1931), pp. 356 ff.

186. Service of low status in public. For comparable case of janitors see Ray Gold, "Janitors versus Tenants: A Status-Income Dilemma," *American Journal of Sociology*, LVII, No. 5 (March, 1952), 486–93. An instructive comparative study would be of mechanics of expensive automobiles. Their salary is comparable to night-club waiters, and they also serve the rich. Like waiters, they scorn their customer's ignorance. But I would guess that this scorn is friendly. The mechanic possesses esoteric skills, and his "dirty" work is performed in privacy. He views himself more as master and less as servant, and he has a strong group of peers to support this view. He is likely to identify himself positively with the work product and with the car-owner.

187. A higher proportion of traitors. The tentative nature of these conclusions must be emphasized. We deal in hypotheses, and a great deal of research would be necessary before definitive statements could be justified. Milton Millon, using a questionnaire devised by me, which he and a group of fellow-students enlarged and improved, tried to find quantitative data to support the strong impressionistic evidence that waiters had a relatively low level of patriotism. The questionnaire consisted of a group of stories in which loyalty to nation was opposed to loyalty to another group, such as family, church, and business, or in which sacrifices for nation were demanded. The waiters showed less inclination to make sacrifices for nation than did a group of YMCA adult leaders who were asked the same questions. The extraordinary difficulty of questionnaire construction, administration, and validation in this field makes it impossible to draw definite conclusions

PAGE

from this work. The only conclusion is that further work needs to be done. Plans are under way to do this at the University of Chicago.

187. Relatively greater willingness of youth. For review of poll data see Otto Klineberg, *Tensions Affecting International Understanding* (Bull. 62 [New York: Social Science Research Council, 1950]), pp. 169–71.

Young people join. For left see Gabriel Almond, *The Appeals of Communism,* pp. 217, 21; for right, Reinhard Bendix, "Social Stratification and Political Power," *American Political Science Review,* XLVI, No. 2 (June, 1952), 357–75. The social base of the radicalism of youth is underlined by the fact that the social position of the *aged* may also produce tendencies toward extremism. As the group of the aged increases absolutely and relatively to the whole population, it is not unlikely that their reaction to deprivation will take the form of political action. This has already happened to some degree, as, for example, in California. In the long run, the radicalism of the aged may become a national problem of greater importance than the delinquency of youth. For some hints of this problem see S. M. Lipset, P. F. Lazarsfeld, A. H. Barton, and Juan Linz, "The Psychology of Voting: An Analysis of Political Behavior," in Gardner Lindzey (ed.), *Handbook of Social Psychology* (Cambridge: Addison-Wesley Publishing Co., Inc., 1954), II, 1148.

188. See Erik H. Erikson's remarkable article, "Identity and Totality," in *Human Development Bulletin, Fifth Annual Symposium* (Chicago: Committee on Human Development, University of Chicago, 1954). This is an advance article on a longer report in preparation. See also Erik H. Erikson's *Childhood and Society* (New York: W. W. Norton & Co., 1950). His article "Wholeness and Totality: A Psychiatric Contribution," in *Totalitarianism,* ed. Carl Friedrich (Cambridge: Harvard University Press, 1954), was not available when this chapter was written.

189. "I would rather be quite insecure. . . ." Erik H. Erikson, "Identity and Totality," *Human Development Bulletin,* p. 65. The next two quotations are from the same article. For an analysis of Hitlerism as the response of German youth to the appeals of a leader whose attractiveness was great as a consequence of deep psychocultural conflicts see Erikson's "Hitler's Imagery and German Youth," *Psychiatry,* V (1942), 475–93.

PAGE

190. "... revolt of discontented. . . ." Robert G. L. Waite, *Vanguard of Nazism* (Cambridge: Harvard University Press, 1952), p. 18.

"They thought that. . . ." Howard Becker, *German Youth: Bond or Free* (London: K. Paul, Trench, Trubner & Co., Ltd., 1946), p. 51.

192. Voting and ethnic groups. See, among many other references, L. H. Bean, F. Mosteller, and F. Williams, "Nationalities and 1944," *Public Opinion Quarterly*, VIII, No. 3 (1944), 368–75; Samuel Lubell, *The Future of American Politics* (New York: Harper & Bros., 1952); B. R. Berelson, P. F. Lazarsfeld, and W. N. McPhee, *Voting*, especially pp. 61–75.

The challenge of religious loyalties. For a crucial period of English history, when the issue of religion became paramount in defining national loyalty, see Charles Howard McIlwain's masterly Introduction to *The Political Works of James I* ("Harvard Political Classics," Vol. I [Cambridge: Harvard University Press, 1918]), pp. xv–cxi. The parallels between the oath of allegiance, required by James's Act of Supremacy, and certain latter-day loyalty oaths deserve detailed inquiry and analysis.

192–93. The Catholic church. The relationships between church and national loyalties have received extensive treatment in Salo Wittmayer Baron, *Modern Nationalism and Religion*, especially chap. iv for discussion of Catholicism; see also Heinrich A. Rommen, *The State in Catholic Thought* (London: B. Herder Book Co., 1945); John Courtney Murray, S.J., *Governmental Repression of Heresy* (Woodstock, Md.: Woodstock College, n.d.).

194. The histories of Christian denominationalism. See H. Richard Niebuhr, *The Social Sources of Denominationalism* (New York: Shoe String Press, 1954); Sydney G. Diamond, *The Psychology of the Methodist Revival* (New York: Oxford University Press, 1926); E. K. Nottingham, *Methodism and the Frontier* (New York: Columbia University Press, 1941).

The emergence of Christianity. See A. D. Nock, *Conversion* (Oxford: Oxford University Press, 1933) and bibliography there provided. ". . . In the expansion of Christianity in its first two centuries within the Roman Empire there was little, if any, direct preaching to the masses. A pagan came in contact with the movement in a number of *casual* ways" (p. 212; italics added).

PAGE

194–97. David G. Mandelbaum, "Social Trends and Personal Pressures: The Growth of a Culture Pattern," in *Language, Culture, and Personality*, ed. L. Spier, A. I. Hallowell, and S. S. Newman (Menasha, Wis.: Sapir Memorial Publication Fund, 1941), pp. 219–38. The quotations, in order, are from pp. 225, 229, 230, 232. Though I have utilized Mr. Mandelbaum's data extensively, the interpretation is my own, and he can be charged with no responsibility for it. For an analogous case of changing religion in primitive societies see Philleo Nash, "The Place of Religious Revivalism in the Formation of the Intercultural Community on Klamath Reservation," in *Social Anthropology of North American Tribes*, ed. Fred Eggan (Chicago: University of Chicago Press, 1937), pp. 377 ff.

CHAPTER 11

198–99. The young man from northern Tennessee. Mr. Louis Brownlow, whose authority is unimpeachable on these matters, vouches for the story. For one version of it see Mr. Brownlow's fine autobiography, *A Passion for Politics* (Chicago: University of Chicago Press, 1955), p. 390.

199. Whittaker Chambers, *Witness* (New York: Random House, 1952).

199–200. Mary McCarthy, "My Confession," *Reporter*, December 22, 1953, pp. 28–34, and January 5, 1954, pp. 27–31.

199–201. Political accidents and loyalty. In a book published after this chapter was written, Oscar Handlin examines a series of incidents crucial to the course of American history and suggests that accidents have a large role in the affairs of nations (see *Chance or Destiny* [Boston: Little, Brown & Co., 1955]).

200. Unrealized by the person concerned. Lincoln Steffens has charted the course of municipal corruption in similar terms. One leading crook did not realize what he was doing until "the Committee's exposure, with the public (and private) horror and press comment on it, exposed him to himself" (Lincoln Steffens, *The Autobiography of Lincoln Steffens* [New York: Harcourt, Brace & Co., 1931], pp. 272–73).

201. The "inner rhythm." Harold D. Lasswell, "The Selective Effect of Personality on Political Participation," in *Studies in the Scope and Method of "The Authoritarian Personality,"* ed. R. Christie and M. Jahoda (Glencoe, Ill.: Free Press, 1954), p. 202.

PAGE

201–2. The "authoritarian" personality and the consistency of personality. T. W. Adorno *et al.*, *The Authoritarian Personality*, p. 971 and *passim.* For incisive methodological criticism see Herbert H. Hyman and Paul B. Sheatsley, " 'The Authoritarian Personality'—a Methodological Critique," in *Studies in the Scope and Method of "The Authoritarian Personality,"* ed. R. Christie and M. Jahoda, pp. 50–122. Despite the criticism, additional research leaves no doubt about the actuality of the syndrome. For an excellent collection of articles and conceptualization of personality see C. Kluckhohn and H. A. Murray (eds.), *Personality in Nature, Society, and Culture* (New York: Alfred A. Knopf, Inc., 1948), especially pp. 3–48.

202. Communism and hostility and isolation. Gabriel Almond, *The Appeals of Communism,* chap. x. For a suggestive but inconclusive study of the appeal of communism in the United States to intellectuals, see Herbert E. Krugman, "The Interplay of Social and Psychological Factors in Political Deviance" (unpublished Ph.D. dissertation, Department of Political Science, Columbia University, 1952).

Personality as predisposition to action. For an attempt to relate personality to voting behavior see Robert E. Lane, "Political Personality and Electoral Choice," *American Political Science Review,* XLIX, No. 1 (March, 1955), 173–90.

Traitors and childhood. The psychoanalytic discussions of treason are rudimentary and unsatisfactory (see Ernest Jones, "The Psychology of Quislingism," *International Journal of Psychoanalysis,* XXII [1941], 1–6; Bingham Dai, "Divided Loyalty in War," *Psychiatry,* VII [November, 1944], 327–40; see also Joost A. M. Meerloo, "The Psychology of Treason and Loyalty," *American Journal of Psychotherapy,* VIII, No. 4 [October, 1954], 648–66).

Biological determinants of political personality. For discussion of recent work on relationships between adrenal hormones and mental illness, indicating some biopsychological influences, see Mary Julian White, "The Recent Literature on Stress and the Adrenocorticotrophic and Adrenocortical Hormones," *Psychiatry,* XIII (August, 1950), 392–95. For ambitious but unpersuasive attempts to relate body type to personality and action see the work of William H. Sheldon, especially *The Varieties of Temperament* (New York: Harper & Bros., 1942) and *Varieties of Delinquent Youth* (New York: Harper & Bros., 1949).

PAGE

202. Personality and course of experience. See George H. Mead, *Mind, Self, and Society*, ed. Charles W. Morris (Chicago: University of Chicago Press, 1934), especially pp. 200–209, 273–80; also an unpublished paper by my colleague and friend, Nelson Foote, on "Developmental Sociology" (I have also profited from conversations with Foote). For this type of analysis applied to the experience of taking narcotics see Howard S. Becker, "Becoming a Marihuana User," *American Journal of Sociology*, LIX, No. 3 (November, 1953), 235–42.

203. What society defines as permissible. I know of no better discussion on this point than the familiar study of Ruth Benedict, *Patterns of Culture* (New York: Mentor Books, 1949).

There is no evidence. See Edward A. Shils, "Authoritarianism: 'Right' and 'Left,'" in *Studies in the Scope and Method of "The Authoritarian Personality,"* ed. R. Christie and M. Jahoda, especially pp. 42–49.

Neither national loyalty nor disloyalty is a necessary personality fulfilment. This statement is not contradicted by the fact that a strong similarity seems to exist between the authoritarian personality described by Adorno and his colleagues and the convinced Nazi described by Henry V. Dicks in an impressive paper, "Personality Traits and National Socialist Ideology," *Human Relations*, III, No. 2 (1950), 111–54.

". . . blind attachment. . . ." T. W. Adorno *et al.*, *The Authoritarian Personality*, pp. 107, 116.

204. He joins those he finds most congenial. Daniel J. Levinson, in T. W. Adorno *et al.*, *The Authoritarian Personality*, p. 206, uses the phrase "selective assimilation" to describe this process. See also G. Murphy, L. B. Murphy, and T. M. Newcomb, *Experimental Social Psychology* (rev. ed.; New York: Harper & Bros., 1937), pp. 1045–46.

Politics as public expressions of private motives. See Harold D. Lasswell, *Psychopathology and Politics* (Chicago: University of Chicago Press, 1930).

205. Other causes . . . to explain their determination. See Charles A. Beard, *An Economic Interpretation of the Constitution of the United States* (New York: Macmillan Co., 1944); John F. Jameson, *The American Revolution Considered as a Social Movement* (New York: P. Smith, 1950).

PAGE

205. Radicals have explicit political demands. The general scheme was first suggested in the early works of Harold D. Lasswell. William Kornhauser, in his unpublished thesis ("Liberal and Radical Political Careers," chap. vii), has shown how radicals and liberals differ in their political expectations, demands, and identifications.

206. ". . . merely refuse to recognize him. . . ." John W. Wheeler-Bennett, *The Nemesis of Power*, p. 526.

207. The psychological wave of the future. The field is now subject to intensive investigation, though the results are by no means consistent. For example, gross categories of class, education, income, and sex do not correlate persuasively with personality factors (Daniel J. Levinson in T. W. Adorno *et al., The Authoritarian Personality*, pp. 199–207); the *occupation* of parents is apparently related consistently with the personality of children (Else Frenkel-Brunswik in *Studies in the Scope and Method of "The Authoritarian Personality,"* ed. R. Christie and M. Jahoda, p. 232); but there is no correlation between the personality of adults and the occupations of their fathers (Daniel J. Levinson, in T. W. Adorno *et al., The Authoritarian Personality*, p. 204).

CHAPTER 12

208–9. The case of Mr. N. is taken from his individual file record in the National Archives. The record contains not only his own several statements (one written during his incarceration at a special camp for "troublemakers") but also an FBI report and several assessments of his conduct and character by officials of the War Relocation Authority. Italics in the quotation on p. 210 are added.

210. The honorable may betray. See John Galsworthy's play, *Loyalties* (New York: Charles Scribner's Sons, 1923), for an example of class loyalties initially triumphing over justice. See also Denis Gwynn, *Traitor or Patriot* (New York: Jonathan Cape and Harrison Smith, Inc., 1931), a biography of Sir Roger Casement. I am indebted to Howard B. White for some of the ideas on which this paragraph is based.

212. New groups demand new living patterns. For analysis of the difficulty of moving upward in class see A. Davis and J. Dollard, *Children of Bondage* (Washington: American Council on Education, 1940); W. Lloyd Warner and P. S. Lunt, *The Social Life of a Modern Community* ("Yankee City Series," Vol. I [New Haven:

Yale University Press, 1941]). For compilation of relevant research see R. Bendix and S. M. Lipset, *Class, Status, and Power* (Glencoe, Ill.: Free Press, 1953).

214. The Soviet idealist . . . careerist . . . conformist. See the case histories in Raymond A. Bauer's unpublished paper, "The Development of Attitudes towards the Soviet Regime: Selected Case Histories" (March 31, 1952).

CHAPTER 13

222. "To have once been dropped. . . ." Testimony of John Von Neumann in *Organization and Administration of the Military Research and Development Programs: Hearings before a Subcommittee of the Committee on Government Operations, House of Representatives* (83d Cong., 2d sess. [Washington: Government Printing Office, 1954]), p. 380. The consequences of loyalty investigations in the short run are accurately described, I think, in Mr. Von Neumann's statement and in the subsequent discussion of my text. I think it not unlikely, however, that in the long run those whose loyalty has been unfairly questioned during the period of the cold war may find themselves in a relatively privileged position—that status and deference may some day be given these persons just because they once faced a congressional committee.

"The shattering financial, psychological. . . ." Walter Gellhorn, *Security, Loyalty, and Science* (Ithaca, N.Y.: Cornell University Press, 1950), p. 157.

223. Norbert Wiener, "Conspiracy of Conformists. . . ," *Nation*, CLXXVIII, No. 18 (May 1, 1954), 375.

On scientists as internationalists see the essay of S. Chandrasekhar, "The Scientist," in *The Works of the Mind*, ed. Robert B. Heywood (Chicago: University of Chicago Press, 1947), pp. 159–79. Chandrasekhar quotes the great physicist, Rutherford, with respect to the co-operative nature of science.

224. On Allan Nunn May see Rebecca West, *The Meaning of Treason*, especially p. 202.

Nigel Balchin, *A Sort of Traitors* (London: Collins, 1949), published in the United States as *Who Is My Neighbor?* (Boston: Houghton Mifflin Co., 1950); Michael Amrine, *Secret* (Boston:

PAGE

Houghton Mifflin Co., 1950), pp. 184–85. The same conflict of scientific versus national loyalties is found in C. P. Snow, *The New Men* (London: Macmillan & Co., Ltd., 1954).

224. Views strengthened as result of Oppenheimer case. See *Bulletin of the Atomic Scientists,* Vol. X, No. 5 (May, 1954), and No. 9 (September, 1954), which contain numerous statements by eminent scientists of faith in Dr. Oppenheimer and criticism of the security rulings.

228. ". . . the scientist as a class. . . ." Don K. Price, *Government and Science* (New York: New York University Press, 1954), p. 57.

Damage to the nation. For an excellent discussion of impact of loyalty-security programs on science and scientists see Edward A. Shils, "Security and Science Sacrificed to Loyalty," *Bulletin of the Atomic Scientists,* XI, No. 4 (April, 1955), 106–9, 130. This number of the *Bulletin* is devoted to "Secrecy, Security, and Loyalty" and contains a number of relevant articles.

229. Civil servants demoralized, suspicious, unhappy. For one report by a group of relatively unwilling witnesses see *Task Force Report on Personnel and Civil Service,* prepared for the Commission on Organization of the Executive Branch of the Government (February, 1955); also Eleanor Bontecou, *The Federal Loyalty-Security Program* (Ithaca, N.Y.: Cornell University Press, 1953). An excellent preliminary study of the social-psychological impact of loyalty-security programs among federal employees and university teachers is M. Jahoda and S. W. Cook, "Security Measures and Freedom of Thought," *Yale Law Review,* XLI, No. 3 (March, 1952), 296–333.

On state legislative committees see Walter Gellhorn (ed.), *The States and Subversion* (Ithaca, N.Y.: Cornell University Press, 1952).

". . . for offenses not always defined. . . ." Robert K. Carr, *The House Committee on Un-American Activities* (Ithaca, N.Y.: Cornell University Press, 1952), p. 452.

The withdrawal of affection. The first quoted statement was made as a government attorney handed his resignation to his superior officer (the latter a member of his department's loyalty review board); the second statement was a spectator's reaction after a friend had been quizzed by a Senate investigating committee.

PAGE

230. The withdrawal of competence. See Alan Barth, *The Loyalty of Free Men* (New York: Viking Press, 1951), pp. 123–30; see also Robert K. Carr, *House Committee on Un-American Activities,* pp. 452–61.

"The conclusion has become inescapable. . . ." Letter to *New York Times,* January 17, 1954, signed by Norman Armour, Robert Woods Bliss, Joseph C. Grew, William Phillips, and G. Howland Shaw, sec. 4, p. 8.

Hans Morgenthau, "The Impact of the Loyalty-Security Measures on the State Department," *Bulletin of the Atomic Scientists,* XI, No. 4 (April, 1955), 139.

231. Governments must guard themselves. I think it may be fairly argued that the excesses of loyalty-security and secrecy regulations during the period of the cold war were a reaction against the relative slothfulness of security during, and immediately after, the real war. The overstringency of many officers during the later period was undoubtedly an expiation of guilt feelings concerning the earlier one. This is an important point for any general history of the problem, but it does not alter in any way the analysis offered in the text.

234. Don K. Price, *Government and Science,* chap. iv. I believe Price's discussion excellent, but I register a dissent to Price's faith in the military bureaucracy as a guardian of democratic method. For more specific suggestions for programs of personnel and information security see J. B. Phelps, R. S. Brown, Jr., and S. A. Goudsmit, "Toward a Positive Security Program," *Bulletin of the Atomic Scientists,* XI, No. 4 (April, 1955), 165–69; also Vannevar Bush, "To Make Our Security System Secure," *New York Times Magazine,* March 20, 1955.

". . . absolute security is likely. . . ." Alan Barth, *Loyalty of Free Men,* pp. 131–46.

235. ". . . a basic concept of our laws. . . ." Francis Biddle, *The Fear of Freedom* (Garden City, N.Y.: Doubleday & Co., Inc., 1951), p. 248.

CHAPTER 14

238. Ferdinand Tönnies in *Gemeinschaft und Gesellschaft* (Leipzig: H. Buske, 1935). An American edition is Ferdinand Tönnies,

PAGE

Fundamental Concepts of Sociology, trans. and supplemented by Charles P. Loomis (New York: American Book Co., 1940).

239. For Weber's views see especially his *The Protestant Ethic and the Spirit of Capitalism,* trans. Talcott Parsons (reprinted by University of Chicago Bookstore for Social Sciences 2, n.d.); also H. H. Gerth and C. W. Mills, in their Introduction to *From Max Weber: Essays in Sociology* (New York: Oxford University Press, 1946), especially pp. 65–74.

Émile Durkheim, *The Division of Labor in Society,* trans. George Simpson (Glencoe, Ill.: Free Press, 1947), especially Preface to the second edition, pp. 1–31; *The Elementary Forms of the Religious Life,* trans. Joseph Wald Swain (Glencoe, Ill.: Free Press, 1947); and *Suicide: A Study in Sociology,* trans. John A. Spaulding and G. Simpson (Glencoe, Ill.: Free Press, 1951).

239–40. For Veblen's views see especially his *The Theory of the Leisure Class* (New York: Macmillan Co., 1908); also his *The Engineers and the Price System* (New York: B. W. Huebsch, Inc., 1921); *The Theory of Business Enterprise* (New York: Charles Scribner's Sons, 1932); and *Essays in Our Changing Order.*

240. For Freud's most explicit statement on this theme see his *Civilization and Its Discontents,* trans. Joan Riviere (New York: J. Cape & H. Smith, 1930).

240–41. C. Wright Mills, *White Collar* (New York: Oxford University Press, 1951), pp. xvi, xvii.

241. Such views are widely shared. Sebastian de Grazia, *The Political Community,* pp. 56, 74, 189; Philip Selznick, *The Organizational Weapon,* chap. vii; Willmoore Kendall, Introduction to A. Rossi, *A Communist Party in Action;* Baker Brownell, *The Human Community* (New York: Harper & Bros., 1950), pp. 4–6, 293. For an influential statement of similar theme see José Ortega y Gasset, *The Revolt of the Masses.*

242. For Mannheim's views see especially *Diagnosis of Our Time;* also his *Man and Society in an Age of Reconstruction* (New York: Harcourt, Brace & Co., 1941).

244. Concerning isolation versus the richness of urban life see Louis Wirth, "Urbanism as a Way of Life," *American Journal of Sociology,* Vol. XLIV, No. 1 (July, 1938); Morris Janowitz, *The Community Press in an Urban Setting* (Glencoe, Ill.: Free Press,

PAGE

1952); J. Smith, W. H. Form, and G. P. Stone, "Local Intimacy in a Middle-sized City," *American Journal of Sociology*, LX, No. 3 (November, 1954), 276–84; Georg Simmel, *The Sociology of Georg Simmel*, pp. 412–22.

245. Voters cannot distinguish important issues. See P. F. Lazarsfeld, B. Berelson, and H. Gaudet, *The People's Choice;* and B. Berelson, P. F. Lazarsfeld, and W. N. McPhee, *Voting*. Note especially the table in the latter work, pp. 331–47, summarizing results of many voting studies.

Extreme beliefs and extreme partisanship. B. Berelson, P. F. Lazarsfeld, and W. N. McPhee, *Voting*, p. 314.

"It was the radicalization. . . ." Reinhard Bendix, "Social Stratification and Political Power," *American Political Science Review*, XLVI, No. 2 (June, 1952), 369.

247. ". . . the only leaders of national scope. . . ." David Riesman, *The Lonely Crowd*, p. 244.

248. The public is competent. See James Bryce, *Modern Democracies* (New York: Macmillan Co., 1921), I, 159; Walter Lippmann, *Public Opinion* (New York: Pelican Books, 1946).

Leaders must always look back. See the two great books by W. Ivor Jennings, *Cabinet Government* (Cambridge: At the University Press, 1937) and *Parliament* (Cambridge: At the University Press, 1939).

251. Socrates' statement is from Plato's *Apology*, trans. B. W. Jowett (New York: Published for the Classics Club by W. T. Black, 1942), p. 84.

252. Edmund Burke, *Reflections on the French Revolution*, ed. Ernest Rhys ("Everyman's Library" [London: J. M. Dent & Sons, 1935]), pp. 44, 193. Italics have been added.

252–53. Criticism may be followed by action. In this paragraph I have, of course, loosely paraphrased, and in some cases used actual words and phrases from, the Declaration of Independence. The point was put more bluntly by Abraham Lincoln in his first inaugural address: "This country with its institutions belongs to the people who inhabit it. Whenever they shall grow weary of the existing government, they can exercise their constitutional right of amending it, or their revolutionary right to dismember or overthrow it."

PAGE

253. For a discussion of international loyalties, see Quincy Wright, "Loyalties and Peace," *Faith and Freedom*, Vol. VIII, Part 2, No. 23 (Spring, 1955), 49–63.

254. "Nationalism and the split atom. . . ." E. B. White, *The Wild Flag*, p. 186. For the argument (rejected in this volume) that national loyalties are synthetic and intellectual and thus different from other loyalties see Hans Kohn, *The Idea of Nationalism*, p. 9, and notes, pp. 579–80. Kohn's conclusion here is similar to mine: that national loyalties lead naturally to international ones.

254–55. Mr. Justice Brandeis in *Olmstead* v. *United States*, 277 U.S. 438 (1928); see also Mr. Justice Douglas in *Public Utilities Commission* v. *Pollak*, 343 U.S. 451, 467 (1952): "The right to be let alone is indeed the beginning of all freedom."

255. ". . . no one who reads our national literature. . . ." Alexander Meiklejohn, *What Does America Mean?* (New York: W. W. Norton & Co., Inc., 1935), p. 71.

Index

The Table of Contents (pp. ix–xii) constitutes a relatively full outline of the book, and the Index does not duplicate the topical headings given there.